ASHAMED OF THE GOSPEL

ASHAMED OF THE GOSPEL

WHEN THE CHURCH BECOMES LIKE THE WORLD

THIRD EDITION

JOHN MACARTHUR

CROSSWAY

WHEATON, ILLINOIS

Ashamed of the Gospel: When the Church Becomes Like the World

Copyright © 1993, 2010 by John MacArthur

Published in association with the literary agency of Wolgemuth and Associates, Inc.

Published by Crossway Books
        a publishing ministry of Good News Publishers
        1300 Crescent Street
        Wheaton, Illinois 60187

Cover design: Tobias' Outerwear for Books

First printing, third edition, 2010

Printed in the United States of America

Unless otherwise indicated, Scripture quotations are taken from the ESV® Bible (*The Holy Bible: English Standard Version®*), copyright © 2001 by Crossway Bibles, a publishing ministry of Good News Publishers. Used by permission. All rights reserved.

Scripture quotations indicated as from NASB are taken from *The New American Standard Bible*, copyright © 1960, 1962, 1963, 1968, 1971, 1972, 1973, 1975, 1977, and 1995 by The Lockman Foundation and are used by permission.

Quotations indicated as from KJV are taken from the King James Version.

Appendix 4, "Carnal vs. Spiritual Wisdom," is an excerpt from "A Soliloquy on the Art of Man-Fishing" by Thomas Boston, adapted for modern readers. This version, © 1993 by Phil Johnson, is used by permission.

ISBN 13: 978-1-4335-0929-2

ISBN 10: 1-4335-0929-6

PDF ISBN: 978-1-4335-0930-8

Mobipocket ISBN: 978-1-4335-0931-5

ePub ISBN: 978-1-4335-2339-7

Library of Congress Cataloging-in-Publication Data
MacArthur, John, 1939–
   Ashamed of the Gospel : when the church becomes like the world /
John MacArthur. – 3rd ed.
     p. cm.
   Includes bibliographical references.
   ISBN-13: 978-1-4335-0929-2 (hc)
   1. Evangelicalism. 2. Church and the world. 3. Modernism (Christian
theology). 4. Spurgeon, C. H. (Charles Haddon), 1834–1892. I. Title.
BR1640.M243   2010
270.8'2—dc22   2009017997

SH		19	18	17	16	15	14	13	12	11	10
15	14	13	12	11	10	9	8	7	6	5	4	3	2	1

To

RICK DRAA

*My faithful and beloved friend and servant of the Lord
on my behalf—who for more than thirty-five years
has recorded my voice and spread it across the globe.*

CONTENTS

I am not ashamed of the gospel, for it is the power of God for salvation to everyone who believes, to the Jew first and also to the Greek.

ROMANS 1:16

Therefore do not be ashamed of the testimony about our Lord, nor of me his prisoner, but share in suffering for the gospel by the power of God . . . which is why I suffer as I do. But I am not ashamed, for I know whom I have believed, and I am convinced that he is able to guard until that Day what has been entrusted to me.

2 TIMOTHY 1:8, 12

Whoever is ashamed of me and of my words in this adulterous and sinful generation, of him will the Son of Man also be ashamed when he comes in the glory of his Father with the holy angels.

MARK 8:38

ACKNOWLEDGMENTS

I first broached the idea of this book to Lane Dennis and Crossway sometime in late 1992. Lane's enthusiasm for the project was immediate and profound. With his encouragement, we shifted into high gear, compiling and editing the first edition within three months after getting the go-ahead from Crossway. No book I have ever written has come together so quickly and so easily. Crossway launched the book in mid-1993 at the Christian Booksellers Association convention in Atlanta. The title has been a mainstay in Crossway's catalog ever since, and they have done a marvelous job of maintaining its visibility in the marketplace. I'm very grateful to Lane and the staff at Crossway for what they did in 1993 to make it possible to publish this book on such a fast schedule and for all that they have done over the years to keep it in the marketplace.

Lance Quinn (then an associate pastor at Grace Church; now senior pastor of The Bible Church of Little Rock) was a major help to me during the writing of the first edition, proofreading and critiquing chapters during the initial editorial process.

Numerous people at Grace to You also contributed to the project. These include Arline Hampton (who transcribed the sermons from which material for the book was drawn), Mike Taylor (who for more than twenty years managed the editorial department at Grace to You, until the Lord took him to heaven in June of 2009), and Tom Pennington, who stepped into the gap to provide leadership at Grace to You while other key staff were working to meet that short deadline. Tom's heightened involvement at Grace to You was one of the most wonderful and far-reaching side effects of the decision to fast-track this book. He spent more than a decade working alongside me—first at Grace to You, then in the role Lance Quinn vacated at Grace Church when he was called to Little Rock. Like Lance, Tom proved too gifted and too valuable to the kingdom to be kept in my side office. He is now senior pastor of Countryside Bible Church in Southlake, Texas.

Major thanks to Phil Johnson, who did the hands-on editorial work in

1993 to compile and edit these chapters, blending material from more than fifty sermons that I had preached over twenty-five years' time. Phil has also edited the updates and the supplementary material for this revised edition. His fingerprints are on every page of the book, and I continue to be thankful for the nearly thirty-year partnership the Lord has given us.

Phil has often reminded me that his well-known interest in Charles Spurgeon began when he edited the first edition of this book. He had never read any of Spurgeon's writings—or even a full biography of Spurgeon—prior to starting the editorial work on this book. While helping assemble the first draft of *Ashamed of the Gospel*, he did some research on the Down-Grade Controversy. Once he began reading Spurgeon's writings and sermons, he found it impossible to stop. In the years since 1993 he has posted reams of Spurgeon material on the Internet, helping to introduce countless people around the world to the Prince of Preachers, showing how supremely *relevant* a Victorian Baptist preacher is to what's happening in the church today. The Internet's Spurgeon Archive is thus one of the enduring legacies of this book. Phil has assembled the material in Appendix 2 for this new edition.

Finally, thanks to Robert Wolgemuth, who had the vision for a revision and rerelease of this book and who brought the idea of a new edition to Crossway.

PREFACE TO THE 2010 EDITION

What marvel if, under some men's shifty talk, people grow into love of both truth and falsehood! People will say, "We like this form of doctrine, and we like the other also." The fact is, they would like anything if only a clever deceiver would put it plausibly before them. They admire Moses and Aaron, but they would not say a word against Jannes and Jambres. We shall not join in the confederacy which seems to aim at such a comprehension.

CHARLES HADDON SPURGEON[1]

Sometime in the summer of 2007, I picked up a copy of *Ashamed of the Gospel* for the first time in fourteen years and started thumbing through it. Before I put the book down again, I had devoured eight chapters. I was pleased and amazed to see the enduring relevance of the book—especially since I wrote it to critique the notion that *relevance* is achieved by dragging the church from fad to fad in a vain effort to stay abreast of the times.

Of course, my passion for the message of this book has not diminished since I first proposed the idea to my publisher, but I was nevertheless surprised and encouraged to see how much of what I wrote in 1993 is expressed exactly as I would want to say it today. While I am disappointed by how accurately (and speedily) the predictions I made have been fulfilled, I am not disheartened, and I intend to keep sounding the warning as long as the Lord gives me breath. In fact, before putting the book down that day, I resolved to do my best to see it released again in a new, expanded edition. You hold the fruit of that resolution in your hands.

Only rarely do I re-read my own books, especially those that were first published more than a decade ago. In this case, "more than a decade ago" was a different century!

---

[1] *The Greatest Fight in the World* (London: Passmore & Alabaster, 1891), 38.

The world of 1993 was another time in many significant ways. That was a unique year, strikingly different from the rest of the twentieth century—but also nothing at all like the Internet era, which was just about to begin.

History will no doubt always remember the early 1990s as a pivotal time in human history. In 1992, conservative op-ed commentator George Will published a compilation of his newspaper columns written over the prior three years. He titled the anthology *Suddenly*, which perfectly captured the spirit of the day. Suddenly, confusingly, *everything* was in flux. Worldly fads and philosophies were changing faster than ever. The changes were global and profound, affecting everything from art to zoology. Ideological changes, societal changes, political changes, and moral changes were the order of the day. The shifting of so many opinions and boundaries all at once was both drastic and disorienting.

No wonder. Every important worldview built on "modern" thought was now utterly discredited. Some of the most basic presuppositions modern secular society had staked out as true and certain were left totally in tatters.

THE END OF THE COLD WAR

A major turning point had occurred on November 9, 1989, when the Berlin Wall fell literally overnight, signaling the failure of European Communism. The end of Lenin's legacy came very quickly—and so did other monumental changes, all with stunning speed. Gorbachev, Glasnost, and the Gulf War dominated the news at the start of the 90s, but the Gulf War ended in early 1991, and the Soviet Union collapsed in August of that same year. Boris Yeltsin boldly defied an attempted coup, took the reins of Russian power, and began the formal dissolution of the Soviet empire.

By 1993, the world was emphatically renouncing the values of the Cold War. We were watching our parents' concept of "modernity" quickly fade in the rearview mirror. The word *postmodernism* was just starting to be used here and there in popular discourse—but the set of ideas it stands for were already evident everywhere. Before most people even realized we had witnessed the end of the *modern* era, *post*modern values had completely altered the way the world thinks and talks about truth.

There was, of course, a positive side to the end of modernity. Many modern presuppositions *needed* to be debunked—starting with the notion that science and human reason are reliable arbiters of truth and falsehood.

Modernity, nicknamed "The Age of Reason" by its earliest advocates, more or less began with a rejection of Scripture's authority and the elevation of the human mind in its place. The fall of every major modern ideology exposed the hubris of that way of thinking, and that was unequivocally a good development.

Besides that, the worldwide remapping of political alliances opened wonderful new opportunities for ministry. I was privileged to make numerous trips to the former Soviet Union, teaching groups of pastors and preaching in Russian and Ukrainian churches. I went at the behest of Soviet Baptists and formed relationships with them that endure strongly to this day. During my earliest visits to that part of the world, I was absolutely amazed to see the strength and vitality of evangelical churches there. Their worship services were the very picture of austere simplicity—just the preaching of the Word and the celebration of the ordinances, totally devoid of the flash and entertainment being touted as essential tools for the times by all the "experts" back home. That got me thinking more deeply than ever about how the Lord builds His church and what it means to be a wise master builder (1 Cor. 3:10–15).

By the early 90s American evangelicalism was shamelessly imitating virtually every worldly fad. Church leaders and church-growth strategists openly described the gospel as a commodity to be sold at market, and the predictable result was a frantic attempt to make the gospel into the kind of product most buyers wanted. The conventional wisdom was that sophisticated marketing strategies were far more effective than gospel proclamation for reaching the "unchurched" multitudes. No one, it seemed, wanted to challenge that notion, which was buttressed with countless opinion polls. And who could argue with the obvious "success" of several entertainment-oriented megachurches?

Western evangelicals had been gradually losing interest in biblical preaching and doctrinal instruction for decades. The church in America had become weak, worldly, and man-centered. Evangelical ears were itching for something more hip and entertaining than biblical preaching (cf. 2 Tim. 4:3), and business-savvy evangelical pundits declared that it was foolish not to give people what they demanded. Without pragmatic methodologies numerical growth would be virtually impossible, they insisted—even though such pragmatism was manifestly detrimental to *spiritual* growth.

Churches were starving spiritually while overdosing on entertainment. A few prosperous megachurches masked the tragedy with incredibly large attendance figures, but anyone who took time to examine the trajectory could see that Western evangelicalism was in serious trouble.

Those trends were exactly what prompted me to write this book in the first place.

By contrast, the beleaguered Iron-Curtain churches were hungry for biblical teaching, steadily gaining spiritual strength, and growing numerically on the strength of bold gospel ministry. After years of Communist oppression, they were finally free to preach Christ openly, and that is precisely what they did. They were flourishing as a result.

Most Russian pastors had no formal training, so they sought help from the West in the areas of biblical interpretation and doctrine. (That's how I got involved with them.) The most mature and discerning leaders in the Iron-Curtain churches were wary of influences from the West. Frankly, I shared their concern and appreciated their caution. I was convinced that even the weakest of *their* churches could teach evangelicals in America a lot about the biblical approach to church growth. They understood that no legitimate church-growth strategy should ever fail to recognize the truth of John 15:19–20: "If you were of the world, the world would love you as its own; but because you are not of the world, but I chose you out of the world, therefore the world hates you. Remember the word that I said to you: 'A servant is not greater than his master.' If they persecuted me, they will also persecute you. If they kept my word, they will also keep yours."

When the Iron Curtain fell, however, "missionaries" from the West flooded the former Soviet Union, not so much with gospel-based resources and Bible-study tools, but with highly questionable evangelistic strategies—and with the same poisonous philosophy of church growth that had made Western evangelicalism so superficial and worldly. Russian church leaders were appalled that so many tawdry trends came into their culture from the West under the pretense of evangelism. I was offended, too—and embarrassed.

I remember watching glitzy American televangelists with comically big hair peddling their health-and-wealth message and other false gospels on Russian television during my earliest trips to Moscow.[2] They probably had little effect on healthy Russian *churches*, but they injected a seriously

---

[2]I've often marveled at how much American evangelicals talk about the importance of "contextualization" compared to how little care they take when real cross-cultural communication is necessary. Head scarves (babushkas) and modest clothing were emblems of submission for Christian women in the persecuted church (as was the case in Corinthian culture—cf. 1 Cor. 11:5–6). Blitzing post-Communist Russia with Western pop culture and televangelist hairdos was probably the most culturally insensitive thing Western Christians could have done to their poor and oppressed brethren just emerging from behind the Iron Curtain.

false gospel into the public perception, totally confusing millions. Soviet people had been indoctrinated with atheism and shielded from the truth of Scripture. They therefore had no means of distinguishing truth from falsehood in religion. So much false Christianity on television no doubt inoculated multitudes against the real gospel.

I also remember seeing a parade of "student missionaries" from America putting on a variety show in a public square in Kiev, using every circus trick from jugglers to clowns and every wordless type of entertainment from mimes to interpretive dance, all claiming to communicate "the gospel"—or *something* spiritual-sounding—across the language barrier. I frankly could not be certain what the actual message was supposed to be. I have a fairly good grasp of the gospel as Scripture presents it, and that was not the message being pantomimed in Independence Square. Again, I was embarrassed for the church in the West.

Back in America, these performances were being reported as serious evangelistic work. Judging from the numbers of supposed converts claimed, we might have expected churches in the Iron-Curtain countries to be doubling and quadrupling on a monthly basis.

Russian and Ukrainian churches were indeed growing, but the evangelistic buskers and street artists from the West had nothing to do with that. Those churches grew because Russian Christians, now free to proclaim the gospel openly, preached repentance from sin and faith in Christ to their neighbors. The response was remarkable. I sat in many Russian worship services for hours at a time, hearing convert after convert publicly repent—renouncing former sins and declaring faith in Christ to the gathered church, always in standing-room-only crowds. It was the polar opposite of what American church growth gurus insisted was absolutely necessary. But it was just like watching the book of Acts unfold in real life.

As a matter of fact, most of the Westerners who rushed to the former Soviet Union when Communism collapsed missed the real signs of church growth in those years because they completely ignored the churches that were already there. They started parachurch organizations, opted for pure media ministry, sponsored Punch-and-Judy shows in the public square, or tried to start new churches modeled on Western worldly styles. Most of the visible results of that sort of "evangelistic" and church-planting activity proved to be blessedly short-lived.

What *did* last was by no means all good. Americans injected into that culture a style of worldly evangelicalism that is now gaining traction and causing confusion within the Russian-speaking churches. Those churches that had weathered decades of government harassment and public ridicule now have to contend with something much subtler but a thousand times worse: trendy methods from American evangelicals—gimmicks and novelties that diminish practically everything truly important in favor of things that appeal to people's baser instincts.

By far the most subtle and dangerous Western influences came in through church growth experts, missiologists, and professional pollsters. Unlike the televangelists and street performers, these academicians and marketers managed to gain a platform within Russian-speaking churches. They were trusted because they were writers, career missionaries, seminary professors with credentials, and pastors with huge churches. They brought loads of books and ideas, virtually all of them advocating a highly pragmatic approach to ministry that was foreign in every sense to a church that had lived under Communist persecution for the better part of a century.

One struggles to imagine anything more grossly inappropriate than the fad-chasing pragmatism that was deliberately injected into Russian and eastern European churches by Westerners tinkering with theories about contextualization. But the influx of shallow evangelicalism into Russia in the early 90s was barely the tip of the iceberg. Thanks to various means of instant, inexpensive mass communications, the stultifying influence of dysfunctional American religion soon inundated the entire world. The Internet in particular suddenly opened the floodgates so that it became impossible to contain and control such nonsense. Within just a few years, evangelical gimmickry became the most visible and influential expression of Western "spirituality" worldwide.

The poison of religious pragmatism is now an enormous *global* problem.

THE DAWN OF THE INTERNET AGE

The World Wide Web had quietly been implemented less than a year after the Soviet Union broke up. Still, by 1993, when this book's first edition hit the shelves, no one but the earliest Internet insiders had even heard about the Web—much less seen it. Most people had no clue how quickly or how drastically the Web would alter the world as we knew it.

I remember being told at a strategic planning retreat in 1996 that the World Wide Web would eventually become the primary vehicle for the dissemination of our radio broadcast and recorded sermons. (At the time, radio and cassette tapes were still the only media we were using for audio content.) When the men at Grace to You who stay abreast of new technologies predicted that within twenty years or so cassette tapes would be a totally dead technology, I thought they were exaggerating. "You can't access the Internet in a car," I pointed out. "Even if you could, who wants to carry a computer on the car seat, when it's so much more convenient to pop in a cassette tape?"

Technology is clearly not my forte.

The speed with which the world has caught on to the new media is mind-boggling. The convenience and velocity of Internet communications have changed almost every facet of how we live. The easy availability of so much information (and *misinformation*) has profoundly altered the way people learn and think and make decisions.

Meanwhile, the ease, immediacy, and affordability of Internet publishing has leveled the playing field between pundits and the proletariat. Anyone can start a blog, for free. Anyone with a computer (or cell phone) and an Internet connection can instantly broadcast his every opinion worldwide. Novices and scholarly authorities alike can employ the same media. Those who are most adept at gathering an audience are the ones who are being heard, not necessarily those most qualified to speak.

So many opinions and so much information all moving so quickly means a simple, off-the-cuff sound bite may be a thousand times more influential than a meticulously researched treatise. In fact, whether something is true or false is usually deemed less important than the way the idea is communicated. (Today's marketing strategies are based on that assumption.) Most people naturally prefer a punchy one-liner to a carefully written essay. So style takes precedence over content in almost every venue. Sound bites are simply easier to swallow than a serious discourse.

That reality is reflected in the way we digest the news, the way our politicians run their campaigns, and even the way people manage personal relationships. Text messages are probably the most common form of communication between individuals. Power dating has replaced courtship. Quality time is seen as a substitute for real parenting. The typical radio talk show invites listeners to call in, but the host invariably cuts callers off rudely if they can't make a cogent point in four seconds or less. Interviewers on network television do the same thing to guests they invite to participate in panel discussions, squandering the panelists' expertise in favor of keeping the show moving at a pace no one can really keep up with anyway. It's the show, not the substance, that matters. The quest for a bigger audience share trumps the truth. (And isn't that exactly like the philosophy that drives so many contemporary churches?)

I've participated in several of those televised panels, and sometimes the panelists are physically scattered across the continent, unable to see one another and barely able to make out the other speakers' sound bites in those discreet earpieces. Even that doesn't matter. As long as the camera gives the *impression* of bringing many points of view face-to-face, the goal has been met. So what if no one gets to say more than half a sentence at a time? Our culture has simply lost patience with reasoned discourse and careful exposition.

It is not without significance that the most popular form of communication on the Internet at the moment is Twitter—an application that lets users broadcast their thoughts to the entire world in pithy quips. Each "Tweet" has a 140-character limit, and millions of them are sent every week. It's the next logical step in the evolution of the new media. Blogs have already begun to fade from the limelight. (The average blog post is three paragraphs. Too wordy.)

Attention spans are getting shorter, literacy has suffered dramatically, and logic itself is frequently dismissed as unnecessarily pedantic. The Web is well-suited to a culture where what we *feel* is deemed more important than what we *think*. The Internet hosts millions of forums where people trade opinions and aphorisms, and these often become the electronic-data equivalent of acrimonious yelling matches. Internet forums are notorious for the profanity and hostility that dominate them. If you want vivid proof of human depravity in abundance, eavesdrop on practically any unmoderated Internet forum, including the ones devoted to discussing theology.

And in case you haven't noticed, our culture has lost the ability to distinguish between what's trivial and what's profound. Evidence of that is abundant in the online forums, too.

The Internet has created an ideal environment for postmodernism to flourish and spread—not in spite of all those shortcomings but precisely *because* of them.

POSTMODERNISM: QUESTION EVERYTHING

I have examined and critiqued postmodernism elsewhere.[3] It should be sufficient for our purposes in this context to summarize the postmodern mindset by describing it as dubiousness about practically everything. As we

---

[3]*The Truth War* (Nashville: Thomas Nelson, 2007), 10–26.

noted, the starting point for *modernity* was a rejection of biblical authority (setting aside belief in the supernatural as an untenable or merely irrelevant opinion). Instead, science and human reason were foolishly treated as reliable and authoritative. In the end, the disastrous failure of so many modern ideologies utterly debunked modern rationalism and delivered a deathblow to modern certitude. *Postmodernism* therefore subjects every idea and every authority to endless skepticism.

Modernity's most basic assumption was that the way to achieve unshakable certainty is through a rigorous application of the scientific method. (Whatever could be tested and proved in the laboratory—or logically deduced from scientific "facts"—was deemed true; everything else was written off as mere superstition.) Moderns were convinced that a basic foundation of settled scientific knowledge would easily provide a trustworthy authority by which *all* truth claims could be tested. That process in turn would eventually bring about a uniform consensus regarding all the fundamental realities of life and human existence.

When those expectations were finally extinguished by countless buckets of cold reality, modernism itself lay utterly discredited amid the smoldering ashes. Whereas the modern mind had sought uniformity, certainty, and order, postmodernism canonized the opposite values: diversity, doubt, and defiance. "Question everything" is the postmodern manifesto.

Combine those values with the ease of Internet communications, and what you get is what you see: the elimination of practically all distinctions between knowledge and ignorance, authority and incompetence, expertise and ineptitude.

Where did this notion of postmodernity come from, and how did it sneak up and take over the whole world (as it seems) so quickly?

The word *postmodern* is older than most people realize. It was commonly applied to artistic, literary, and architectural styles as early as the end of World War I. From the mid-1960s through the 1980s, the term was used with increasing frequency to describe a way of thinking about truth and interpreting language. Jacques Derrida (who coined the term *deconstruction* to describe postmodern hermeneutics) was writing his postmodern perspectives on the implications of language and philosophy in the 1960s. Michel Foucault and Jean-François Lyotard explored the political ramifications of oppressive language and meta-narratives in the 1970s. In the 1980s, spurred on by writers like Richard Rorty and Jean Beaudrillard, postmodernism's trademark contempt for rationalistic certitude dominated much of the academic world. By 1990 *postmodernism* had already become a familiar buzzword in most college literature and philosophy classes. Students resonated with this way of thinking about truth; their thoroughly modern parents were baffled by it.

By the late 1990s, young evangelicals began to discover postmodernism. Already more than a decade late to the party, they were determined not to be left behind. Coming from the age group then known as Generation X, these postmodernized youth were mostly products of a ministry style that had kept young people sequestered in the youth ministry, away from adults. They and their peers had learned to "do church" in settings where the focus was mostly on games and activities. Their music was a whole generation newer than the supposedly contemporary stylings their parents favored. They sported fashions that were even more cutting edge than the slickest seeker-sensitive church would ever think to feature. And the attitudes of youth and youth leader alike were shaped to fit the postmodern style: deeply cynical.

The main problem for those young people was that their parents' churches were indeed pathologically shallow and worldly. The students had grown up being entertained far more than they were spiritually fed. When they began to move out of the youth group into the adult world, they were turned off by churches that simply could not keep up with changing styles. In reality, even the trendiest seeker-sensitive churches were still wedded to the tastes and convictions of a modern, not a postmodern, generation.

That is what inevitably happens when churches abandon biblical ministry in favor of worldly trends. "He who marries the spirit of the age soon finds himself a widower." I don't know who first coined that saying, but it perfectly describes what has happened again and again to churches and denominations that chase fads. By the early 1990s, most mainstream evangelicals had completely bought into the idea that stylishness is paramount. But they were finding it extremely hard to keep up with the times. Even the most culturally obsessed churches were still trying to come to grips with the fads and worldly values of the 80s (or earlier). That became a major source of embarrassment and frustration to young evangelicals who had been taught that cultural relevance was everything. They understood better than their parents did how the world was changing, and they could see very clearly that the church was not keeping in step.

Since their parents' own example had *taught* them to embrace worldly trends and to leverage pop culture for church growth, they followed the same pragmatic pattern, with even more zeal than their parents had shown. Their concept of "relevance" was just as superficial and culture-bound as their parents' had been. But the culture they were determined to blend with their religion was worse by magnitudes, because it was hostile to the very ideas of truth and assurance. Of course, the experts and strategists who had originally championed market-driven strategies nevertheless continued to feed and encourage the pragmatism.

All those developments were already discernible in the early 1990s, and that is precisely what prompted me to write this book in the first place. Evangelicalism's growing superficiality, a spiraling loss of confidence in the power of Scripture, the relentless pursuit of worldly fads, and a steady drift away from historic evangelical convictions were already widespread and serious problems. Those trends were all driven by evangelicals' obsession with pleasing the world. It was obvious (to anyone with eyes to see) that the market-driven approach to evangelism and church growth was headed for disaster.

The discovery of postmodernism by Gen-Xers in seeker-sensitive youth groups culminated in precisely the kind of disaster this book foretold. It was a recipe for the perfect apostasy: thousands of young people had been indoctrinated with pragmatism as a way of life, raised with the idea that worship must be tailored to please "Unchurched Harry" in order to be relevant, and taught to regard truth as unattainable. Now they were embracing all those errors at once and attempting to blend them all into A New Kind of Christianity.

The earliest conscientiously postmodern evangelicals soon found one another and formed a network. Zondervan signed some of the network's most provocative voices as authors and started an imprint specifically for their books. The result was the Emerging Church movement. Prominent figures in the movement soon discarded the terms *church* and *movement* and began referring to themselves as participants in "the Emerging Conversation." It was a typically postmodern, Internet-era "conversation"—sound bites without substance, passions devoid of principle, and zeal without knowledge. It was a movement full of sound and fury, signifying nothing.

Emerging mainly from the shallow end of the evangelical movement, the new post-evangelical subculture simply lacked any solid doctrinal moorings. It's hard to think of a tenet of historic Christianity that has not been questioned or openly attacked by people who are currently leading the Conversation. That goes for truths as basic as the doctrine of the Trinity, as important as the authority of Scripture, and as precious as the doctrine of substitutionary atonement.

Predictably, the Emerging movement fragmented within its first decade.

The most prolific authors and leading figures in the network seemed to take their ideas and arguments straight from the original modernist playbook—despite all their talk about being *post*modern. A handful of early participants who were theological conservatives recognized the dangers of such neo-liberal theology and eventually repudiated the movement completely. Several of the moderates in the original Emerging network still seem to be trying to work out where to go from here.

All those developments have followed the very same pattern of doctrinal and spiritual erosion that Charles Spurgeon described more than a hundred years ago and labeled "the Down-Grade." It is the same broad path to destruction I warned about in this book's first edition. The church still desperately needs to hear and heed the same plea. (Perhaps today more than ever.) That fact alone explodes the typical evangelical notion about what makes a message "relevant."

I've altered as little as possible of the original work, merely cleaning up a sentence here and there. I decided to leave as many of the anecdotes, illustrations, and citations intact as possible, even though some of them might at first glance seem somewhat dated. All of them could easily have been replaced and perhaps amplified with more recent examples. But one of the main reasons for reissuing this book was to underscore the fact that its message is not out-of-date. It has *never* been out-of-date. There's a clear line of philosophical continuity that ties the modernists of Spurgeon's era to the champions of seeker-sensitivity in the twentieth century and the scions of postmodernity in the current generation. As Spurgeon and his colleagues pointed out in the articles that launched the Down-Grade Controversy, the patterns of such thinking extend *backward* in history, too. In one way or another, the same underlying doctrinal paradigm and pragmatic rationale has greased the slide for every season of apostasy the church has ever known.

With that in mind, I've tried to let what I originally wrote speak for itself, commenting via the footnotes when I wanted to expand on a point or explain something in more detail than I did the first time around.

I've also added two new chapters (11 and 12) and an additional appendix consisting of material quoted from Spurgeon's sermons and writings. In the original edition, Chapter 10 was titled "Epilogue." I've changed that to "Interlude" because the chapter (which was brief anyway) now ties the content of the original book to the new chapters. The new appendix seemed to fit best between the first and second appendixes of the first edition, so I put it there and renumbered the remaining appendixes.

PREFACE TO THE 1993 EDITION

Everywhere there is apathy. Nobody cares whether that which is preached is true or false. A sermon is a sermon whatever the subject; only, the shorter it is the better.

CHARLES HADDON SPURGEON[1]

Those words from Spurgeon were written in 1888. He might have been describing the state of evangelicalism at the start of the twenty-first century.

In 1992—exactly a hundred years after the great preacher's death—I stood by his tomb in London—a heavy stone vault, nondescript and blended into the cemetery between a road and a large building. If I hadn't had someone to lead me there, I would not have found it. Spurgeon's and his wife's names are engraved in stone, but there is no information on the tomb itself about who he was. The average sightseer might miss the stone vault (there are larger, more impressive ones all around), or on seeing it, not realize it is the burial place of a man who in his time was perhaps more well-known and more influential than England's Prime Minister.

As I stood by Spurgeon's grave, I couldn't help thinking how much the church needs men like him today. Spurgeon was not afraid to stand boldly for the truth, even when it meant he stood alone. Preaching the Word of God was his sole passion. He believed the church's tolerance of preaching was beginning to decline, while some ministers were experimenting with alternative approaches and abbreviated messages. He saw in that a great danger, and his concern thrust him into a battle that ultimately led to his death. He had been placed in that grave one hundred years—almost to the day—before my visit.

Contrast Spurgeon's attitude toward preaching with the prevailing opinion of our day. In fact, Spurgeon's lament is diametrically opposite the per-

---

[1] "Preface," *The Sword and the Trowel* (1888 complete volume), iii.

spective expressed in a column I read a few years ago in a popular Christian magazine. A well-known preacher was venting his own *loathing* for long sermons. January 1 was coming, so he resolved to do better in the coming year. "That means wasting less time listening to long sermons and spending much more time preparing short ones," he wrote. "People, I've discovered, will forgive even poor theology as long as they get out before noon."[2]

Unfortunately, that perfectly sums up the predominant attitude behind much of contemporary ministry. Bad doctrine is tolerable; a long sermon most certainly is not. The timing of the benediction is of far more concern to the average churchgoer than the content of the sermon. Sunday dinner and the feeding of our mouths takes precedence over Sunday school and the nourishment of our souls. Long-windedness has become a greater sin than heresy.

The church has imbibed the worldly philosophy of pragmatism, and we're just beginning to taste the bitter results.

WHAT IS PRAGMATISM?

Pragmatism is the notion that meaning or worth is determined by practical consequences. It is closely akin to *utilitarianism*, the belief that usefulness is the standard of what is good. To a pragmatist/utilitarian, if a technique or course of action has the desired effect, it is good. If it doesn't seem to work, it must be wrong.

Pragmatism as a philosophy was developed and popularized at the end of the last century by philosopher and psychologist William James, along with other noted intellectuals such as John Dewey and George Santayana. It was James who gave the new philosophy its name and shape. In 1907, he published a collection of lectures entitled *Pragmatism: A New Name for Some Old Ways of Thinking*[3] and thus defined a whole new approach to truth and life.

Pragmatism has roots in Darwinism and secular humanism. It is inherently relativistic, rejecting the notion of absolute right and wrong, good and evil, truth and error. Pragmatism ultimately defines truth as that which is useful, meaningful, and helpful. Ideas that don't seem workable or relevant are rejected as false.

---

[2]Jamie Buckingham, "Wasted Time," *Charisma* (December 1988), 98.
[3](New York: Longmans, Green, & Co, 1907). From the start, James stressed the implications of pragmatism for matters of faith. The final chapter of his book was titled "Pragmatism and Religion." In it, he essentially acknowledged that faith and pragmatism are contradictory values. "On pragmatic principles we cannot reject any hypothesis if consequences useful to life flow from it" (273). Pragmatism, to James's way of thinking, argues decisively for pluralism in religion (276–278). Modern and postmodern pragmatists, even in evangelical circles, have moved steadily toward that same conclusion.

What's wrong with pragmatism? After all, common sense involves a measure of legitimate pragmatism, doesn't it? If a dripping faucet works fine after you replace the washers, it is reasonable to assume that bad washers were the problem. If the medicine your doctor prescribes produces harmful side effects or has no effect at all, you need to ask if there's a remedy that works. Such simple pragmatic realities are generally self-evident.

But when pragmatism is used to make judgments about right and wrong, or when it becomes a guiding philosophy of life, theology, or ministry, it inevitably clashes with Scripture. Spiritual and biblical truth is not determined by testing what "works" and what doesn't. We know from Scripture, for example, that the gospel often does not produce a positive response (1 Cor. 1:22–23; 2:14). On the other hand, Satanic lies and deception can be quite effective (Matt. 24:23–24; 2 Cor. 4:3–4). Majority reaction is no test of validity (cf. Matt. 7:13–14), and prosperity is no measure of truthfulness (cf. Job 12:6). Pragmatism as a guiding philosophy of ministry is inherently flawed. Pragmatism as a test of truth is nothing short of satanic.

Nevertheless, an overpowering surge of ardent pragmatism is sweeping through evangelicalism. Traditional methodology—most notably preaching—is being discarded or downplayed in favor of newer means, such as drama, music, dance, comedy, variety, side-show histrionics, pop psychology, and other entertainment forms. The new methods supposedly are more "effective"—that is, they draw a bigger crowd. And since the chief criterion for gauging the success of a church has become attendance figures, whatever pulls in the most people is accepted without further analysis as *good*. That is pragmatism.

Perhaps the most visible signs of pragmatism are seen in the convulsive changes that have revolutionized the church worship service in the past decade. Some of evangelicalism's largest and most influential churches now boast Sunday services that are deliberately designed to be rollicking rather than reverent.

Even worse, *theology* now takes a back seat to *methodology*. One author has written, "Formerly, a doctrinal statement represented the reason for a denomination's existence. Today, methodology is the glue that holds churches together. A statement of ministry defines them and their denominational existence."[4] Incredibly, many believe this is a positive trend, a major advance for the contemporary church.

Some church leaders evidently think the four priorities of the early

---

[4]Elmer L. Towns, *An Inside Look at 10 of Today's Most Innovative Churches* (Ventura, CA: Regal, 1990), 249.

church—the apostles' teaching, fellowship, the breaking of bread, and prayer (Acts 2:42)—make a lame agenda for the church in this day and age. Churches are allowing drama, recreation, entertainment, self-help programs, sex-education seminars, and similar enterprises to eclipse the importance of God-centered, Bible-based Sunday worship and fellowship. In fact, everything seems to be in fashion in the church today *except* biblical preaching. The new pragmatism sees preaching—particularly expository preaching—as passé. Plainly declaring the truth of God's Word is regarded as unsophisticated, offensive, and utterly ineffective. We're now told we can get better results by first amusing people, giving them pop psychology or impressing them with a high-tech, special-effects smoke-and-light show—thus wooing them into the fold. Once they know we are cool and feel they are comfortable, they'll be ready to receive biblical truth in small, diluted doses.

Pastors have drawn their ministry philosophies from books on marketing methods. Many young ministers devour such resources in search of new techniques to help their churches grow. Major seminaries have shifted their pastoral training emphasis from Bible curriculum and theology to counseling technique and church-growth theory. All these trends reflect the church's growing commitment to pragmatism.

Martyn Lloyd-Jones saw this coming and responded to it a generation ago. He pointed out that the ideas driving these trends are not really innovative at all. It's been done before, always with disastrous results:

> These proposals that we should preach less, and do various other things more, are of course not new at all. People seem to think that all this is quite new, and that it is the hallmark of modernity to decry or to depreciate preaching, and to put your emphasis on these other things. The simple answer to that is that there is nothing new about it. The actual form may be new, but the principle is certainly not a new one at all; indeed it has been the particular emphasis of this present century.[5]

IS PRAGMATISM REALLY A SERIOUS THREAT?

I am convinced that pragmatism poses precisely the same subtle threat to the church in our age that modernism represented nearly a century ago. Modernism was a movement that embraced higher criticism[6] and liberal theology while denying nearly all the supernatural aspects of Christianity. Modernists gained ground early and easily among evangelicals by decrying the importance of doctrine (which was deemed divisive and unnecessarily

[5]*Preaching and Preachers* (Grand Rapids, MI: Zondervan, 1971), 33.
[6]An approach to Scripture that discards all faith that the Bible is God's Word.

pedantic) while championing the importance of charity and good works. Truths as vital to Christianity as the deity of Christ and bodily resurrection were declared relatively unimportant—treated as secondary, optional articles of faith—compared to the duties of loving one's neighbor and performing good works.

Of course, it is not necessary (or even possible) to denigrate sound doctrine in order to embody Christ's love. But in those Victorian times, the dominant forces in secular society had made an artificial brand of "politeness" into an idol. Christians steeped in that culture's false standards of virtue had imbibed the notion that there was something inherently uncharitable and unseemly about polemical dialogues over doctrinal differences. In such a climate, the modernists' plea seemed very persuasive.

So modernism did not first surface as an overt attack on orthodox doctrine. The earliest modernists seemed concerned primarily with interdenominational unity. They merely wanted to *downplay* doctrine for the sake of harmony. They uncritically accepted the notion that doctrine is inherently divisive. And they were fearful that a fragmented church would become irrelevant in the modern age.

They did not grasp that the only thing even remotely relevant about the church is the gospel message we are commissioned to proclaim. The modernists had already given up their confidence in the power of the gospel, the importance of sound doctrine, and the authority of God's Word. Therefore, in a misguided effort to enhance the church's "relevance," modernists sought to synthesize Christian teachings with the latest insights from science, philosophy, and literary criticism.

That is how modernism began as a methodology but soon evolved into a unique theology.

Bear in mind that modernists viewed doctrine itself as a secondary issue. The brotherhood and good works that grow out of Christian charity were the only truly primary things; everything else was negotiable. *Especially* doctrine. They believed doctrine must be considered fluid and adaptable—certainly not something worth fighting for. In 1935 John Murray gave this assessment of the typical modernist:

> The modernist very often prides himself on the supposition that he is concerned with life, with the principles of conduct and the making operative of the principles of Jesus in all departments of life, individual, social, ecclesiastical, industrial, and political. His slogan has been that Christianity is life, not doctrine, and he thinks that the orthodox

Christian or fundamentalist, as he likes to name him, is concerned simply with the conservation and perpetuation of outworn dogmas of doctrinal belief, a concern which makes orthodoxy in his esteem a cold and lifeless petrification of Christianity.[7]

When harbingers of modernism began to appear in the late 1800s, few Christians were troubled. The most heated controversies in those days were relatively small backlashes against men like Charles Spurgeon—men who were trying to warn the church about the threat. Most Christians—particularly church leaders—were completely unreceptive to such warnings. Spurgeon in particular was accused of overreacting, and his motives were impugned. After all, it wasn't as if *outsiders* were imposing new teachings on the church; these were people from within the denominations—and scholars at that. Certainly they had no agenda to undermine the core of orthodox theology or attack the heart of Christianity itself. Divisiveness and schism seemed far greater dangers than apostasy.

But however benign the modernists' intentions may have seemed at the very first, their ideas *did* represent a grave threat to orthodoxy, as history has amply proved. The movement spawned teachings that decimated practically all the mainline denominations in the first half of the twentieth century. By downplaying the importance of doctrine, modernism opened the door to theological liberalism, moral relativism, and rank unbelief. Most evangelicals today tend to equate the word *modernism* with full-scale denial of the faith. It is often forgotten that the aim of the early modernists was simply to make the church more "modern," more unified, more relevant, and more acceptable to a skeptical modern age.

Just like the pragmatists today.

Like the church of a hundred years ago, we live in a world of rapid changes—major advances in science, technology, world politics, and education. Like the brethren of that generation, Christians today are open, even eager, for change in the church. Like them, we yearn for unity among the faithful. And like them, we are sensitive to the hostility of an unbelieving world.

Unfortunately, there is at least one other parallel between the church today and the church in the late nineteenth century: many Christians seem completely unaware—if not unwilling to see—that serious dangers threaten the church from within. Yet if church history teaches us anything, it teaches

---

[7]"The Sanctity of the Moral Law," *Collected Writings of John Murray*, 4 vols. (Edinburgh: Banner of Truth, 1976), 1:193.

us that the most devastating assaults on the faith have always begun as subtle errors arising from within.

Living in an unstable age, the church cannot afford to be vacillating. We minister to people desperate for answers, and we cannot soft-pedal the truth or extenuate the gospel. If we make friends with the world, we set ourselves at enmity with God. If we trust worldly devices, we automatically relinquish the power of the Holy Spirit.

These truths are repeatedly affirmed in Scripture: "Do you not know that friendship with the world is enmity with God? Therefore whoever wishes to be a friend of the world makes himself an enemy of God" (Jas. 4:4). "Do not love the world or the things in the world. If anyone loves the world, the love of the Father is not in him" (1 John 2:15).

"The king is not saved by his great army; a warrior is not delivered by his great strength. The war horse is a false hope for salvation, and by its great might it cannot rescue" (Ps. 33:16–17). "Woe to those who go down to Egypt for help and rely on horses, who trust in chariots because they are many and in horsemen because they are very strong, but do not look to the Holy One of Israel or consult the LORD!" (Isa. 31:1). "Not by might, nor by power, but by my Spirit, says the LORD of hosts" (Zech. 4:6).

The whole point about Israel's being a light to the world (Isa. 42:6; 49:6) is that they were supposed to be *different*. They were explicitly forbidden to imitate the Gentiles' manner of dress, grooming, foods, religion, and other aspects of the culture. God told them, "You shall not do as they do in the land of Egypt, where you lived, and you shall not do as they do in the land of Canaan, to which I am bringing you. You shall not walk in their statutes" (Lev. 18:3). And as Martyn Lloyd-Jones pointed out, "Our Lord attracted sinners because He was different. They drew near to Him because they felt that there was something different about Him. . . . And the world always expects us to be different. This idea that you are going to win people to the Christian faith by showing them that after all you are remarkably like them, is theologically and psychologically a profound blunder."[8]

IS WORLDLINESS STILL A SIN?

Worldliness is rarely even mentioned today, much less identified for what it is. The word itself is beginning to sound quaint. Worldliness is the sin of allowing one's appetites, ambitions, or conduct to be fash-

---

[8]Lloyd-Jones, *Preaching and Preachers*, 140.

ioned according to earthly values. "All that is in the world—the desires of the flesh and the desires of the eyes and pride in possessions—is not from the Father but is from the world. And the world is passing away along with its desires, but whoever does the will of God abides forever" (1 John 2:16–17).

Yet today we have the extraordinary spectacle of church programs deliberately designed to cater to fleshly desire, sensual appetites, and human pride—"the desires of the flesh and the desires of the eyes and pride in possessions." To achieve this worldly appeal, church activities often go beyond the merely frivolous. For several years a colleague of mine has been collecting a "horror file" of clippings that report how churches are employing innovations to keep worship services from becoming dull. Since the late 1970s, some of America's largest evangelical churches have been employing worldly gimmicks like slapstick, vaudeville, wrestling exhibitions, and even mock striptease to spice up their Sunday meetings. No brand of horseplay, it seems, is too outrageous to be brought into the sanctuary. Burlesque has become the liturgy of the pragmatic church.

Moreover, many in the church believe this is the *only* way we will ever reach the world. We're told that if the unchurched multitudes don't want classic hymns, serious doctrine, and biblical preaching, we must give them what they want. Hundreds of churches have followed precisely that theory, actually surveying unbelievers to learn what it would take to get them to attend.

Acceptability in the culture and increased church attendance have subtly but steadily usurped holiness and true worship as the primary objectives of our church gatherings. Preaching the Word and boldly confronting sin are seen as archaic, ineffectual means of winning the world. After all, those things actually drive most people away. Why not entice people into the fold by offering what they want, creating a friendly, comfortable environment, and catering to the very desires that drive their strongest urges? As if we might get unconverted worldlings to accept Jesus by somehow making Him more likable or making His message less offensive.

That kind of thinking badly skews the mission of the church. The Great Commission is not a marketing manifesto. True evangelism does not require salesmen but prophets. It is the Word of God, not any earthly enticement, that plants the seed for the new birth (1 Pet. 1:23). We gain nothing but God's displeasure if we seek to remove the offense of the cross (cf. Gal. 5:11).

IS ALL INNOVATION WRONG?

Please do not misunderstand my concern. It is not innovation per se that I oppose. I recognize that styles of worship are always in flux. I also realize that if the typical seventeenth-century Puritan walked into Grace Community Church (where I am pastor) he might be shocked by our music, probably dismayed to see men and women seated together, and quite possibly disturbed that we use a public address system. Spurgeon himself would not appreciate our organ.

I am not in favor of a stagnant church. And I am not bound to any particular musical or liturgical style. Those things in and of themselves are not issues Scripture even addresses. Nor do I think my own personal preferences in such matters are necessarily superior to the tastes of others. I have no desire to manufacture some arbitrary rules that govern what is acceptable or not in church services. To do so would be the essence of legalism.

My complaint is with a philosophy that relegates God and His Word to a subordinate role in the church. I believe it is unbiblical to elevate entertainment over preaching and to put public relations ahead of worship in our church services. And I stand in opposition to those who believe salesmanship can bring people into the kingdom more effectively than a sovereign God. That philosophy has opened the door wide for worldliness to infiltrate the church.

"I am not ashamed of the gospel," the apostle Paul wrote (Rom. 1:16). Unfortunately, "ashamed of the gospel" seems more and more apt as a description of some of the most visible and influential churches of our age.

I see many striking parallels between what is happening in the church today and what happened more than a hundred years ago. The more I read about that era, the more my conviction is reinforced that we are seeing history repeat itself. Throughout this book, I will highlight features of late nineteenth-century evangelicalism that correspond to contemporary issues. I will particularly focus on an episode from the life of Spurgeon that has come to be known as "The Down-Grade Controversy." And I will quote frequently from Spurgeon's writings on these matters.

I share at least two things in common with Charles Spurgeon: Both of us were born on June 19, and like me, he pastored one congregation for virtually all of his ministry. The more I read of his writing and preaching, the more I sense a kindred spirit.

By no means, however, do I view myself as Spurgeon's equal. Surely no preacher in the history of the English language has had Spurgeon's facility with words, his ability to convey the authority of the divine message, his passion for truth, or his grasp of preaching combined with such knowledge of theology. He was also a churchman par excellence, innately gifted as a leader. Pastoring in troubled times, Spurgeon filled his 5,500-seat auditorium several times a week. His own flock's esteem for him remained undiminished until his death. I sit at his feet, not by his side.

Furthermore, I do not desire to ignite the kind of altercation Spurgeon touched off in the Down-Grade Controversy. Spurgeon himself blamed the conflict for his death. Departing for a rest on the French Riviera in 1891, he told friends, "The fight is killing me."[9] Three months later word came back from France that Spurgeon was dead. He had not sought a fight. But refusing to compromise his biblical convictions, he could not avoid the controversy that ensued.

In all candor, controversy is immensely distasteful to me. Those who know me personally will affirm that I do not enjoy any kind of dispute. Yet there is a fire in my bones that constrains me to speak plainly regarding my biblical convictions. I cannot keep silent when so much is at stake.

It is in that spirit that I offer this book. I hope no one will perceive it as an attack on any person or ministry in particular. It is not. It is a plea to the whole church regarding matters of principle, not personalities. And while I expect there will be widespread disagreement with much of what I say, I have tried to write without being disagreeable.

These are issues about which many people have deep convictions. When such matters are broached—particularly when contrary opinions are stated forthrightly—people sometimes become angry. I do not write in anger, and I would ask readers to receive what I write with the spirit in which it is offered.

My prayer is that this book will challenge your thinking in a way that will drive you to the Scriptures "to see if these things [are] so" (cf. Acts 17:11). And I pray that the Lord will deliver His church from the same kind of downhill slide into worldliness and unbelief that devoured the church and exhausted her spiritual stamina exactly a hundred years ago.

---

[9]Iain Murray, *The Forgotten Spurgeon* (Edinburgh: Banner of Truth, 1966), 163.

1

CHRISTIANITY ON THE DOWN-GRADE

Doth that man love his Lord who would be willing to see Jesus wearing a crown of thorns, while for himself he craves a chaplet of laurel? Shall Jesus ascend to his throne by the cross, and do we expect to be carried there on the shoulders of applauding crowds? Be not so vain in your imagination. Count you the cost, and if you are not willing to bear Christ's cross, go away to your farm and to your merchandise, and make the most of them; only let me whisper this in your ear, "What shall it profit a man if he gain the whole world and lose his own soul?"

CHARLES HADDON SPURGEON[1]

If you're familiar with the life of Charles Haddon Spurgeon, you have probably heard of "the Down-Grade Controversy." Spurgeon spent the final four years of his life at war against the trends of early modernism, which he rightly saw as a threat to biblical Christianity.

The name by which history remembers the controversy comes from the title of a series of articles Spurgeon published in his monthly magazine, *The Sword and the Trowel*. (See Appendix 1 for an overview of the "Down-Grade" articles and a fuller account of the ensuing controversy.) Spurgeon wanted to admonish his flock about the dangers of moving away from the historic positions of biblical Christianity. Biblical truth is like the pinnacle of a steep, slippery mountain, Spurgeon suggested. One step away, and you find yourself on the down-grade. Once a church or individual Christian starts moving down the precipitous incline, Spurgeon said, momentum

---

[1] "Holding Fast the Faith," *The Metropolitan Tabernacle Pulpit*, Vol. 34 (London: Passmore and Alabaster, 1888), 78. This sermon was preached February 5, 1888, at the outset of the Down-Grade Controversy, just after Spurgeon's censure by the Baptist Union (see Appendix 1).

takes over. Recovery is unusual and occurs only when Christians get on the "Up-line" through spiritual revival.

In the controversy that transpired, Spurgeon resigned from the Baptist Union. Later he was the subject of an official censure by the Union. Within a few years the Baptist Union was hopelessly lost to the new theology and Spurgeon was dead. In 1900, Spurgeon's wife, Susannah, wrote,

> So far as the Baptist Union was concerned, little was accomplished by Mr. Spurgeon's witness-bearing and withdrawal. . . . But, in other respects, I have had abundant proofs that the protest was not in vain. Many, who were far gone on the 'Down-grade,' were stopped in their perilous descent, and, by God's grace, were brought back to the 'Up-line'; others, who were unconsciously slipping, were made to stand firmly on the Rock; while, at least for a time, in all the churches, Evangelical doctrines were preached with a clearness and emphasis which had long been lacking.[2]

She believed the Lord would ultimately make clear how right her husband had been in his "protest against false doctrine and worldliness."[3]

To this day, church historians debate whether Spurgeon was right to withdraw from the Union. Many believe he should have stayed and fought to keep it orthodox. He considered that option but concluded it would have been futile. I am inclined to believe Spurgeon was right to withdraw. But whether we agree with his course of action or not, we have no choice but to acknowledge that history *has* vindicated Spurgeon's warnings about the deadly dangers of the down-grade. In the early part of the twentieth century, the spreading "false doctrine and worldliness"—theological liberalism and modernism—ravaged denominational Christianity. Most of the mainline denominations were violently if not fatally altered by these influences. The result in Spurgeon's own England was particularly devastating. A hundred years after Spurgeon sounded the alarm, most theological education in England is rank liberal. Church attendance is a small fraction of what it was then. Evangelicals are a tiny minority, true biblical preaching is uncommon even in supposedly Bible-believing churches, and the evangelical movement has been dangerously susceptible to almost every theological fad exported from America. In short, evangelicalism in England never recovered from the modernist/liberal assault that began a century ago.

A hundred years later, history is repeating itself. The church has

---

[2]*The Autobiography of Charles H. Spurgeon*, 4 vols. (London: Passmore and Alabaster, 1897), 4:255.
[3]Ibid., 4:257.

become worldly—and not just worldly, but studiously so. Winds of doctrinal compromise are beginning to stir.

"False doctrine and worldliness"—the same two influences Spurgeon attacked—*always* go hand in hand, with worldliness leading the way. Christians today tend to forget that modernism did not come on the scene with a theological agenda but a methodological one. Early modernists were not trying to hit at the core of biblical faith; they were simply trying to make Christianity more palatable to a cynical world.

The same spirit is abroad in the church today. I am convinced that most of those behind it would not deliberately undermine biblical Christianity. Nevertheless, they have introduced into the church a philosophy of pragmatism and a spirit of worldliness that if left unchecked will eventually reap the same bitter harvest as the modernism of a hundred years ago.

MARKET-DRIVEN MINISTRY?

The new philosophy is straightforward: The church is in competition against the world, and the world is very good at capturing people's attention and affections. The church, on the other hand, tends to be very poor at "selling" its product. Evangelism should therefore be viewed as a marketing challenge, and the church should market the gospel in the same way all modern businesses sell their products. That calls for some fundamental changes. The goal in all marketing is "to make both the producer and consumer satisfied."[4] So anything that tends to leave the "consumer" unsatisfied must be jettisoned. Preaching—particularly preaching about sin, righteousness, and judgment—is too confrontive to be truly satisfying. The church must learn to couch the truth in ways that amuse and entertain.

One best-selling author has written, "I believe that developing a marketing orientation is precisely what the Church needs to do if we are to make a difference in the spiritual health of this nation for the remainder of this century."[5] He adds, "My contention, based on careful study of data and the activities of American churches, is that the major problem plaguing the Church is its failure to embrace a marketing orientation in what has become a marketing-driven environment."[6]

That all may sound very modern, very shrewd—but it is not biblical. And it has given the church a hard push onto the slippery slope. Marketing principles have become the arbiter of the church's message and agenda.

---

[4]George Barna, *Marketing the Church* (Colorado Springs: NavPress, 1988), 41.
[5]Ibid., 13.
[6]Ibid., 23.

Whatever elements of the biblical message don't fit the promotional plan simply must be omitted. Marketing savvy demands that the offense of the cross must be downplayed. Salesmanship requires that negative subjects like divine wrath be avoided. Consumer satisfaction means that the standard of righteousness cannot be raised too high. The seeds of a watered-down gospel are thus sown in the very philosophy that drives many ministries today. And in some churches, the preaching of the gospel has been throttled completely.

Make no mistake: the new philosophy is profoundly altering the message the church conveys to the world, although many who propound these ideas think of themselves as loyal to biblical doctrine.

Evangelical Christianity is on the down-grade again.

TOWARD A BIBLICAL PHILOSOPHY OF MINISTRY

How does market-driven ministry compare with the biblical model? How do you think Timothy would have fared under Paul's tutelage if he had followed the advice of twentieth-century marketeers?

We have a thorough answer to that question from the two epistles Paul wrote to Timothy in the New Testament. Paul had personally mentored the young pastor, but Timothy encountered severe trials when he got into a pastorate of his own. He struggled with fear and human weakness. He was evidently tempted to soften his preaching in the face of persecution. At times he seemed ashamed of the gospel. Paul had to remind him to stand up for the faith with boldness, even if it meant suffering: "Do not be ashamed of the testimony about our Lord, nor of me his prisoner; but share in suffering for the gospel" (2 Tim. 1:8). The two rich epistles from Paul to Timothy outline a ministry philosophy that challenges the prevailing wisdom of today.

Paul instructed Timothy that he must:
• Correct those teaching false doctrine and call them to a pure heart, a good conscience, and a sincere faith (1 Tim. 1:3–5).
• Fight for divine truth and for God's purposes, keeping his own faith and a good conscience (1:18–19).
• Pray for the lost and lead the men of the church to do the same (2:1–8).
• Call women in the church to fulfill their God-given role of submission and to raise up godly children, setting an example of faith, love, and sanctity with self-restraint (2:9–15).
• Carefully select spiritual leaders for the church on the basis of their giftedness, godliness, and virtue (3:1–13).

• Recognize the source of error and those who teach it, and point these things out to the brethren (4:1–6).
• Constantly be nourished on the words of Scripture and its sound teaching, avoiding all myths and false doctrines (4:6).
• Discipline himself for the purpose of godliness (4:7–11).
• Boldly command and teach the truth of God's Word (4:11).
• Be a model of spiritual virtue that all can follow (4:12).
• Faithfully read, explain, and apply the Scriptures publicly (4:13–14).
• Be progressing toward Christlikeness in his own life (4:15–16).
• Be gracious and gentle in confronting the sin of his people (5:1–2).
• Give special consideration and care to those who are widows (5:3–16).
• Honor faithful pastors who work hard (5:17–21).
• Choose church leaders with great care, seeing to it that they are both mature and proven (5:22).
• Take care of his physical condition so he is strong to serve (5:23).
• Teach and preach principles of true godliness, helping his people discern between true godliness and mere hypocrisy (5:24—6:6).
• Flee the love of money (6:7–11).
• Pursue righteousness, godliness, faith, love, steadfastness, and gentleness (6:11).
• Fight for the faith against all enemies and all attacks (6:12).
• Keep all the Lord's commandments (6:13–16).
• Instruct the rich to do good, to be rich in good works, and to be generous (6:17–19).
• Guard the Word of God as a sacred trust and a treasure (6:20–21).

In his second epistle, Paul reminded Timothy that the pastor's duty is to:

• Keep the gift of God in him fresh and useful (2 Tim. 1:6).
• Not be timid but powerful (1:7).
• Never be ashamed of Christ or anyone who serves Christ (1:8–11).
• Hold tightly to the truth and guard it (1:12–14).
• Be strong in character (2:1).
• Be a teacher of apostolic truth so that he may reproduce himself in faithful men (2:2).
• Suffer difficulty and persecution willingly while making the maximum effort for Christ (2:3–7).
• Keep his eyes on Christ at all times (2:8–13).
• Lead with authority (2:14).
• Interpret and apply the Scripture accurately (2:15).
• Avoid useless conversation that leads only to ungodliness (2:16).
• Be an instrument of honor, set apart from sin and useful to the Lord (2:20–21).

- Flee youthful lusts and pursue righteousness, faith, love, and peace (2:22).
- Refuse to be drawn into philosophical and theological wrangling (2:23).
- Not be an arguer but kind, teachable, gentle, and patient even when he is wronged (2:24–26).
- Face dangerous times with a deep knowledge of the Word of God (3:1–17).
- Understand that Scripture is the basis and content of all legitimate ministry (3:16–17).
- Preach the Word—in season and out of season—reproving, rebuking, and exhorting with great patience and instruction (4:1–2).
- Be sober in all things (4:5).
- Endure hardship (4:5).
- Do the work of an evangelist (4:5).

Nothing in that list hints at a market-driven philosophy. In fact, some of those commands are impossible to harmonize with the theories that are so popular today. To sum it all up in five categories, Paul commanded Timothy 1) to be faithful in his preaching of biblical truth; 2) to be bold in exposing and refuting error; 3) to be an example of godliness to the flock; 4) to be diligent and work hard in the ministry; and 5) to be willing to suffer hardship and persecution in his service for the Lord.

Of course, the practical significance of this goes beyond those who are pastors. *Every* Christian is called to a life of ministry, and Paul's instructions to Timothy contain principles that apply to every believer in every form of ministry. When the church is on the down-grade, it means that multitudes of individuals are carried along on the spiritual decline. "False doctrine and worldliness" in the church infects every member of the body. Paul's instructions to Timothy are by no means meant only for the "elite" in Christian leadership or professional ministry. That is to say that ministry philosophy—and the issues we are addressing in this book—should be the concern of every Christian; these matters are by no means the exclusive domain of professional "clergy."

Recently I spent some time reading a dozen or so of the latest books on ministry and church growth. Most of those books had long sections devoted to defining a philosophy of ministry. *Not one* of them referred to the instructions Paul outlined so carefully for Timothy. In fact, none of them drew any element of their ministry philosophy from the New Testament pastoral epistles! Most drew principles from modern business, marketing techniques, management theory, psychology, and other similar sources. Some tried to *illustrate* their principles using biblical anecdotes. But not one of them drew their philosophy from Scripture—although much of the New Testament was explicitly written to instruct churches and pastors in these matters!

MINISTERING IN AN AGE OF ITCHING EARS

Unfortunately, the market-driven ministry philosophy appeals to the very worst mood of our age. It caters to people whose first love is themselves and who care not for God—unless they can have Him without disrupting their selfish lifestyles. Promise such people a religion that will allow them to be comfortable in their materialism and self-love, and they will respond in droves.

Paul foresaw such a time. Near the end of his second epistle to Timothy, after outlining the principles we have listed above, Paul abridged his advice to Timothy in this well-known verse: "preach the word; be ready in season and out of season; reprove, rebuke, and exhort, with complete patience and teaching" (2 Tim. 4:2). Then the apostle added this prophetic warning: "For the time is coming when people will not endure sound teaching, but having itching ears they will accumulate for themselves teachers to suit their own passions, and will turn away from listening to the truth and wander off into myths" (4:3–4). The King James Version translates the passage like this: "After their own lusts shall they heap to themselves teachers, having itching ears; and they shall turn away their ears from the truth."

Clearly there was no room in Paul's philosophy of ministry for the give-people-what-they-want theory that is so prevalent today. He did not urge Timothy to conduct a survey to find out what his people wanted. He did not suggest that he study demographic data or do research on the "felt needs" of his people. Paul would not have approved in any way if Timothy had catered to the demands of his audience. On the contrary, Paul commanded his protégé to preach the Word—faithfully, reprovingly, patiently—and confront the spirit of the age head-on.

HOW DO WE DEFINE SUCCESS?

Notice that Paul said nothing to Timothy about how people might respond. He did not lecture Timothy on how large his church was, how much money it took in, or how influential it was. He did not suggest that the world was supposed to revere, esteem, or even accept Timothy. In fact, Paul said nothing whatsoever about external success. Paul's emphasis was on *commitment*, not success.

Contemporary ministry philosophy is infatuated with worldly standards of success. The churches most often judged "successful" are the large, rich, megachurches with multimillion-dollar facilities, spas, handball courts, day-care centers, special-effects systems, and so on. But not one church in a thousand falls into that category. That means one of two things: most churches are pitiful failures, or the gauge of success in ministry must be something besides material prosperity.

The answer is obvious to anyone who knows Scripture. External criteria such as affluence, numbers, money, or positive response have never been the biblical measure of success in ministry. Faithfulness, godliness, and spiritual commitment are the virtues God esteems—and such qualities should be the building blocks of any ministry philosophy. That is true in both small and large churches. Size does not signify God's blessing. And popularity is no barometer of success. In fact, it can be a reason for condemnation. God told Jeremiah, "An appalling and horrible thing has happened in the land: the prophets prophesy falsely, and the priests rule at their direction; my people love to have it so" (Jer. 5:30–31).

Look again at Paul's instructions to Timothy. Instead of urging Timothy to devise a ministry that would garner accolades from the world, he warned him about suffering and hardship—hardly the stuff of modern church growth experts' aspirations! In Scripture big budgets, affluent members, and large membership rolls are *never* portrayed as valid goals. Paul was not telling Timothy how to be "successful"; he was not instructing him in techniques for increasing attendance figures; he was encouraging him to pursue the divine standard.

That, of course, is what defines true success. Real success is not getting results at any cost. It is not prosperity, power, prominence, popularity, or any of the other worldly notions of success. Real success is doing the will of God regardless of the consequences.

Or, using the terms as the world often employs them, the appropriate goal is not success but excellence.[7] Paul was encouraging Timothy to be all that God had called and gifted him to be. He was not advising Timothy to seek success; he was urging him to pursue excellence.

---

[7] A helpful contrast between *success* and *excellence* may be found in Jon Johnston, *Christian Excellence: Alternative to Success* (Grand Rapids, MI: Baker, 1985).

THE FOUNDATION OF AN EXCELLENT MINISTRY

Let's look a little more closely at these few verses from the beginning of 2 Timothy 4:

> I charge you in the presence of God and of Christ Jesus, who is to judge the living and the dead, and by his appearing and his kingdom: preach the word; be ready in season and out of season; reprove, rebuke, and exhort, with complete patience and teaching. For the time is coming when people will not endure sound teaching, but having itching ears they will accumulate for themselves teachers to suit their own passions, and will turn away from listening to the truth and wander off into myths. As for you, always be sober-minded, endure suffering, do the work of an evangelist, fulfill your ministry. (vv. 1–5)

That brief passage defines biblical ministry. It includes nine reminders from Paul to Timothy that no minister dare disregard. Those who are derelict in these duties are on the down-grade, whether they realize it or not.

Remember Your Calling

"I charge you in the presence of God and of Christ Jesus, who is to judge the living and the dead, and by his appearing and his kingdom"—thus Paul begins this final section of the last inspired epistle he ever wrote. He was near the end of his own life, anticipating his own execution. He knew he would stand before God to give an account. These thoughts were heavy on his mind. And so he reminded Timothy of the seriousness of the young pastor's own commission.

He counseled Timothy to live and work in light of impending judgment. Timothy needed to concern himself with what *God* thought of his ministry, not what *people* thought. Notice that Paul invoked "the *presence* of God and of Christ Jesus, who is to judge the living and the dead." He wanted Timothy to understand that the One who would judge him is the One in whose presence he was then ministering. God is our audience. God judges by His own criteria, not by what people think.

Elsewhere Paul says, "We will all stand before the judgment seat of God. . . . So then each one of us will give an account of himself to God" (Rom. 14:10, 12). That is the point he wants to make with Timothy. He is not ministering to please men, but to please God.

Preach the Word

What kind of ministry pleases God? "Preach the word" (v. 2). Obedience to that simple command *must* be the centerpiece of every truly biblical ministry philosophy. The preacher's task is to proclaim Scripture and give the sense of it (cf. Neh. 8:8). All other content is extraneous to the message.

My father was a pastor, and when I first told him that I felt God had called me to a life of ministry, he gave me a Bible in which he had written, "Dear Johnny, preach the Word. 2 Timothy 4:2." That simple statement became the compelling stimulus in my heart. I have never forgotten that simple biblical instruction from my dad—preach the Word. What else is there to preach?

Preaching the Word is not always easy. The message we are required to proclaim is often offensive. Christ Himself is a stone of stumbling and a rock of offense (Rom. 9:33; 1 Pet. 2:8). The message of the cross is a stumbling block to some (1 Cor. 1:23; Gal. 5:11), mere foolishness to others (1 Cor. 1:23). "The natural person does not accept the things of the Spirit of God, for they are folly to him, and he is not able to understand them because they are spiritually discerned" (1 Cor. 2:14). Why do you suppose Paul wrote, "I am not ashamed of the gospel" (Rom. 1:16)? Surely it is because so many Christians *are* ashamed of the very message we are commanded to proclaim.

As we have noted, Timothy evidently struggled with the sin of being ashamed. He was "ashamed of the testimony about our Lord," and even ashamed of Paul (2 Tim. 1:8). Timothy seems to have been a timid soul, not at all like the strong and courageous apostle Paul. He was young, and some people demeaned him because of that (1 Tim. 4:12). He knew full well that even being associated with Paul was dangerous. Publicly proclaiming God's truth could land him in prison with Paul. At the very least, he was sure to incur hostility and debates from Jews who were antagonistic to the gospel.

What is more, Timothy apparently struggled with the impulses of youthful lust (2 Tim. 2:22). He may have felt he was not all he should be.

Those were some compelling reasons for Timothy to silence his proclamation. So when Paul commanded him to preach, he was demanding that he go against his own natural inclinations and inhibitions.

What was the Word that Timothy was to preach? Paul had made this clear at the end of chapter 3: "*All Scripture* is breathed out by God and profitable for teaching, for reproof, for correction, and for training in righteousness" (2 Tim. 3:16, emphasis added). This is the Word to be preached: "the whole counsel of God" (Acts 20:27). In chapter 1 Paul had told Timothy, "Follow the pattern of the sound words that you have heard from me" (v. 13). He was speaking of the revealed words of Scripture—all of it. He urged Timothy to "Guard the good deposit entrusted to you" (v. 14). Then in chapter 2 he told him to study the Word and handle it accurately (v. 15). Now he is telling him to proclaim it. So the entire task of the faithful minister revolves around the Word of God—guarding it, studying it, and proclaiming it.

In Colossians 1 the apostle Paul, describing his own ministry philosophy, writes, "I became a minister according to the stewardship from God that was given to me for you, *to make the word of God fully known*" (v. 25, emphasis added). In 1 Corinthians he goes a step further: "And I, when I came to you, brothers, did not come proclaiming to you the testimony of God with lofty speech or wisdom. For I decided to know nothing among you except Jesus Christ and him crucified" (2:1–2). In other words, his goal as a preacher was not to entertain people with his rhetorical style or to amuse them with cleverness, humor, novel insights, or sophisticated methodology—he simply preached Christ crucified.

There have always been men in the pulpit who gather crowds because they are gifted orators, interesting storytellers, entertaining speakers, dynamic personalities, shrewd crowd-manipulators, rousing speech-makers, popular politicians, or erudite scholars. Such preaching may be *popular*, but it is not necessarily *powerful*. No one can preach with power who does not preach the Word. And no faithful preacher will water down or neglect the whole counsel of God. Proclaiming the Word—all of it—is the pastor's calling.

And so preaching the Word *must* be the very heart of our ministry philosophy. Any other philosophy replaces the voice of God with human wisdom. Philosophy, politics, humor, psychology, homespun advice, and human opinion can never accomplish what the Word of God does. Those things may be interesting, informative, entertaining, and sometimes even helpful—but they are not the business of the church. The preacher's task is not to be a conduit for human wisdom; he is God's voice to speak to the congregation. No human message comes with the stamp of divine authority—only the Word of God. I frankly do not understand preachers who are willing to abdicate this solemn privilege. Moral lectures and motivational talks are no substitute for God's Word. Why should we proclaim the wisdom of men when we have the privilege of preaching the Word of God?

Be Faithful in and out of Season

Paul next reminds Timothy that he is called to a never-ending task. Not only is he to preach the Word, he is to do it regardless of the climate of opinion around him. He is to be faithful when such preaching is tolerated—but also when it is not.

Let's face it—right now preaching the Word is out of season. Humanity is experiencing God's wrath as He gives people over to the consequences of sinful choices (Rom. 1:24, 26, 28), "the due penalty for their error" (v. 27). Society may be feeling this divine abandonment in our age more than ever before. And the decline of preaching in the church can actually contribute to people's sense of helplessness. Martyn Lloyd-Jones argued that "in many ways it is the departure of the Church from preaching that is responsible in a large measure for the state of modern society. . . . The Church, having abandoned her real task, has left humanity more or less to its own devices."[8]

This is certainly no time for weak men, weak messages, and weak ministries. What is needed is moral strength and courage and uncompromising proclamation of the truth that can set people free. "So far from saying that we must have less preaching and turn more and more to other devices and expedients, I say that we have a heaven-sent opportunity for preaching."[9]

The market-driven philosophy currently in vogue says that plainly declaring biblical truth is outmoded. Biblical exposition and theology are seen as antiquated and irrelevant. This philosophy is rooted in the belief that contemporary churchgoers will not tolerate being preached to. People today won't just sit in the pew while someone up front preaches. They are products of a media-driven culture, and they need a church experience that will satisfy them on their own terms. "Preaching is broken," we're told. And the subsequent rationale for abandoning preaching is more high-sounding, philosophical mumbo-jumbo about the church's need to give people what they demand: "The church has failed to take the cultural shifts of postmodernity seriously. In today's culture . . . people are increasingly distrustful of authority figures, especially preachers, with overarching explanations of how the world works."[10]

But Paul says the excellent minister must be faithful to preach the Word even when it is not in fashion. The expression he uses is "be ready." The Greek term (*ephistēmi*) literally means "to stand beside." It has the idea of

---

[8]Martyn Lloyd-Jones, *Preaching and Preachers* (Grand Rapids, MI: Zondervan, 1971), 35.
[9]Ibid., 42.
[10]Tom Allen, "Younger Pastors Ask: Is Preaching out of Touch?" Associated Baptist Press release, February 20, 2004.

eagerness. It was often used to describe a military guard, always at his post, prepared for duty. Paul was speaking of an explosive eagerness to preach, like that of Jeremiah, who said that the Word of God was a fire in his bones. That's what he was demanding of Timothy. Not reluctance but readiness. Not hesitation but fearlessness. Not cool talk but the Word of God.

Reprove, Rebuke, and Exhort

Paul also gives Timothy instructions about the *tone* of his preaching. He uses two words that carry negative connotations and one that is positive: reprove, rebuke, and exhort (2 Tim. 4:2). All valid ministry must have a balance of positive *and* negative. The preacher who fails to reprove and rebuke is not fulfilling his commission.

I recently listened to a radio interview with a preacher well-known for his emphasis on positive thinking. This man had stated in print that he assiduously avoids any mention of sin in his preaching because he feels people are burdened with too much guilt anyway. The interviewer asked how he could justify such a policy. The pastor replied that he had made the decision early in his ministry to focus on meeting people's *needs*, not attacking their *sin*.

But people's deepest need is to confess and overcome their sin. So preaching that fails to confront and correct sin through the Word of God does *not* meet people's need. It may make them feel good, and they may respond enthusiastically to the preacher, but that is not the same as meeting real needs.

Reproving, rebuking, and exhorting is the same as preaching the Word, for those are the very same ministries Scripture accomplishes: "All Scripture is breathed out by God and profitable for teaching, for reproof, for correction, and for training in righteousness" (2 Tim. 3:16). Notice the same balance of positive and negative admonition. Reproof and correction are negative; teaching and training are positive.

Although the reproofs of God's Word are essential and must never be neglected, the positive part of instruction is, for obvious reasons, where the majority of our energies ought to be invested. The word "exhort" is *parakaleō*, a word that means "encourage." The excellent preacher confronts sin and then encourages repentant sinners to behave righteously. He is to do this "with complete patience and teaching" (4:2). In 1 Thessalonians 2:11–12, Paul talks about how, "like a father with his children, we exhorted each one of you and encouraged you and charged you to walk in a manner worthy of God." This often requires great patience and much instruction. But the excellent minister cannot neglect these aspects of his calling.

Don't Compromise in Difficult Times

There is an urgency in Paul's charge to young Timothy: "For the time is coming when people will not endure sound teaching, but having itching ears they will accumulate for themselves teachers to suit their own passions" (2 Tim. 4:3). That is a prophecy reminiscent of those found in 2 Timothy 3:1 ("understand this, that in the last days there will come times of difficulty") and 1 Timothy 4:1 ("the Spirit expressly says that in later times some will depart from the faith"). This, then, is Paul's third prophetic warning to Timothy about the difficult times that were to come. Note the progression: The first one said that the time would come when people will depart from the faith. The second one warned Timothy that dangerous times were coming for the church. Now the third one suggests that the time would come when those *in the church* would not endure sound doctrine but desire instead to have their ears tickled.

Fearless preaching is all the more necessary in such dangerous times. When people will not tolerate the truth, that's when courageous, outspoken preachers are most desperately needed to speak it.

Why are people unwilling to endure sound teaching? Their love of sin. Sound preaching, as we have seen, confronts and rebukes sin, and people in love with sinful lifestyles will not tolerate such teaching. They want to have their ears tickled (v. 3).

Paul employs the expression "sound teaching" in 1 Timothy 1 as well. In verses 9 and 10 of that chapter, he speaks of the law as being "for the lawless and disobedient, for the ungodly and sinners, for the unholy and profane, for those who strike their fathers and mothers, for murderers, the sexually immoral, men who practice homosexuality, enslavers, liars, perjurers, and w*hatever else is contrary to sound doctrine*" (emphasis added). A society filled with and influenced by liars, perjurers, murderers, and homosexuals is by no means tolerant of sound teaching.

Notice that Paul does *not* suggest that the way to reach such a society is to soften or adapt the message so that such people will be comfortable with it. Just the opposite is true. Such ear-tickling is abominable. Paul urges Timothy to be willing to suffer for the truth's sake and to keep preaching the Word boldly and faithfully. That's the only way intolerant people can be exposed to the truth, which alone can soften their hearts.

Incidentally, the interpretive question raised by this passage hinges on the words "they" in verse 3. To whom does the word refer? To the world? Or to the church? Surely this statement is true of the world's attitude— unregenerate people seldom are willing to tolerate sound teaching. But here Paul is speaking specifically of the people to whom Timothy preaches. This seems to refer primarily to people in the church. It suggests that a time would come when professing Christians in Ephesus would not stand for sound preaching.

Isn't that precisely the state of the church in our society today? In fact, this is the very thing marketing experts are pointing out to church leaders. The whole basis of their philosophy is that people don't want to hear the truth proclaimed; they want to be entertained. The marketing plan says give them what they want. Scripture says otherwise.

There are thousands of supposedly evangelical churches worldwide that cannot stomach sound doctrine. They would not tolerate for two weeks strong biblical teaching that refutes their doctrinal error, confronts their sin, convicts them, and calls them to obey the truth. They don't want to hear healthy teaching. Why? Because people in the church want to own God without giving up sinful lifestyles, and they will not endure someone telling them what God's Word says about it.

What *do* they want to hear? "Having itching ears they will accumulate for themselves teachers to suit their own passions" (v. 3). Ironically, they seek out *teachers*. In fact, they *heap to themselves* teachers—but not sound ones. They choose the teachers who tell them what they want to hear. They want what tickles their ears and feeds their lusts. They want what makes them feel good about themselves. Preachers who offend them, they reject. They accumulate a mass of teachers who feed their insatiable selfish appetites. And the preacher who brings the message they most need to hear is the one they least like to hear.

Unfortunately, preachers with ear-tickling messages are all too abundantly available. "In periods of unsettled faith, scepticism, and mere curious speculation in matters of religion, teachers of all kinds swarm like the flies in Egypt. The demand creates the supply. The hearers invite and shape their own preachers. If the people desire a calf to worship, a ministerial calf-maker is readily found."[11]

This appetite for ear-tickling preaching has a terrible end. Verse 4 says these people will ultimately "turn away from listening to the truth and wander off into myths." They become the victims of their own refusal to hear

---

[11]Marvin R. Vincent, *Word Studies in the New Testament*, 4 vols. (New York: Scribner's, 1900), 4:321.

the truth. "They will turn away" is in the active voice. The people willfully choose this action. "Will be turned aside to myths" is in the passive voice. It describes what happens to them. Having turned from the truth, they become victims of deception. As soon as they turn away from the truth, they become pawns of Satan.

That is happening on a very wide scale in the church today. Evangelicalism has lost its tolerance for confrontive preaching. Now the floodgates have opened for serious doctrinal error. Christians madly pursue extrabiblical revelation in the form of prophecies and dreams. Preachers deny or ignore the reality of hell. The modern gospel promises heaven apart from holiness. Churches ignore the biblical teaching on women's roles, homosexuality, and other politically charged issues. The human medium has overtaken the divine message. The result has been serious doctrinal compromise on a far-reaching scale. If the church does not repent and return to the up-line (as Spurgeon would say), these errors and others like them will become epidemic.

Look again at the key phrase in verse 3: "having itching ears." Why will not they endure sound doctrine? Why do they heap to themselves teachers? Why do they turn away from the truth? Because down deep inside they simply want to have their ears tickled. They don't want to be confronted. They don't want to be convicted. They want to be entertained. They want preaching that produces pleasant sensations. They want to feel good. They want their ears to be amused and electrified with anecdotes, humor, psychology, motivational lectures, reassurance, positive thinking, self-congratulation, ego-massaging sermonettes, and agreeable small talk. Biblical reproof, rebuke, and exhortation are unacceptable.

But the truth of God does not tickle our ears, it boxes them. It burns them. It *first* reproves, rebukes, convicts—*then* exhorts and encourages. Preachers of the Word must be careful to maintain that balance.

In John 6, after Jesus had delivered a particularly hard message, Scripture tells us, "After this many of his disciples turned back and no longer walked with him" (v. 66). As the crowds left, our Lord turned to His disciples and asked, "Do you want to go away as well?" (v. 67). Peter's reply on behalf of the Twelve is significant: "Lord, to whom shall we go? You have the words of eternal life" (v. 68). That was the right response. It revealed the difference between true disciples and hangers-on: their hunger for *the Word.* Jesus said, "If you abide in my word, you are truly my disciples" (John 8:31). People seeking to be entertained or fed, curiosity-seekers, and people who just follow the crowd are by no means true disciples. Those who love the Word are the true followers of Christ. They will not desire preachers who tickle their ears.

Be Sober in All Things

The attitude of the excellent minister must be one of thoughtful sobriety. "Always be sober-minded" (v. 5) is not merely a warning against drunkenness. Nor is Paul suggesting that Timothy should be somber, joyless, gloomy, morose, or angry all the time. *Sober* means self-controlled, steady, attentive. It describes a state of mental alertness and control of one's faculties.

This is a solid person, a stable person, like an athlete who has brought all his passions and appetites and nerves under complete control to perform at a maximum level. To put it in the negative, a preacher is not to be flaky, not to be trendy, not to be a pursuer of whims. In the face of a changing world, in the midst of a vacillating church, in the context of a rocking and reeling society, ministers had better be rooted, steadfast, stable—rock-solid. We cannot compromise when the pressure is on.

The church has had enough erratic, trendy, whimsical preachers who flip-flop depending on the tide of the mob. What is most needed now are spiritual men who remain totally steadfast in an unstable world and who know their priorities. We need ministers whose heads are clear of deceit, false teaching, and unorthodox notions. We need preachers who will courageously declare the whole counsel of God. How wearisome it must be to God to hear insipid, innocuous pabulum dribbled out of pulpits instead of His Word!

The noble preacher is balanced, consistent, solid. He is unmoved by the cries of those who beg to have their ears tickled.

Endure Hardship

Obviously, excellent ministers cannot be those who yearn for earthly applause. Neither can they be lovers of earthly comfort. The life of ministry is not a life of leisure. Timothy needed to be willing to endure hardship (v. 5). He could not have the kind of ministry God desired of him unless he was willing to go through some suffering.

No ministry of any value ever comes without pain. I often encounter young men headed for ministry who are looking for a church without problems, a ministry without challenges, a congregation that will make life easy. There is no such place for the faithful preacher of the Word. The notion that ministry can be both effective and painless is a lie. You *will* encounter hardship if you preach the unadulterated Word. And when adversity strikes, you have two choices. You can endure and remain steadfast, or you can compromise. The faithful minister holds the line for the truth. You cannot do that and escape suffering. "Indeed, all who desire to live a godly life in Christ Jesus will be persecuted" (2 Tim. 3:12). Thus faithfulness and hardship go hand in hand.

This is a repeated theme in Paul's epistles to his young protégé. In 2 Timothy 2:1–3, he wrote, "You then, my child, be strengthened by the grace that is in Christ Jesus. . . . Share in suffering as a good soldier of Christ Jesus." Now he reminds Timothy again that suffering is as much a part of the faithful minister's duty as any other aspect of the work.

Did Timothy follow Paul's counsel? Evidently he did. Hebrews 13:23, an obscure little verse, says, "You should know that our brother Timothy has been released, with whom I shall see you if he comes soon." The writer of Hebrews obviously knew Timothy well and loved him. He tells the Hebrews that Timothy had been "released." Released from what? The Greek word used there suggests that Timothy had been released from prison. We can assume that when the suffering came, Timothy endured it. He did not compromise. He remained faithful, even though it evidently meant imprisonment. He did not try to find a cheap way out.

Do the Work of an Evangelist

At first glance it might seem that the command "do the work of an evangelist" is an abrupt change of direction. But it is not. Paul was encouraging Timothy to reach out beyond the comfort level of his own flock and boldly proclaim the Word to unbelievers. Paul was not suggesting that Timothy's *office* was that of an evangelist. He was telling him that part of his duty as a pastor was to evangelize unbelievers.

Again, Paul was commanding Timothy to declare the truth boldly. Timothy may have been tempted to seek a haven in the comfort of the flock. Paul was urging him to minister instead on the front line. He wanted Timothy to face the world courageously and preach Christ crucified. He wanted him to proclaim sin, righteousness, judgment, and God's law. He wanted him to declare the depravity, not the dignity, of mankind. He wanted him to herald the Second Coming and warn of eternal judgment. He wanted him to magnify the cross, the resurrection, the atonement, grace, and faith. He was urging Timothy to be solemn and persuasive in confronting unbelief.

Fulfill Your Ministry

This brief charge to Timothy ends with a final imperative: "Fulfill your ministry" (v. 5). "Fulfill" means "accomplish, fill it up, do it all." He might have said, "Don't serve God halfheartedly; do it with all your might." Paul was coming to the end of his own life, and he was able to say, "For I am already being poured out as a drink offering, and the time of my departure has come. I have fought the good fight, I have finished the race, I have kept the faith. Henceforth there is laid up for me the crown of righteousness, which the Lord, the righteous judge, will award to me on that Day, and not only to me but also to all who have loved his appearing" (2 Tim. 4:6–8). He wanted Timothy to reach the same point someday.

Remember, this charge from Paul to Timothy has implications for every Christian. We are all to be ministers in whatever sphere of service divine providence places us. Whether you are a mother ministering to her own children or the pastor of a 15,000-member congregation, these principles apply to you. There is no room for compromise. There is no place for timidity. There is no time for delay. There is no need for fear. Fill up your service to the Lord; accomplish it all. That is possible only if the ministry is done right.

HOLDING FAST THE FAITH

At the height of the Down-Grade Controversy, two weeks after he was censured by the Baptist Union, Charles Spurgeon preached a message entitled "Holding Fast the Faith," in which he said:

> We must never hide our colours. There are times when we must dash to the front and court the encounter, when we see that our Captain's honour demands it. Let us never be either ashamed or afraid. Our Lord Jesus deserves that we should yield ourselves as willing sacrifices in defence of his faith. Ease, reputation, life itself, must go for the name and faith of Jesus. If in the heat of the battle our good name or our life must be risked to win the victory, then let us say, "In this battle some of us must fall; why should not I? I will take part and lot with my Master, and bear reproach for his sake." Only brave soldiers are worthy of our great Lord. Those who sneak into the rear, that they may be comfortable, are *not* worthy of the kingdom. . . .
>
> Brethren, we must be willing to bear ridicule for Christ's sake, even that peculiarly envenomed ridicule which "the cultured" are so apt to pour upon us. We must be willing to be thought great fools for Jesus'

sake. . . . For my part, I am willing to be ten thousand fools in one for my dear Lord and Master, and count it to be the highest honour that can be put upon me to be stripped of every honour, and loaded with every censure for the sake of the grand old truth which is written on my very heart. . . .

Before I could quit my faith . . . I should have to be ground to powder, and every separate atom transformed.[12]

Spurgeon closed with these words:

Everybody admires Luther! Yes, yes; but you do not want any one else to do the same to-day. When you go to the Zoological Gardens you all admire the bear; but how would you like a bear at home, or a bear wandering loose about the street? You tell me that it would be unbearable, and no doubt you are right.

So, we admire a man who was firm in the faith, say four hundred years ago; the past ages are a sort of bear-pit or iron cage for him; but such a man to-day is a nuisance, and must be put down. Call him a narrow-minded bigot, or give him a worse name if you can think of one. Yet imagine that in those ages past, Luther, Zwingli, Calvin, and their compeers had said, "The world is out of order; but if we try to set it right we shall only make a great row, and get ourselves into disgrace. Let us go to our chambers, put on our night-caps, and sleep over the bad times, and perhaps when we wake up things will have grown better."

Such conduct on their part would have entailed upon us a heritage of error. Age after age would have gone down into the infernal deeps, and the pestiferous bogs of error would have swallowed all. These men loved the faith and the name of Jesus too well to see them trampled on. Note what we owe them, and let us pay to our sons the debt we owe our fathers.

It is to-day as it was in the Reformers' days. Decision is needed. Here is the day for the man, where is the man for the day? We who have had the gospel passed to us by martyr hands dare not trifle with it, nor sit by and hear it denied by traitors, who pretend to love it, but inwardly abhor every line of it. The faith I hold bears upon it marks of the blood of my ancestors. Shall I deny their faith, for which they left their native land to sojourn here? Shall we cast away the treasure which was handed to us through the bars of prisons, or came to us charred with the flames of Smithfield?

Personally, when my bones have been tortured with rheumatism, I have remembered Job Spurgeon, doubtless of my own stock, who in

---

[12]"Holding Fast the Faith," 78, 83.

Chelmsford Jail was allowed a chair, because he could not lie down by reason of rheumatic pain. That Quaker's broad-brim overshadows my brow. Perhaps I inherit his rheumatism; but that I do not regret if I have his stubborn faith, which will not let me yield a syllable of the truth of God.

When I think of how others have suffered for the faith, a little scorn or unkindness seems a mere trifle, not worthy of mention. An ancestry of lovers of the faith ought to be a great plea with us to abide by the Lord God of our fathers, and the faith in which they lived. As for me, I must hold the old gospel: I can do no other. God helping me, I will endure the consequences of what men think obstinacy.

Look you, sirs, *there are ages yet to come.* If the Lord does not speedily appear, there will come another generation, and another, and all these generations will be tainted and injured if we are not faithful to God and to his truth to-day. We have come to a turning-point in the road. If we turn to the right, mayhap our children and our children's children will go that way; but if we turn to the left, generations yet unborn will curse our names for having been unfaithful to God and to his Word. I charge you, not only by your ancestry, but by your posterity, that you seek to win the commendation of your Master, that though you dwell where Satan's seat is, you yet hold fast his name, and do not deny his faith. God grant us faithfulness, for the sake of the souls around us! How is the world to be saved if the church is false to her Lord? How are we to lift the masses if our fulcrum is removed? If our gospel is uncertain, what remains but increasing misery and despair? Stand fast, my beloved, in the name of God! I, your brother in Christ, entreat you to abide in the truth. Quit yourselves like men, be strong. The Lord sustain you for Jesus' sake. Amen.[13]

Spurgeon did his part. He passed the baton to another generation, and they passed it to another. They finished their course having kept the faith, and now it is our turn. Will we keep the faith? Will we fulfill our ministry? Are we willing to suffer hardship for being faithful? Are we committed to a biblical ministry of preaching the Word without shame?

We who love the Lord and His church must not sit by while the church gains momentum on the down-grade of worldliness and compromise. Men and women before us have paid with their blood to deliver the faith intact to us. Now it is our turn to guard the truth. It is a task that calls for courage, not compromise. And it is a responsibility that demands unwavering devotion to a very narrow purpose.

---

[13]Ibid., 83–84.

In the same sermon I have been quoting from, Spurgeon included this reminder:

> Dear friends, this name, this faith, these are our *message*. Our only business here below is to cry, "Behold the Lamb." Are any of you sent of God with any other message? It cannot be. The one message which God has given to his people to proclaim is salvation through the Lamb—salvation by the blood of Jesus. . . . To tell of Jesus is our occupation, we have nothing to say which is not comprised in the revelation made to us by God in Jesus Christ. He who is our comfort is our one theme.[14]

That echoes Paul's words to Timothy. "Preach the Word." We have nothing else worth saying. There is no other message. There is no other valid ministry. Until the church recovers that truth and that single-minded commitment to our calling, evangelicalism will continue to be pulled relentlessly further into the down-grade.

---

[14]Ibid., 81.

2

THE USER-FRIENDLY CHURCH

At a certain meeting of ministers and church officers, one after another doubted the value of prayer-meetings; all confessed that they had a very small attendance, and several acknowledged without the slightest compunction that they had quite given them up. What means this? Are churches in a right condition when they have only one meeting for prayer in a week, and that a mere skeleton?

CHARLES HADDON SPURGEON[1]

The contemporary church is undergoing a revolution in worship styles unprecedented since the Protestant Reformation. Ministry has married marketing philosophy, and this is the natural product. It is a studied effort to change the way the world perceives the church. Church ministry is being completely revamped in an attempt to make it more appealing to unbelievers.

The experts are now telling us that pastors and church leaders who want to be successful must concentrate their energies in this new direction. Provide non-Christians with an agreeable, inoffensive environment. Give them freedom, tolerance, and anonymity. Always be positive and benevolent. If you must have a sermon, keep it brief and amusing. Don't be preachy or authoritative. Above all, keep everyone entertained. Churches following this pattern will see numerical growth, we're assured; those that ignore it are doomed to decline.

The kinds of innovation being tried are extraordinary, even radical. For example, some churches now offer their largest services on Friday or Saturday night instead of Sunday morning. These services are usually heavy on music and entertainment, offering people an alternative to the theater or social circuit. Church members can now "get church out of the way"

[1]"Another Word Concerning the Down-Grade," *The Sword and the Trowel* (August 1887), 397–398.

early, then have the rest of the weekend to use as they wish. One Saturday churchgoer explained why these alternative services are so important: "If you go to Sunday school at 9:00 A.M., then to the 11 A.M. service and leave about 1 P.M., your day is pretty well shot."[2]

Judging from attendance figures, *lots* of church members feel spending the Lord's Day in church is tantamount to blowing the whole day. Non-Sunday alternative services in some churches are more heavily attended than traditional Sunday worship services.

That's not all. Many of these services offer no preaching whatsoever. Instead they rely on music, skits, multimedia, and other means of communication to convey the message. "This is the generation that grew up on television," one pastor told *Time* magazine. "You have to present religion to them in a creative and visual way."[3] Some churches are taking that philosophy a step further, cutting out preaching on Sunday morning as well.

Even the music and skits are carefully chosen to try to make unbelievers comfortable. Almost nothing is dismissed as inappropriate: rock 'n' roll oldies, disco tunes, heavy metal, rap, dancing, comedy, clowns, mime artists, stage magic, martial arts, cage fighting, and (more recently) explicit sex education have all become part of the evangelical repertoire. In fact, one of the few things judged out of place in church these days is clear and forceful preaching.

The whole point is to make the church "user-friendly." That is a term borrowed from the computer industry. It was first employed to describe software and hardware that is easy for the novice to operate. Applied to the church, it usually describes a ministry that is benign and utterly non-challenging. In practice, it has become an excuse for importing worldly amusements into the church in an attempt to try to attract non-Christian "seekers" or "unchurched Harrys" by appealing to their fleshly interests. The obvious fallout of this preoccupation with the unchurched is a corresponding de-emphasis on those who *are* the true church. The spiritual needs of believers are being neglected to the hurt of the body.

POUNDING THE PULPIT?

Not that preaching has been entirely abandoned. Some of the user-friendly churches offer at least one service a week (often a midweek service) where a spoken message is the centerpiece. But even in those meetings the style is

---

[2]Cited in John Dart, "Protestant Churches Join the Fold, Fill Pews with Saturday Services," *Los Angeles Times* (September 15, 1991), B3.
[3]Barbara Dolan, "Full House at Willow Creek," *Time* (March 6, 1989), 60.

more psychological and motivational than biblical. Above all, the emphasis is on user-friendliness. I recently read through a stack of newspaper and magazine articles about the user-friendly phenomenon, and a common thread began to emerge. Here are some quotations from some of these clippings describing the preaching in user-friendly churches:

- "There is no fire and brimstone here. No Bible-thumping. Just practical, witty messages."
- "Services at [the church featured in the article] have an informal feeling. You won't hear people threatened with hell or referred to as sinners. The goal is to make them feel welcome, not drive them away."
- "As with all clergymen [this pastor's] answer is God—but he slips Him in at the end, and even then doesn't get heavy. No ranting, no raving. No fire, no brimstone. He doesn't even use the H-word. Call it Light Gospel. It has the same salvation as the Old Time Religion, but with a third less guilt."
- "The sermons are relevant, upbeat, and best of all, short. You won't hear a lot of preaching about sin and damnation and hell fire. Preaching here doesn't sound like *preaching*. It is sophisticated, urbane, and friendly talk. It breaks all the stereotypes."
- "[The pastor] is preaching a very upbeat message. . . . It's a salvationist message, but the idea is not so much being saved from the fires of hell. Rather, it's being saved from meaninglessness and aimlessness in this life. It's more of a soft-sell."
- "The idea, [the pastor] says, is to get people through the front doors, then disprove the stereotype of the sweating, loosened necktied, Bible-thumping preacher who yells and screams about burning in hell for eternity."

So the new rules may be summed up as follows: Be clever, informal, positive, brief, and friendly. Never loosen your necktie. Never let them see you sweat. And never, never use the h-word.

(Perhaps it should be noted that in recent years the h-word has made something of a comeback among younger preachers who have adopted mild profanity in their preaching as a way of connecting with "the culture.")

I realize most of the above quotations represent what outside observers have said about user-friendly churches, not how they portray their own ministries. Many of them would vehemently deny that they downplay or deny any point of evangelical doctrine. In fact, George Barna's best-selling book *User-Friendly Churches* includes this disclaimer twice: "None of the successful churches described in this book is interested in being user friendly in the sense of compromising the gospel or the historic faith of the church just to make friends with the age."[4]

But in fact the truth of Scripture is being compromised when it is relegated to a footnote in someone's sermon. The historic Christian faith *has* been abandoned when—in order to forge a friendship with the world— hard truths are avoided, vapid amusements are set in place of sound teaching, and semantic gymnastics are employed to avoid mention of the difficult truths of the Bible. If the design is to make the seeker comfortable, isn't that rather incompatible with the biblical teaching on sin, judgment, hell, and several other important topics? And so the biblical message is inevitably distorted by the philosophy. And what about the believer who should be fed?

Please understand, I'm not suggesting preachers *ought* to be sweaty, unkempt ranters and ravers who scream, yell, pound the pulpit, and thump the Bible. But let's face it, such preachers are hardly in abundance these days. The imagery of the angry Bible-thumper has become an easy stereotype that is often used against those who simply believe straightforward proclamation of truth is more important than making "unchurched Harry" comfortable.

The weakness of the pulpit today does not stem from frantic cranks who harangue about hell; it is the result of men who compromise and who fear to speak God's Word powerfully, with conviction. The church is certainly not suffering from an overabundance of forthright preachers; rather, it seems glutted with men-pleasers (cf. Gal. 1:10).

THE CUSTOMER IS SOVEREIGN

At the heart of the market-driven, user-friendly church is the goal of giving people what they want. Advocates of the philosophy are quite candid about this. I noted in Chapter 1 that consumer satisfaction is the stated goal of the new philosophy. One key resource on market-driven ministry says, "This is what marketing the church is all about: providing our product (relationships) as a solution to people's felt need."[5]

Felt needs thus determine the road map for the modern church-marketing plan. The idea is a basic marketing principle: you satisfy an existing desire rather than trying to persuade people to buy something they don't want.

---

[4](Ventura, CA: Regal, 1991), 1, 15–16.
[5]George Barna, *Marketing the Church* (Colorado Springs: NavPress, 1988), 51.

Accurately assessing people's felt needs is therefore one of the keys to modern church growth theory. Church leaders are advised to poll potential "customers" and find out what they are looking for in a church, then offer that. Demographic information, community surveys, door-to-door polls, and congregational questionnaires are the new tools. Information drawn from such sources is considered *essential* to building a workable marketing plan. Ministers today are told they cannot reach people effectively without it.

Worst of all, it seems people's felt needs are taken more seriously than the real but unfelt human deficiencies that are consistently highlighted in Scripture. Felt needs include issues like loneliness, fear of failure, feelings of inadequacy, codependency, a poor self-image, eating disorders, depression, anger, resentment, and similar inward-focused inadequacies. The *real* problem—the root of all these other feelings—is human depravity, an issue that is carefully skirted (and sometimes in recent years overtly denied) in the teaching of the typical user-friendly church.

No longer are pastors taught to declare to people what God demands of them. Instead, they are counseled to find out what the people's demands are, then do whatever is necessary to cater to popular opinion. The audience is regarded as "sovereign," and the wise preacher will "shape his communications according to their needs in order to receive the response he [seeks]."[6]

The effect of such a philosophy is apparent; men-pleasers are filling the pulpits of our churches. Moreover, Scripture is no longer the authoritative guide for ministry; the marketing plan is. One textbook on church marketing includes this statement: "The marketing plan is the Bible of the marketing game; everything that happens in the life of the product occurs because the plan wills it."[7] Applied to church ministry, that means a human strategy—not the Word of God—becomes the fountain of all church activity and the standard by which ministry is measured.

That approach to ministry is so obviously convoluted and so grossly unbiblical that I am amazed so many pastors are swayed by it. But it has become an extremely influential philosophy. Thousands of churches have overhauled their entire ministry and are now attempting to cater to the masses.

In fact, the user-friendly church movement has become so large that many secular newspapers have begun to take note of the trend. One article in the *Los Angeles Times* described how a megachurch grew out of a

---

[6]Ibid., 33.
[7]Ibid., 45.

door-to-door survey conducted for a "marketing study" when this church was not yet formed. "Customer Poll Shapes a Church" was the title of the article—and it is fitting. The story described how the pastor "tailored the church's program to the needs and gripes people registered in his door-to-door survey."[8] Of course, the article said, his messages are brief, low-key, upbeat, and topical, with titles like "The Changing American Dream." He spices his sermonettes with quotations from news and financial magazines.

Another Southern California newspaper ran an article entitled, "Marketing the Maker." It describes several local churches that have employed the market-driven philosophy—and seem to be booming. One church "bought time on classic rock stations for an ad that sounded more like a pitch for a social club than an invitation to join a church. And newspaper ads were placed in the entertainment section, not the religion section."[9]

There is nothing wrong, of course, with a church placing ads in the entertainment section. But it *is* wrong for a church to promise—and deliver—a "church service" that is merely a religious form of entertainment. And that is precisely what many of these churches are doing. "A *celebration*—not a service" is how this particular church promotes its meetings, held, appropriately, in a movie theater.

In many churches today, you'll never see a live pastor who can look you in the eye. Services are streamed from a remote location to a giant video screen—or if you choose, to your home computer. You even can partake in the worship in your pajamas, without even getting out of bed. Amazingly, some churches actually advertise their Internet webcasts in a way that seems to suggest those are benefits their viewers are welcome to enjoy. ("You can literally worship with us anywhere. It's a different kind of church community and another way to stay connected.")

There's nothing inherently wrong with webcasting or telecasting a church worship service, of course. Internet live-streaming or televised worship services can be a great benefit for people who physically *cannot* be there (such as a sick person or someone who is on a business trip and thus away from home for the weekend). We stream our church services for the benefit of shut-in foreign missionaries who want to keep up with what's happening at home. Plus we have broadcast our recorded sermons by radio for many years and now broadcast on television as well. So I am by no means criticizing mass media or Internet streaming as means of getting the message out to more people.

---

[8]Russell Chandler (December 11, 1989), A1.
[9]Mike McIntyre, *The San Diego Union* (November 6, 1988), D8.

But the ease of those kinds of communication means that pastors must begin to stress more than ever the importance of fellowship, accountability, and participation in the body of Christ at the local level. A streaming Internet worship service is not an adequate way "to get connected" with Christ's body. People who are inclined to duck personal involvement in the church now have a smorgasbord of online alternatives. They can salve their consciences with the impression of church participation but not the reality.

And with so many options, the most casual customer has achieved ultimate sovereignty. If he doesn't like what he sees, he can simply change the channel. Pastors must resist the temptation to tailor their messages to the whims and short attention spans of drive-by listeners like that. Catering to the sound bite surfer is the surest way to empty one's message of real substance.

TURNING CHURCH GROWTH THEORY UPSIDE DOWN

Scripture says the early Christians "turned the world upside down" (Acts 17:6). In our generation the world is turning the church upside down. Biblically, God is sovereign, not "unchurched Harry." *The Bible*, not a marketing plan, is supposed to be the sole blueprint and final authority for all church ministry. Ministry should meet people's real needs, not indulge their selfishness. Above all, we must bear in mind that the Lord of the church is Christ, not some couch potato with the remote control in his hand.

I never hear the term "user-friendly church" without thinking of Acts 5 and Ananias and Sapphira. What happened there flies in the face of almost all contemporary church growth theory. The Jerusalem church certainly wasn't very user-friendly. In fact, it was exactly the opposite. Luke tells us this episode inspired "great fear . . . upon the whole church and upon all who heard of these things" (v. 11). The church service that day was so disturbing that none of the unchurched people "dared to associate with them." The thought of attending such a church struck terror in their hearts, even though "the people held them in high esteem" (v. 13). The church was definitely not a place for sinners to be comfortable—it was a frightening place!

Let's look carefully at this passage and try to understand it in the proper context. To do that we must go back into Acts 4. Remember, the church was newborn, in all its pristine beauty and freshness and vitality. It was yet unstained by gross sin or human failure. The people were intensely studying the apostles' doctrine. Those early days of church history were bright, happy days, full of love and real fellowship. The joy was overwhelming, and the love was deep and all-inclusive; consequently their testimony was loud and clear. The results were that some fifteen to twenty thousand had come to faith in Jesus Christ in just a few weeks' time. Already Satan had tried by persecution to thwart the purpose of the church. It made no difference; the believers only prayed for more boldness. God answered that prayer, and even more people were saved. God was very real; Christ was very much alive; and the Holy Spirit was displayed in great power in those days.

But Satan was already plotting a more dangerous attack. If he couldn't destroy the church by an external assault of persecution, he would try the more subtle internal approach. And that is exactly what happened.

SIN IN THE CAMP

This is the first recorded occasion of sin in the church. Of all the firsts in Acts, it is the saddest. Satan's strategy of infiltrating the church began at this time, and it is still continuing today.

This entire account is a classic example of the Bible's stubborn honesty. God could have given us a soft-focus picture of the early church with all the imperfections hidden. But Scripture never leaves the truth out—even when it is painful and ugly. The church is not perfect and never has been. Some people use that as an excuse to stay away: "I'd go to church, but there are too many hypocrites." I always think, *Well, we have room for one more.* The objection itself is hypocritical. Of course there are hypocrites in the church. That's one of the truths we glean from this account in Acts 5.

There's a sense in which a passage like this can be an encouragement. Not that we are encouraged by sin. But it is encouraging to know that the early church grappled with exactly the same kind of problems we have today.

Even the apostle Paul must have sometimes been discouraged by problems he encountered in the churches. In 2 Corinthians 11:24–27, he gave a list of all the kinds of trials and persecution he had endured:

> Five times I received at the hands of the Jews the forty lashes less one. Three times I was beaten with rods. Once I was stoned. Three times I was shipwrecked; a night and a day I was adrift at sea; on frequent journeys, in danger from rivers, danger from robbers, danger from my own people, danger from Gentiles, danger in the city, danger in the wilderness, danger at sea, danger from false brothers; in toil and

hardship, through many a sleepless night, in hunger and thirst, often without food, in cold and exposure.

Then in conclusion he adds this, the supreme trial of all: "And, apart from other things, there is the daily pressure on me of my anxiety for all the churches" (v. 28). He wasn't talking about the stress of paperwork and administrative details; he was speaking of the battle to bring believers to maturity.

Beginning with this incident in Acts 5, the sins of the saints became a perpetual problem for the church. Every epistle Paul wrote in the New Testament included something of major consequence about sin in the church. In Romans 16:17–18 he wrote, "I appeal to you, brothers, to watch out for those who cause divisions and create obstacles contrary to the doctrine that you have been taught; avoid them. For such persons do not serve our Lord Christ, but their own appetites, and by smooth talk and flattery they deceive the hearts of the naive." The Corinthian church was overrun with problems: divisions, strife, immorality, misuse of spiritual gifts, and so on. The Galatians were tolerant of false teaching and legalism (cf. Gal. 3:1–4). Paul had to entreat the Ephesians to walk in a manner worthy of their calling, to be humble and gentle, patiently showing forbearance to one another in love, being diligent to preserve the unity of the Spirit in the bond of peace (4:1–4). He had to urge the Philippians to be like-minded, united in peace, intent on one purpose (2:1–2). He even named two women, Euodia and Syntyche, whom he wanted to get along with one another (4:2–3). In Colossians 3 he repeats a whole list of spiritual deficiencies, capped by a command for the Colossians to clean up their lives. He unrelentingly waged war against sin in the church.

A SHARING COMMUNITY

The church had begun as a sharing community. Acts 4:32–37 says,

> Now the full number of those who believed were of one heart and soul, and no one said that any of the things that belonged to him was his own, but they had everything in common. And with great power the apostles were giving their testimony to the resurrection of the Lord Jesus, and great grace was upon them all. There was not a needy person among them, for as many as were owners of lands or houses sold them and brought the proceeds of what was sold and laid it at the apostles' feet, and it was distributed to each as any had need. Thus Joseph, who was also called by the apostles Barnabas (which means

son of encouragement), a Levite, a native of Cyprus, sold a field that belonged to him and brought the money and laid it at the apostles' feet.

They Had True Spiritual Unity

The congregation had already burgeoned and blossomed to include thousands of people, and they were continually multiplying. Nevertheless, they "were of one heart and soul." It was not just that they all belonged to the same organization, but that they had true spiritual unity. They believed as one. They thought as one. They were in the truest sense a body, a single organism with one heartbeat and one soul (cf. Phil. 1:27). They were preoccupied with each other and with winning the world. They were too busy with those priorities to worry about their own selves. Everyone was caring for everyone else, so everyone's needs were met. Selfishness was therefore rendered unnecessary. What a beautiful kind of preoccupation that was! How rich and sweet their fellowship must have been!

They Shared All Their Possessions

Many people misunderstand this passage. "They had everything in common" does not mean these people lived in a commune. Remember, at Pentecost, Jerusalem was filled with pilgrims who came for the feast. During religious feasts, as many as a million people would come to Jerusalem. They obviously needed housing and food, and there weren't enough inns to accommodate everyone. So it was customary for believers to open their homes and allow people to live with them. Suddenly, at Pentecost on this particular year, hundreds of these people embraced Christ and then began to win their friends and families to Him. Surely many of them remained in Jerusalem to sit under the apostles' teaching.

The financial pressures on these people and their hosts must have been tremendous. In addition, there were many poor people in Jerusalem. And some believers' income may have been cut off when they testified of their faith in Christ. To deal with all this, all believers were willing to share what they had.

This was not a commune. People did not drop out of society, quit their jobs, pool their money, and live in a common building or camp. Acts 2 describes what they were doing:

> And all who believed were together and had all things in common. And they were selling their possessions and belongings and distributing the proceeds to all, as any had need. And day by day, attending the temple

together and breaking bread in their homes, they received their food with glad and generous hearts, praising God and having favor with all the people. And the Lord added to their number day by day those who were being saved. (vv. 44–47)

This was a spiritual community, not a cloister. Christians still owned their own houses—they continued "breaking bread in their homes" (v. 46). That is, they broke bread, or had communion, in private homes. "Selling" and "distributing" in verse 45 are perfect-tense verbs. That suggests that the selling and sharing were going on all the time. There was no one point when the community of believers sold all they had and pooled their funds. A continuous process was going on whereby people who had resources were sharing them with believers who did not. They did not live in a communal shelter or put up barracks to accommodate everyone. That would have undermined the God-ordained priority of the family unit, which God designed to be independent and to function as the building block of society and the means of passing truth and righteousness from generation to generation.

People were selling their possessions—their land holdings and their portable goods—and sharing the proceeds when they knew others had needs. Paul commanded giving in this same spirit. He urged the Corinthians to be generous in giving to the needs of the saints in Macedonia—"your abundance at the present time should supply their need, so that their abundance may supply your need, that there may be fairness" (2 Cor. 8:14). Is that any different from what we do today? Not if our churches are healthy. Christians who see a brother or sister in need should have a natural desire to supply the need (cf. 1 John 3:17). That's what these early Christians were doing. Those who sold possessions did so completely voluntarily. This becomes a crucial point when we examine the sin of Ananias and Sapphira.

They Were Nourished by Powerful Preaching

"With great power the apostles were giving their testimony to the resurrection of the Lord Jesus" (4:33). The preaching was bold and powerful. They were not ashamed of the gospel, though there was much persecution in those days. In fact, it specifically says they were preaching about the resurrection. That is the very truth that got them in the most trouble. At the beginning of this same chapter we learn that the priests, the captain of the temple guard, and the Sadducees, "greatly annoyed because they were teaching the people and proclaiming in Jesus the resurrection from the dead" (v. 2), seized Peter and John and threw them in jail. Peter and John weren't trying to win approval from the Sadducees and priests by preaching a message they wanted to hear! They boldly proclaimed the very thing that most offended them! They refused to tone down the great doctrines of the Word of God to eliminate the offense. They never suppressed their message because someone might be offended.

The apostles' preaching ministry included teaching as well as evangelism. Acts 2:42 says that those who believed "devoted themselves to the apostles' teaching." This was a well-fed but voracious flock.

The Jerusalem church would have been a wonderful place for fellowship. They did not follow any of the contemporary user-friendly marketing techniques, but the brotherhood was warm and real. They lovingly met one another's actual needs. And they had rich and ample teaching. Acts 2:42 tells us, "And they devoted themselves to the apostles' teaching and the fellowship, to the breaking of bread and the prayers." None of that was designed to attract unbelievers. Nevertheless, new people kept coming, because the Lord kept adding to the church day by day those who were being saved (v. 47).

A POSITIVE ROLE MODEL

Luke records *how* resources were shared among needy believers. Those with resources sold them, then placed the proceeds at the apostles' feet (vv. 34–35). The apostles distributed the funds to those who had needs. Through that simple system, all the needs were met (v. 34). That is essentially the same system we use today when we take an offering in the church. The money goes into a common fund, where the leaders of the church have the responsibility for stewardship of it.

Barnabas is the specific example Luke chose to show a positive role model. *Barnabas* was a nickname, meaning "son of encouragement." Apparently this man, "Joseph . . . a Levite, a native of Cyprus" (v. 36), had the gift of exhortation, so he was given a nickname that fit. Barnabas later accompanied the apostle Paul on his first missionary journey.

Barnabas was a Levite, a member of the priestly tribe of Israel. It is unlikely that he, a priest, would have been a very wealthy man. But somehow he had acquired a piece of property. He sold it. Then he brought the money to the apostles to be distributed. He didn't ask for recognition. He didn't try to control how the money was used. He just turned it over. What is clear from Acts 4 is that Barnabas gave from love out of a pure heart—

just for the blessedness of giving. And we can assume that a whole lot of others in the Jerusalem church did the same thing.

A NEGATIVE ROLE MODEL

But not everyone. The story that follows makes a startling contrast to the tone of Acts 4. It is shocking to see sin in this church. It is appalling to see the brazen falsehood that Ananias and Sapphira conspired to tell. Most of all, it is astonishing to see how severely the Lord dealt with their sin:

> But a man named Ananias, with his wife Sapphira, sold a piece of property, and with his wife's knowledge he kept back for himself some of the proceeds and brought only a part of it and laid it at the apostles' feet. But Peter said, "Ananias, why has Satan filled your heart to lie to the Holy Spirit and to keep back for yourself part of the proceeds of the land? While it remained unsold, did it not remain your own? And after it was sold, was it not at your disposal? Why is it that you have contrived this deed in your heart? You have not lied to men but to God." When Ananias heard these words, he fell down and breathed his last. And great fear came upon all who heard of it. The young men rose and wrapped him up and carried him out and buried him.
>
> After an interval of about three hours his wife came in, not knowing what had happened. And Peter said to her, "Tell me whether you sold the land for so much." And she said, "Yes, for so much." But Peter said to her, "How is it that you have agreed together to test the Spirit of the Lord? Behold, the feet of those who have buried your husband are at the door, and they will carry you out." Immediately she fell down at his feet and breathed her last. When the young men came in they found her dead, and they carried her out and buried her beside her husband. And great fear came upon the whole church and upon all who heard of these things. (Acts 5:1–11)

As generous and sacrificial and selfless as the saints at Jerusalem were, there was an exception. What Ananias did was spawned by the seeds of greed and deceit. His sin is to the book of Acts what Achan's sin is to the book of Joshua. Both were deceitful, miserly, selfish acts that interrupted the victorious progress of God's people and brought sin into the camp at the height of great triumph.

The saints in Jerusalem were giving out of a Spirit-filled heart. Ananias's sin revealed a Satan-filled heart (v. 3). The contrast between the end of chapter 4 and the beginning of chapter 5 could hardly be more dramatic.

Ananias's name means "the Lord is gracious"; *Sapphira* means "beautiful." Their deed was anything but gracious or beautiful. Seeing that others were selling property and giving the money to the apostles, they pledged to do the same. Verse 2 tells us, however, that when the time came to give, they "kept back . . . part of the proceeds." It is clear that both of them were in on the plot.

THE LEAVEN OF THE PHARISEES

What was their motive? They wanted a little spiritual prestige. They wanted to *appear* to be giving sacrificially, yet keep some of the money for themselves. That suggests they loved money. And "the love of money is a root of all kinds of evil," Paul wrote Timothy. "Through this craving . . . some have wandered away from the faith and pierced themselves with many pangs" (1 Tim. 6:10). That was certainly true of Ananias and Sapphira. The book of Hebrews says, "Keep your life free from love of money, and be content with what you have, for he has said, 'I will never leave you nor forsake you'" (13:5).

Here were two characters so tainted with the love of money that they were willing to conspire together to commit the grossest kind of hypocrisy. They sold their land, but rather than giving all the proceeds to the Lord as they had promised, they gave half to the Lord under the pretense that it was the whole price. They must have thought they could gain spiritual esteem *and* some cash along with it.

Their sin was not that they did not give everything. There was no divine requirement that they give everything. They had a perfect right to keep or give whatever they desired. They didn't even have to sell their property. It was all voluntary, as is all giving spoken of in the New Testament.

The sin was their lie. They had made their vow to the Holy Spirit publicly in front of the congregation. They lied to the entire congregation, but worse still, they lied to God (v. 4). Perhaps they thought of this as a secret sin, but it didn't stay secret long. God Himself exposed it to the entire congregation.

Now let's be honest. This kind of hypocrisy is not a particularly uncommon sin. Nor is it the kind of evil we tend to think of as heinous. Lots of people give money under false pretenses. This is the moral equivalent of the man who rolls up a few dollar bills so it will look like he's putting a large wad into the collection plate. Or the woman who makes a great show of depositing an offering envelope, when there's only a quarter inside. It's like the Pharisees who had someone blow a trumpet in the synagogues and streets when they did alms, so everyone would notice (Matt. 6:2).

Jesus says of such people, "they have received their reward" (vv. 2, 5, 16). They want people to see their show of good works, and people notice. That's their reward. They seek glory from people, not from God, so the human recognition is the only reward they will ever get. "But when you give to the needy, do not let your left hand know what your right hand is doing, so that your giving may be in secret. And your Father who sees in secret will reward you" (Matt. 6:3–4). This sin may seem petty to us, but not to God. God hates hypocrisy and feigned holiness. Jesus called it "the leaven of the Pharisees" (Luke 12:1).

Now this leaven was threatening to infect the infant church. God would deal with it harshly and abruptly, sending signals to everyone about the seriousness of life in the church.

PETER'S RESPONSE

Peter, under the inspiration of the Spirit of God, saw through their hypocrisy. Imagine the shock that hit Ananias! He comes before the apostles, lays his money at their feet, and smugly tells them it is the money he got from selling his property. He probably stood there a moment, basking in what he thought was their approval. He must have assumed that they were looking at him as a spiritual giant, a generous and godly man.

But Peter looked him in the eye and said to him, "Ananias, why has Satan filled your heart to lie to the Holy Spirit and to keep back for yourself part of the proceeds of the land?" (Acts 5:3).

In many churches Ananias would have received the approval he sought, no matter what his motives. A pragmatic church leader might reason, *After all, this is a substantial sum of money. OK, his motives aren't pure, but, hey, he's not a bad guy, and we can use the money. We can't embarrass him in front of all the people. If we do that, we'll never get another dime from him.*

Not Peter. He confronted the sin directly. "Why has Satan filled your heart?" Notice that Peter was putting the blame on Ananias, not on Satan. "Why?" he asked. Then again in verse 4: "Why is it that you have contrived this deed in your heart?"

Peter also made it clear that the sin was Ananias's hypocrisy, not his keeping half the money: "While it remained unsold, did it not remain your own? And after it was sold, was it not at your disposal?" (v. 4). Ananias could have done whatever he wanted with the money. He could have kept his land. There was no requirement for him to do otherwise. It would not have been sinful if he had said, "I sold my property, and here is half the money." He had every right to give as much or as little as he wanted. But he sinned by claiming he was giving everything when he had actually kept some for himself.

And he lied to God, not just to men. More specifically, this was a blatant lie to the Holy Spirit.[10] How had he lied to the Holy Spirit? He had vowed to give the full value of his property and failed to follow through. The Old Testament sage wrote, "When you vow a vow to God, do not delay paying it, for he has no pleasure in fools. Pay what you vow. It is better that you should not vow than that you should vow and not pay" (Eccl. 5:4–5). Moses' law contained a similar warning: "If you make a vow to the LORD your God, you shall not delay fulfilling it, for the LORD your God will surely require it of you, and you will be guilty of sin. But if you refrain from vowing, you will not be guilty of sin. You shall be careful to do what has passed your lips, for you have voluntarily vowed to the LORD your God what you have promised with your mouth" (Deut. 23:21–23).

GOD'S JUDGMENT

God's response to the situation was immediate, severe, and final. He struck Ananias dead on the spot. "When Ananias heard these words, he fell down and breathed his last" (Acts 5:5). This was a judicial act of the Most Holy God. Perhaps Ananias's heart simply stopped out of sheer terror. Right in front of the entire church.

User-friendly? Hardly. Seeker-sensitive? Not in the least. In fact, the effect was that "great fear came upon all who heard of it" (v. 5). God had made Ananias an example to others who might be tempted to trifle with Him and taint the purity of the church.

Does God always judge sin this way? Obviously not, but when He does, it is terrifying. Like Nadab and Abihu (Lev. 10), Korah (Num. 16), Achan (Josh. 7), Herod (Acts 12), and others throughout Scripture, Ananias was immediately judged for his sin and paid with his life. God sovereignly chose to strike him dead summarily. He thus became an example to all. The truth is, God *could* judge every sin this way. "The wages of sin is death" (Rom. 6:23). It is only because of the Lord's infinite mercy that we are not all consumed (cf. Lam. 3:22, KJV). Sometimes God does judge sin with physical

---

[10]This passage is one of the proofs for the deity and personality of the Holy Spirit. In verse 3 Peter said Ananias had lied to the Holy Spirit. In verse 4 he tells Ananias, "You have not lied to men, but to God." The Holy Spirit *is* God. By lying to the apostles about what he was doing, Ananias had committed an even greater offense against the Holy Spirit.

death. Paul wrote to the Corinthians who were disrupting and defiling the Lord's Table, "He who eats and drinks, eats and drinks judgment to himself if he does not judge the body rightly. For this reason many among you are weak and sick, and a number sleep" (1 Cor. 11:29–30, NASB). "Sleep" there refers to physical death. God was actually judging the Corinthians by making them physically ill, and some were even dying.

With Ananias, however, there was no illness, no time lapse. He dropped dead on the spot. God's judgment was swift and terrifying.

SAPPHIRA'S SIN

Scripture says, "The young men rose and wrapped him up and carried him out and buried him" (Acts 5:6). Sapphira was not present when her husband died. "After an interval of about three hours his wife came in, not knowing what had happened" (v. 7). Sapphira was oblivious to her husband's fate, perhaps thinking she would make a grand entrance, with everyone admiring her for the great act of generosity she and Ananias had done.

Peter immediately confronted her: "Tell me whether you sold the land for so much." And she said, "Yes, for so much" (v. 8). This was a deliberate lie, proving that she and her husband had conspired together to commit a premeditated act of hypocrisy.

Peter was as direct as he had been with Ananias: "How is it that you have agreed together to test the Spirit of the Lord? Behold, the feet of those who have buried your husband are at the door, and they will carry you out" (v. 9). She never even had the opportunity to respond. "Immediately she fell down at his feet and breathed her last. When the young men came in they found her dead, and they carried her out and buried her beside her husband" (v. 10).

JUDGMENT MUST BEGIN AT THE HOUSE OF GOD

God is serious about the purity of the church. This was an early and unforgettable lesson about how God views sin among the fellowship of believers. In essence, God was saying, "I am not playing church. I will not trifle with sinners. I am not interested in user-friendliness. I desire righteousness, truth, and sincere hearts." He thus served notice that He is deadly serious. The church is no social gig.

What was the result of this episode? Again, "Great fear came upon the whole church" (v. 11). You can be certain there was a lot of careful self-examination going on in the Jerusalem church that day. And that was the point. God was purifying His church. He wanted His people to take sin seriously. He wanted to discourage shallow commitment. He wanted the people to fear Him. The church meets to worship God, and that demands the confrontation of sin. Here the Lord gives us the very basic model for the church's meeting—sin is dealt with fiercely. The issue is not what unbelievers think about such severity; it is what God thinks about such iniquity.

Surely in first-century Jerusalem there were a lot more contemptible sinners than Ananias and Sapphira. What about Herod, for example? Why didn't God strike him dead? As a matter of fact, He ultimately did (cf. Acts 12:18–23). But as Peter wrote, "It is time for judgment to begin at the household of God" (1 Pet. 4:17). God judges His own people before He turns His wrath on pagans.

Can the church avoid God's judgment? Yes, by purifying herself. After warning the Corinthians that God was already judging sinning church members with sickness and death, Paul told them, "If we judged ourselves truly, we would not be judged" (1 Cor. 11:31). In other words, it is the job of faithful church members to maintain the church's purity. Frankly, the careful, consistent exercise of church discipline is a far more powerful word to unbelievers about reality than some bland and lighthearted talk intended to make them feel welcome and accepted. This lets the unbeliever know that the church is a holy people and is not for unrepentant sinners but for the redeemed ones who love righteousness.

We do that by following the process Jesus outlined in Matthew 18: "If your brother sins against you, *go and tell him his fault, between you and him alone*. If he listens to you, you have gained your brother. But if he does not listen, *take one or two others along with you*, that every charge may be established by the evidence of two or three witnesses. If he refuses to listen to them, tell it to the church. And if he refuses to listen even to the church, *let him be to you as a Gentile and a tax collector*" (vv. 15–17, emphasis added). We refer to this process as church discipline. It may not seem like a very user-friendly concept, but it is what God commands. His design is to purify the church and thus to protect His people from His wrath. Paul wrote, "When we are judged by the Lord, we are disciplined so that we may not be condemned along with the world" (1 Cor. 11:32).

Jesus went on to say, "Truly, I say to you, whatever you bind on earth shall be bound in heaven, and whatever you loose on earth shall be loosed in heaven. Again I say to you, if two of you agree on earth about anything they ask, it will be done for them by my Father in heaven. For where two or three are gathered in my name, there am I among them" (Matt. 18:18–20). Remember, in this context our Lord was describing how to deal with sin in the fellowship. The point is that Christ carries out His own will in the church *through the discipline process.* "There am I among them" means He personally works in and through believers to purify His church as they follow the steps He outlined. The effect is that repentant believers are restored (their sin is "loosed" from them), and hard-hearted sinners are exposed and ousted from the fellowship (their sin is "bound" to them). If we don't follow this process and keep the church pure, He will intervene in judgment (1 Cor. 11:30).

KNOWING THE TERROR OF THE LORD, WE PERSUADE MEN

Here is the salient point for this book: God's judgment against Ananias and Sapphira had an effect beyond the fellowship of believers: "great fear came upon . . . all who heard of these things" (Acts 5:11). Verse 13 says unbelievers did not dare associate with them! This is precisely the opposite of the user-friendly philosophy that is so popular today. Instead of luring people to church by making them feel comfortable and secure, God used fear to keep unbelievers away.

The fear of God was a central doctrine in the early church. Believers and unbelievers alike were taught to fear Him. None but a rank fool would deal frivolously with God. It was that very fear that drew people for salvation and kept them obedient. Whenever the Holy Spirit is genuinely drawing someone to salvation, that person's heart cries out for deliverance from sin! The gospel call is not an invitation to join the fun and end emotional pain.

The contemporary user-friendly movement seems to miss that vital point. Rather than arousing fear of God, it attempts to portray Him as fun, jovial, easygoing, lenient, and even permissive. Haughty sinners who ought to approach God in terror (cf. Luke 18:13) are emboldened to presume on His grace. Sinners hear nothing of divine wrath. That is as wrong as preaching rank heresy.

As we learn from the account of Ananias and Sapphira, God's wrath is not to be taken lightly. Peter wrote, "If [judgment] begins with us, what will be the outcome for those who do not obey the gospel of God?" (1 Pet. 4:17). Paul spoke of divine wrath as one of the primary motivations for evangelism: "Therefore, knowing the fear of the Lord, we persuade others" (2 Cor. 5:11).

WHERE IS USER-FRIENDLINESS TAKING THE CHURCH?

The user-friendly philosophy is a sharp turn down a wrong road for the church. I am convinced that the downgrading of worship, Scripture, and theology will ultimately usher in serious doctrinal compromise. In fact, that may already be happening. Christian leaders who identify themselves as evangelical are beginning to question cardinal doctrines such as hell and human depravity.

One of the most popular movements afoot today embraces a doctrine known as "conditional immortality," similar to annihilationism.[11] It is the idea that unredeemed sinners are simply eradicated rather than spending eternity in hell. A perfect fit for the user-friendly philosophy, this view teaches that a merciful God could not possibly consign created beings to eternal torment. Instead, he obliterates them completely.

"Conditional immortality"—annihilationism—is not a new idea. History shows, however, that most people and movements who adopt anni-hilationist views do not remain orthodox. Denying the eternality of hell is tantamount to a running start on the down-grade. But recently, especially within certain sectors of the Emerging Church movement, conditional immortality and even less sophisticated denials of hell have become fairly commonplace. Unfortunately, even those who say they do believe in hell are happy—in the name of unity and charity, of course—to join hands with those who deny it. They don't seem to care that the doctrine is being undermined in a way that diminishes the gravity and urgency of the gospel message. These days most evangelicals simply yawn at such deviations from biblical orthodoxy.

Spurgeon attacked "conditional immortality" as one of the great errors of the nineteenth-century down-grade. He said that those who deny the eternality of hell "have pretty nearly obliterated the hope of such a heaven as we have all along expected. Of course, the reward of the righteous is to be of no longer continuance than the punishment of the wicked. Both are described as 'everlasting' in the same verse [Matt. 25:46], spoken by the same sacred lips; and as the 'punishment' is made out to be only 'age-lasting,' so must the 'life' be."[12]

Scripture says, "The devil who had deceived them was thrown into the lake of fire and sulfur where the beast and the false prophet were, and they

---

[11]*Conditional immortality* teaches that human souls are not inherently immortal; thus those damned in the judgment pass into oblivion, while the righteous are given immortality. *Annihilationism* is the view that all souls are immortal, but the wicked lose their immortality in the judgment.
[12]"Progressive Theology," *The Sword and the Trowel* (1888), 158.

will be tormented day and night forever and ever" (Rev. 20:10). Jesus told of the rich man who "in Hades, being in torment . . . lifted up his eyes and saw Abraham far off and Lazarus at his side. And he called out, 'Father Abraham, have mercy on me, and send Lazarus to dip the end of his finger in water and cool my tongue, for I am in anguish in this flame'" (Luke 16:23–24). It was also Jesus who said, "If your eye causes you to sin, tear it out. It is better for you to enter the kingdom of God with one eye than with two eyes to be thrown into hell, 'where their worm does not die and the fire is not quenched'" (Mark 9:47–48). And Revelation 14:11 describes the eternal state of those who follow Antichrist in the Tribulation: "The smoke of their torment goes up forever and ever, and they have no rest, day or night, these worshipers of the beast and its image, and whoever receives the mark of its name." The most prolific teacher on hell in all of Scripture was the Lord Jesus Himself. He had more to say about the subject than all the apostles, prophets, and evangelists of Scripture put together.

Preaching that downplays God's wrath does not enhance evangelism; it undermines it. The solemnity of the gospel and the fear of God are utterly trampled when the preacher denies the reality and severity of eternal punishment. The authority of Scripture is compromised when so much of Christ's clear message must be denied or explained away. The seriousness of sin is depreciated by this teaching. And therefore the gospel itself is subverted.

How deeply has the tendency to deny hell penetrated evangelicalism? One survey of evangelical seminary students revealed that nearly half—46 percent—feel that preaching about hell to unbelievers is in "poor taste."[13] Worse, three out of every ten self-professed "born again" people surveyed believe "good" people will go to heaven when they die—even if they've never trusted Christ.[14] One in every ten evangelicals say they believe the concept of sin is outmoded. A 2002 article on the front page of the *Los Angeles Times* said this:

> In churches across America, hell is being frozen out as clergy find themselves increasingly hesitant to sermonize on [the subject]. . . .
> Hell's fall from fashion indicates how key portions of Christian theology have been influenced by a secular society that stresses individualism over authority and the human psyche over moral absolutes. The rise of psychology, the philosophy of existentialism and the consumer culture have all dumped buckets of water on hell. . . .

---

[13]James Davison Hunter, *Evangelicalism: The Coming Generation* (Chicago: University of Chicago, 1987), 40.
[14]George Barna, *The Barna Report* (Ventura, CA: Regal, 1992), 52.

> "It's just too negative," said [one] professor of church history. . . .
> "Churches are under enormous pressure to be consumer-oriented.
> Churches today feel the need to be appealing rather than demanding."[15]

The article also quoted a pastor who told why he thought hell was omitted in the contemporary church: "It isn't sexy enough anymore."

Too many who have embraced the user-friendly trend have not carefully pondered how user-friendliness is incompatible with true biblical theology. It is, at its heart, a pragmatic, not a biblical, outlook. It is based on precisely the kind of thinking that is eating away at the heart of orthodox doctrine. It is leading evangelicalism into neo-modernism and putting churches in the fast lane on the down-grade.

The answer, of course, is not an *un*friendly church, but a vibrant, loving, honest, committed, worshiping fellowship of believers who minister to one another like the church in Acts 4—but who eschew sin, keep one another accountable, and boldly proclaim the full truth of Scripture. People who have no love for the things of God may not find such a place very user-friendly. But God's blessing will be on the fellowship, because that is what He ordained the church to be like. And He *will* add to the church, as He promised.

---

[15]Mike Anton and William Lobdell, "Hold the Fire and Brimstone," *Los Angeles Times* (June 19, 2002), A1.

3

GIMME THAT SHOW-TIME RELIGION

The fact is, that many would like to unite church and stage, cards and prayer, dancing and sacraments. If we are powerless to stem this torrent, we can at least warn men of its existence, and entreat them to keep out of it. When the old faith is gone, and enthusiasm for the gospel is extinct, it is no wonder that people seek something else in the way of delight. Lacking bread, they feed on ashes; rejecting the way of the Lord, they run greedily in the path of folly.

CHARLES HADDON SPURGEON[1]

Toward the end of the nineteenth century . . . the Age of Exposition began to pass, and the early signs of its replacement could be discerned. Its replacement was to be the Age of Show Business."[2]

While Charles Spurgeon was doing battle in the Down-Grade Controversy, a worldwide trend was beginning to emerge that would set the course of human affairs for all of the twentieth century. It was the emergence of entertainment at the very center of family and cultural life. This trend saw the decline of what Neil Postman terms "the Age of Exposition"—marked by the thoughtful exchange of ideas through print and verbal means (preaching, debates, lectures). And it gave rise to "the Age of Show Business"—in which amusements and entertainment have become the most important and time-consuming aspects of human discourse. Drama, film, and finally television have moved show business into the center of our lives—ultimately right into the middle of our family rooms.

---

[1] "Another Word Concerning the Down-Grade," *The Sword and the Trowel* (August 1887), 398.
[2] Neil Postman, *Amusing Ourselves to Death* (New York: Penguin, 1985), 63.

In show business, truth is irrelevant; what really matters is whether we are entertained. Substance counts for little; *style* is everything. In the words of Marshall McLuhan, the medium is the message. Unfortunately, that kind of thinking now rules the church as surely as it does the world.

A. W. Tozer wrote these words in 1955:

> For centuries the Church stood solidly against every form of worldly entertainment, recognizing it for what it was—a device for wasting time, a refuge from the disturbing voice of conscience, a scheme to divert attention from moral accountability. For this she got herself abused roundly by the sons of this world. But of late she has become tired of the abuse and has given over the struggle. She appears to have decided that if she cannot conquer the great god Entertainment she may as well join forces with him and make what use she can of his powers. So today we have the astonishing spectacle of millions of dollars being poured into the unholy job of providing earthly entertainment for the so-called sons of heaven. Religious entertainment is in many places rapidly crowding out the serious things of God. Many churches these days have become little more than poor theaters where fifth-rate "producers" peddle their shoddy wares with the full approval of evangelical leaders who can even quote a holy text in defense of their delinquency. And hardly a man dares raise his voice against it.[3]

By today's standards, the issues that so inflamed Tozer's passions seem trifling. For example, churches were attracting people to Sunday evening services by showing Christian films. Young people's rallies featured up-tempo music and speakers whose specialty was humor. High-energy games and activities were beginning to play a key role in church youth work. Looking back, it may seem difficult to understand Tozer's distress. Hardly anyone these days would be shocked or concerned about any of the methods that seemed radically innovative in the fifties. Most of them are generally regarded as conventional today.

Tozer, however, was not condemning games, music styles, or movies per se. He was concerned with the philosophy underlying what was happening in the church. He was sounding an alarm about a deadly change of focus. He saw evangelicals using entertainment as a tool for church growth, and he believed that was subverting the church's priorities. He feared that frivolous diversions and carnal amusements in the church would eventually destroy people's appetites for real worship and the preaching of God's Word.

---

[3]A. W. Tozer, *The Root of the Righteous* (Harrisburg, PA: Christian Publications, 1955), 32–33.

He was right about that. In fact, Tozer's rebuke is more fitting than ever for the church of the current generation. Tozer—and Spurgeon before him—were identifying a budding trend that now seems to have come into full bloom. What the church was flirting with a hundred years ago became an infatuation in Tozer's time. It is now an obsession.

An article in the *Wall Street Journal* described one well-known church's bid "to perk up attendance at Sunday evening services." The church "staged a wrestling match, featuring church employees. To train for the event, 10 game employees got lessons from Tugboat Taylor, a former professional wrestler, in pulling hair, kicking shins and tossing bodies around without doing real harm."[4] No harm to the staff members perhaps, but what is the effect of such an exhibition on the church's message? Is not the gospel itself clouded and badly caricatured by such tomfoolery? Can you imagine what Spurgeon or Tozer would have thought?

That wrestling match is not an obscure example from some eccentric church on the fringe. It took place in the Sunday evening service of one of America's five largest churches. Similar examples could be drawn from many of the leading churches supposedly in the mainstream of evangelical orthodoxy.

Some will maintain that if biblical principles are presented, the medium doesn't matter. That is nonsense. If an entertaining medium is the key to winning people, why not go all out? Why not have a real carnival? A tattooed acrobat on a high wire could juggle chain saws and shout Bible verses while a trick dog balances on his head. That would draw a crowd. And the *content* of the message would still be biblical. It's a bizarre scenario, but one that illustrates how the medium can cheapen and corrupt the message.

And sadly, it's not terribly different from what is actually being done in some churches. There seems no limit to what modern church leaders will do to entice people who aren't interested in worship and preaching. Too many have bought the notion that the church must win people by offering an alternative form of entertainment.

There seems no limit to how far some churches will go in competing with Hollywood. Some churches now have special-effects directors on their staffs to choreograph the fireworks in the Sunday morning services. A large church in the southwestern United States helped start this trend almost twenty years ago by installing a half-million-dollar special-effects system that would produce smoke, fire, sparks, and laser lights in the

---

[4]R. Gustav Niebuhr, "Mighty Fortresses: Megachurches Strive to Be All Things to All Parishioners," *The Wall Street Journal* (May 13, 1991), A6.

auditorium. The church sent staff members to study live special effects at Bally's Casino in Las Vegas. The pastor ended one service by ascending to "heaven" via invisible wires that drew him up out of sight while the choir and orchestra added a musical accompaniment to the smoke, fire, and light show.[5] It was just a typical Sunday show for that pastor: "He packs his church with such special effects as . . . cranking up a chain saw and toppling a tree to make a point . . . the biggest Fourth of July fireworks display in town and a Christmas service with a rented elephant, kangaroo and zebra. The Christmas show features 100 clowns with gifts for the congregation's children."[6] Those things are nothing by twenty-first-century standards. Things like confetti pyrotechnics, "flame projectors," and audioanimatronics (for the children's ministry, of course) have become fairly common, and churches pay millions for such equipment.

Shenanigans such as exploding confetti and flaming special effects would have been the stuff of Spurgeon's worst nightmares. Even Tozer could not have foreseen the extreme to which evangelicals would go in paying homage to the great god Entertainment.

DRIVEN BY PRAGMATISM

There's no denying that these antics seem to work—that is, they draw a crowd. Many churches that have experimented with such methods report growing attendance figures. A handful of megachurches—those that can afford first-class productions, effects, and facilities—have been able to stimulate enormous numerical growth. Some of them fill huge auditoriums with thousands of people several times every week.

A few of these megachurches resemble elegant country clubs or resort hotels. They feature impressive facilities with bowling lanes, movie theaters, health spas, restaurants, ballrooms, roller-skating rinks, and state-of-the-art multi-court gymnasiums. Recreation and entertainment are inevitably the most visible aspects of these enterprises. Such churches have become meccas for students of church growth.

Evangelicals everywhere are frantically seeking new techniques and new forms of entertainment to attract people. Whether a method is biblical or not scarcely seems to matter to the average church leader—or church-goer—today. Does it *work*? That is the new test of legitimacy. And so raw pragmatism has become the driving force in much of the professing church.

---

[5]Robert Johnson, "Heavenly Gifts: Preaching a Gospel of Acquisitiveness, a Showy Sect Prospers," *The Wall Street Journal* (December 11, 1990), A1–8.
[6]Ibid., A8.

IT'S SHOWTIME!

When Charles Spurgeon warned about those who "would like to unite church and stage, cards and prayer, dancing and sacraments," he was belittled as an alarmist. But Spurgeon's prophecy has been fulfilled before our eyes. Modern church buildings are constructed like theaters ("playhouses," Spurgeon called them). Instead of a pulpit, the focus is a stage. Churches are hiring full-time media specialists, programming consultants, stage directors, drama coaches, special-effects wizards, pyrotechnicians, and choreographers.

This is all the natural extension of a market-driven church philosophy. If the church is only in business to promote a product, church leaders had *better* pay attention to the methods of Madison Avenue. After all, the church's chief competition is a world filled with secular amusements and a host of worldly goods and services. Therefore, the marketing experts say, we will never win people until we develop effective alternative forms of entertainment to capture people's attention and loyalty away from the world's offerings. That goal thus establishes the nature of the marketing campaign.

What's wrong with that? For one thing, the church has no business marketing its ministry as an alternative to secular amusements (1 Thess 3:2–6). That corrupts and cheapens the church's real mission. We are not auctioneers, peddlers, showmen, used car salesmen, or commercial pitchmen. We are Christ's ambassadors (2 Cor. 5:20). Knowing the terror of the Lord (v. 11), motivated by the love of Christ (v. 14), utterly made new by Him (v. 17), we implore sinners to be reconciled to God (v. 20).

Moreover, instead of confronting the world with the truth of Christ, the market-driven megachurches are enthusiastically promoting the worst trends of secular culture. Feeding people's appetite for entertainment only exacerbates the problems of mindless emotion, apathy, and materialism. Quite frankly, it is difficult to conceive of a ministry philosophy more contradictory to the pattern our Lord gave us.

Proclaiming the gospel message of redemption for sinners and teaching the Word for the maturing and holiness of believers should be the heart of every church's ministry. If the world looks at the church and sees an entertainment center or a country club, we're sending the wrong message. If Christians view the church as an amusement parlor, the church will die.

Nothing in Scripture indicates the church should lure people to Christ by presenting Christianity as an attractive option. In the first place, nothing about the gospel is *optional*: "There is salvation in no one else . . . there is no other name under heaven that has been given among men by which we must be saved" (Acts 4:12). In the second place, the gospel is not meant to be *attractive* in the sense of modern marketing. As we have noted, the message of the gospel is often "a stone of stumbling, and a rock of offense" (Rom. 9:33; 1 Pet. 2:8). It is disturbing, revolting, upsetting, confrontive, convicting, and offensive to human pride. There's no way to "market" that. Those who try to erase the offense by making it entertaining inevitably corrupt and obscure crucial aspects of the message. The church must realize that its mission has never been public relations or sales; we are called to live holy lives and declare God's raw truth—lovingly but uncompromisingly—to an unbelieving world.

IS NUMERICAL GROWTH A LEGITIMATE GOAL?

Perhaps I should say that I am no opponent of large churches or of church growth. Grace Community Church was founded in the 1950s and grew exponentially in its first decade, before I ever arrived. By God's grace, the church has continued to see steady growth through most of its history. In a typical week, more than ten thousand people attend our services. We experienced cycles of growth followed by plateaus for several years, until our parking and facilities reached maximum capacity. Neither our attendance nor our people's enthusiasm has diminished one bit since then. As a matter of fact, we keep having to find new ways to accommodate the continuing growth. We send people out for ministry, and in such a transient society, we lose people to job transfers and major life changes. Meanwhile, we still add new members to the church—a hundred or more every month. We also baptize new converts virtually every week. So we are still seeing steady, strong growth, and of course we see that as a good and healthy thing.

What I oppose is the pragmatism often advocated by church growth specialists who elevate numerical growth over spiritual growth and who believe they can induce that numerical growth by following whatever techniques seem to be working at the moment. The faddism bred by that philosophy is becoming more and more unruly. It is diverting many churches from biblical priorities, while producing a handful of megachurches whose growth is dependent on their ability to anticipate and respond to the next cultural trend. The church has been drawn away from true revival and is being seduced by those who advocate the *popularization* of Christianity.

Tragically, most Christians seem oblivious to the problem, satisfied with a Christianity that is fashionable and highly visible.

Is numerical growth a legitimate goal in church ministry? Certainly no worthy church leader would seriously argue that numerical growth is inherently undesirable. And no one believes stagnation or numerical decline are to be sought. But is numerical growth always the best gauge of a church's health?

I agree with George Peters, who wrote,

> Quantitative growth . . . can be deceptive. It may be no more than the mushrooming of a mechanically induced, psychological or social movement, a numerical count, an agglomeration of individuals or groups, an increase of a body without the development of muscle and vital organs. It may be Christendom in the making but not Christianity breaking through. Many mass movements of the past and community and tribal movements have been just that. An example is found in the mass accessions in Europe, particularly in France and Russia, when many were driven to baptism and drawn into the church, resulting in a mass of people professing Christendom but not in a dynamic, vibrant, growing, and responsible church of Jesus Christ. . . . It must be admitted . . . that to a great extent this expansion of the form, profession, and name of Christendom has little resemblance to the Christianity defined in the New Testament and the church portrayed in the book of Acts.
>
> In many ways the expansion of Christendom has come at the expense of the purity of the gospel and true Christian order and life. The church has become infested with pagan beliefs and practices, and is syncretistic in theology. . . . Large segments have become Christo-pagan.[7]

Nothing in Scripture indicates that church leaders should set numerical goals for church growth.[8] Here's how the apostle Paul described the growth process: "I planted, Apollos watered, but *God gave the growth*. So neither he who plants nor he who waters is anything, but only *God who gives the growth*" (1 Cor. 3:6–7, emphasis added).

If we concern ourselves with the *depth* of our ministry, God will see

---

[7]George W. Peters, *A Theology of Church Growth* (Grand Rapids, MI: Zondervan, 1981), 23–24.
[8]Cf. C. Peter Wagner, in *Understanding Church Growth*, ed. Donald A. McGavran, third edition (Grand Rapids, MI: Eerdmans, 1990), 265–281. Here Wagner and McGavran argue that numerical goal setting is an essential part of a biblical approach to church growth: "Setting membership goals is in accordance with God's eternal purpose. Goal setting in the service of the Great Commission is pleasing to God. . . . Scripture is solidly on the side of careful planning for church growth" (270). Yet the only passage of Scripture they cite in support of that statement is Acts 18:4–5, 9, which says nothing about the setting of goals, numerical or otherwise.

to the *breadth* of it. If we minister for spiritual growth, numerical growth will take care of itself.

What good, after all, is numerical expansion that is not rooted in commitment to the lordship of Christ? If people come to church primarily because they find it entertaining, they will surely leave as soon as they stop being amused or something comes along to interest them more. And so the church is forced into a hopeless cycle where it must constantly try to eclipse each spectacle with something bigger and better.

THE PRAGMATIC ROOTS OF THE CHURCH GROWTH MOVEMENT

Pragmatism as a philosophy of ministry has gained impetus from the church growth movement that has flourished over the past fifty years or so. Donald McGavran, the father of the modern church growth movement, was an unabashed pragmatist:

> We devise mission methods and policies in the light of what God has blessed—and what He has obviously not blessed. Industry calls this "modifying operation in light of feedback." Nothing hurts missions overseas so much as continuing methods, institutions, and policies which ought to bring men to Christ—but don't; which ought to multiply churches—but don't. We teach men to be ruthless in regard to method. If it does not work to the glory of God and the extension of Christ's church, throw it away and get something which does. As to methods, we are fiercely pragmatic—doctrine is something else.[9]

As a young missionary in India and son of missionary parents, McGavran had noticed that it was not unusual for missions organizations to labor in India for years and have little or no fruit to show for it. McGavran's own agency had planted only twenty or thirty small churches in several decades of missionary work.[10] McGavran determined to devise a strategy of missions that took note of which methods seemed to work and which ones didn't. "As he declared in the preface to a book he co-authored in the 1930s, he had dedicated himself to 'discarding theories of church growth which do not work, and learning and practicing productive patterns. . . .'"[11]

McGavran's pragmatism seems to have been initially prompted by a

---

[9]Donald McGavran, "For Such a Time as This" (unpublished address, 1970), cited in C. Peter Wagner, "Pragmatic Strategy for Tomorrow's Mission," in ed. A. R. Tippett, *God, Man and Church Growth* (Grand Rapids, MI: Eerdmans, 1973), 147.
[10]Wagner, ed., *Understanding Church Growth*, viii–ix.
[11]Ibid., ix.

legitimate concern for stewardship. He "became alarmed when he saw all too many of God's resources—personnel and finances—being used without asking whether the kingdom of God was being advanced by the programs they were supporting."[12] But pragmatism became the philosophical basis for nearly all that McGavran taught, and that in turn set the agenda for the whole church growth movement.

McGavran founded the Institute of Church Growth, which in 1965 united with the Fuller School of World Mission. From there the pragmatic precepts of the church growth movement have reached into virtually every mission field worldwide.

C. Peter Wagner, professor of church growth at the Fuller School of World Mission, is Donald McGavran's best-known student. Wagner is the most prolific, if not the most influential spokesman in the church growth movement today. He writes of the movement's inherent pragmatism:

> The Church Growth Movement has always stressed pragmatism, and still does even though many have criticized it. It is not the kind of pragmatism that compromises doctrine or ethics or the kind that dehumanizes people by using them as means toward an end. It is, however, the kind of consecrated pragmatism which ruthlessly examines traditional methodologies and programs asking the tough questions. If some sort of ministry in the church is not reaching intended goals, consecrated pragmatism says there is something wrong which needs to be corrected.[13]

Wagner, like most in the church growth movement, claims that the "consecrated pragmatism" he advocates does not allow compromise of doctrine or ethics. "The Bible does not allow us to sin that grace may abound or to use whatever means that God has prohibited in order to accomplish those ends He has recommended," he notes correctly.[14]

"But with this proviso," Wagner continues, "we ought to see clearly that the end *does* justify the means. What else possibly could justify the means? If the method I am using accomplishes the goal I am aiming at, it is for that reason a good method. If, on the other hand, my method is not accomplishing the goal, how can I be justified in continuing to use it?"[15]

Is that true? Certainly not. Especially if "the goal I am aiming at" is a numerical goal with no biblical warrant, or if "my method . . . not accom-

---

[12]Ibid.
[13]C. Peter Wagner, *Leading Your Church to Growth* (Ventura, CA: Regal, 1984), 201.
[14]C. Peter Wagner, *Your Church Can Grow* (Ventura, CA: Regal, 1976), 160–161.
[15]Ibid., 161 (emphasis in original).

plishing the goal" is the clear preaching of God's Word. That is precisely the kind of thinking that is moving biblical exposition out of Christian ministry and replacing it with vaudeville.

One recent best seller goes even further:

> It is . . . critical that we keep in mind a fundamental principle of Christian communication: the audience, not the message, is sovereign. If our advertising is going to stop people in the midst of hectic schedules and cause them to think about what we're saying, *our message has to be adapted to the needs of the audience.* When we produce advertising that is based on the take-it-or-leave-it proposition, rather than on a sensitivity and response to people's needs, people will invariably reject our message.[16]

What if the Old Testament prophets had subscribed to such a philosophy? Jeremiah, for example, preached forty years without seeing any significant positive response. On the contrary, his countrymen threatened to kill him if he did not stop prophesying (Jer. 11:19–23); his own family and friends plotted against him (12:6); he was not permitted to marry and so had to suffer agonizing loneliness (16:2); plots were devised to kill him secretly (18:20–23); he was beaten and put in stocks (20:1–2); he was spied on by friends who sought revenge (v. 10); he was consumed with sorrow and shame—even cursing the day he was born (vv. 14–18); and finally, falsely accused of being a traitor to the nation (37:13–14), Jeremiah was beaten, thrown into a dungeon, and starved many days (vv. 15–21). If an Ethiopian Gentile had not interceded on his behalf, Jeremiah would have died there. In the end, tradition says he was exiled to Egypt, where he was stoned to death by his own people. He had virtually no converts to show for a lifetime of ministry.

Suppose Jeremiah had attended a church growth seminar and learned a pragmatic philosophy of ministry. Do you think he would have changed his style of confrontive ministry? Can you imagine him staging a variety show or using comedy to try to win people's affections? He may have learned to gather an appreciative crowd, but he certainly would not have had the ministry to which God called him.

The apostle Paul didn't use a system based on merchandising skill either, though some self-appointed experts have tried to make him a model of the new pragmatism. Reading into the Bible's white space, one advocate of marketing technique asserts, "Paul was one of the all time great tacti-

---

[16]Barna, *Marketing the Church*, 145 (emphasis added).

cians. He perpetually studied strategies and tactics to identify those that would enable him to attract the most 'prospects' and realize the greatest number of conversions."[17] Of course, the Bible says nothing like that. On the contrary, the apostle Paul shunned clever methods and gimmicks that might proselyte people to false conversions through fleshly persuasion. Paul himself wrote,

> And I, when I came to you, brothers, did not come proclaiming to you the testimony of God with lofty speech or wisdom. For I decided to know nothing among you except Jesus Christ and him crucified. And I was with you in weakness and in fear and much trembling, and my speech and my message were not in plausible words of wisdom, but in demonstration of the Spirit and of power, that your faith might not rest in the wisdom of men but in the power of God. (1 Cor. 2:1–5)

He reminded the church at Thessalonica,

> For our appeal does not spring from error or impurity or any attempt to deceive, but just as we have been approved by God to be entrusted with the gospel, so we speak, not to please man, but to please God who tests our hearts. For we never came with words of flattery, as you know, nor with a pretext for greed—God is witness. Nor did we seek glory from people, whether from you or from others, though we could have made demands as apostles of Christ. (1 Thess. 2:3–6)

Biblical correctness is the *only* framework by which we can evaluate ministry methods.

Any end-justifies-the-means philosophy of ministry inevitably *will* compromise doctrine, despite any proviso to the contrary. If we make effectiveness the gauge of right and wrong, how can that fail to color our doctrine? Ultimately the pragmatist's notion of truth is shaped by what seems effective, not by the objective revelation of Scripture.

A look at the methodology of the church growth movement shows how this occurs. The movement studies *all* growing churches—even those with false doctrine at the core of their teaching. Liberal denominational churches, extreme charismatic sects, and militant hyper-fundamentalist dictatorships all are held up to the specialist's scrutiny. Sometimes principles of growth are gleaned even from Mormon assemblies and Jehovah's Witness Kingdom Halls. The church growth expert looks for characteristics

---

[17]Ibid., 31–32.

common to all growing churches and advocates whatever methods seem
to work.

Are we to believe that growth in non-Christian congregations is proof
that God is at work? Why would we want to duplicate the methodology
of religious groups that deny the gospel? Isn't it fair to question whether
any growth resulting from such methods is illegitimate, engineered by
fleshly means? After all, if a method works as well for a cult as it does for
the people of God, there's no reason to assume that positive results signify
God's blessing.

Utterly missing from most of the church growth literature is any critical analysis of the faulty doctrinal platform on which much contemporary
church growth is built. One author has said of Peter Wagner:

> Wagner makes negative assessments about nobody. He has made a
> career out of finding what is good in growing churches, and affirming
> it—without asking many critical questions. This enables him to hold
> up as models of church life not only Wimber's Vineyard, but Schuller's
> Crystal Cathedral, the entire Southern Baptist denomination, and just
> about any other church that is growing.[18]

The fact that a church is growing is often mistaken for divine sanction.
After all, people reason, why be critical of any teaching that God is blessing with numerical growth? Is it not better to tolerate doctrinal flaws and
lapses of orthodoxy for the sake of growth and unity? Thus pragmatism
molds and shapes one's doctrinal outlook.

Wagner himself, for example, has embraced the signs and wonders of
the Third Wave movement for reasons that are largely pragmatic. He is
very candid about this:

> I am proud to be among those who are advocating power evangelism
> as an important tool for fulfilling the great commission in our day.
> One of the reasons I am so enthusiastic is that *it is working*. Across the
> board, the most effective evangelism in today's world is accompanied
> by manifestations of supernatural power.[19]

Obviously, then, Wagner's pragmatic perspective *has* shaped his doctrine,
not vice versa.

Wagner virtually concedes this point. He says the methodology of the
church growth movement is "phenomenological," not theological. That

---

[18]Tim Stafford, "Testing the Wine from John Wimber's Vineyard," *Christianity Today* (August 8, 1986), 18.
[19]C. Peter Wagner, *The Third Wave of the Holy Spirit* (Ann Arbor, MI: Vine, 1988), 87.

approach "may appear altogether too subjective to many traditional theologians," he admits.[20] He continues, "As a starting point, church growth often looks to the 'is' previous to the 'ought.' . . . What Christians experience about God's work in the world and in their lives is not always preceded by careful theological rationalizations. Many times the sequence is just the opposite: theology is shaped by Christian experience."[21]

That being the case, isn't Wagner's assertion that his pragmatism "is not the kind . . . that compromises doctrine"[22] rendered meaningless? After all, if experience suggests that signs and wonders are effective tools for church growth, and if it is legitimate to allow our experience to shape our theology, it is quite logical to amend one's doctrine—as Wagner himself did—to accommodate some pragmatic, heuristic observation. One must then simply find a way to reinterpret or adapt Scripture to fit whatever doctrinal scheme pragmatism seems to dictate.

It is folly to think one can be both pragmatic *and* biblical. The pragmatist wants to know *what works now*. The biblical thinker cares only about *what the Bible mandates*. The two philosophies oppose each other at the most basic level.

THE AGE OF PRAGMATISM

Nevertheless, philosophical pragmatism has never been more popular in evangelical churches. The church growth movement, which for years was a major factor in world missionary activity, is now having enormous influence in the backyard of Western evangelicalism. The chickens of pragmatism are coming home to roost. North American churches by the hundreds are experimenting with pragmatic methodologies, and the result has been an explosion of interest in innovative church growth techniques. The church growth movement has formed an unofficial alliance with those who believe evangelism is primarily a marketing venture.

Pragmatism in the church reflects the spirit of our age. Books with titles like *Marketing Your Ministry*, *Marketing the Church*, and *The Development of Effective Marketing and Communication Strategies for Churches* have set the tone for ministry for twenty years now. Dozens of Web sites devoted to church-marketing techniques vie for pastors' attention online. For decades now the Christian publishing industry has been producing more advice for church leaders drawn from secular fields of

---

[20]C. Peter Wagner, ed., *Church Growth: State of the Art* (Wheaton, IL: Tyndale, 1986), 33.
[21]Ibid.
[22]*Leading Your Church to Growth*, 201.

study—psychology, marketing, management, politics, entertainment, and business—than all the commentaries, Bible study helps, and books on biblical issues put together.

The role model for contemporary pastors is not the prophet or the shepherd—it is the corporate executive, the politician, or worst of all, the talk-show host. The contemporary church is preoccupied with audience ratings, popularity polls, corporate image, statistical growth, financial profit, opinion surveys, demographic charts, census figures, fashion trends, celebrity status, top-ten lists, and other pragmatic issues. Gone is the church's passion for purity and truth. No one seems to care, as long as the response is enthusiastic.

Tozer noticed that pragmatism had crept into the church of his day, too. He wrote, "I say without hesitation that a part, a very large part, of the activities carried on today in evangelical circles are not only influenced by pragmatism but almost completely controlled by it."[23] Tozer described the danger posed to the church by even so-called "consecrated" pragmatism:

> The pragmatic philosophy . . . asks no embarrassing questions about the wisdom of what we are doing or even about the morality of it. It accepts our chosen ends as right and good and casts about for efficient means and ways to get them accomplished. When it discovers something that works it soon finds a text to justify it, "consecrates" it to the Lord and plunges ahead. Next a magazine article is written about it, then a book, and finally the inventor is granted an honorary degree. After that any question about the scripturalness of things or even the moral validity of them is completely swept away. You cannot argue with success. The method works; *ergo*, it must be good.[24]

A BANKRUPT PHILOSOPHY

Do you see how the new philosophy necessarily undermines sound doctrine? It discards Jesus' own methods—preaching and teaching—as the primary means of ministry. It replaces them with methodologies utterly devoid of substance. It exists independently of any creed or canon. In fact, it avoids dogma or strong convictions as divisive, unbecoming, or inappropriate. It dismisses doctrine as academic, abstract, sterile, threatening, or simply impractical. Rather than teaching error or denying truth, it does something far more subtle, but just as effective from the enemy's point of view. It jettisons content altogether. Instead of attacking orthodoxy

---

[23]A. W. Tozer, *God Tells the Man Who Cares* (Harrisburg, PA: Christian Publications, 1970), 71.
[24]Ibid., 70.

head-on, it gives lip service to the truth while quietly undermining the foundations of doctrine. Instead of exalting God, it denigrates the things that are precious to Him. In that regard, pragmatism poses dangers more subtle than the liberalism that threatened the church in the first half of the century.

Liberalism attacked biblical preaching. One of the most notorious liberal figures in early twentieth-century America was Harry Emerson Fosdick, who wrote, "Preachers who pick out texts from the Bible and then proceed to give their historic settings, their logical meaning in the context, their place in the theology of the writer, with a few practical reflections appended, are grossly misusing the Bible."[25] Fosdick was driven to his hatred of biblical exposition by the same pragmatic concern that has invaded evangelicalism today:

> Could any procedure be more surely predestined to dullness and futility? Who seriously supposes that, as a matter of fact, one in a hundred of the congregation cares, to start with, what Moses, Isaiah, Paul, or John meant in those special verses, or came to church deeply concerned about it? Nobody who talks to the public so assumes that the vital interests of the people are located in the meaning of words spoken two thousand years ago.[26]

Fosdick's suggestion was that preachers start with the audience's felt needs: "Let them not end but start with thinking of the auditors' vital needs, and then let the whole sermon be organized around their constructive endeavor to meet those needs."[27]

"All this is good sense and good psychology," Fosdick wrote, appealing to pragmatism as his justification. "Everybody else is using it from first-class teachers to first-class advertisers. Why should so many preachers continue in such belated fashion to neglect it?"[28]

That is exactly the conventional wisdom of the user-friendly, market-driven philosophy. It starts with felt needs and addresses them with topical messages. If Scripture is used at all, it is only for illustrative purposes. Precisely as Fosdick advocated. It is sheer accommodation to a society addicted to entertainment. Only now that advice comes from *within* evangelicalism. It follows what is fashionable but reveals little concern for what is true. It was well-suited for the liberalism from whence it came. But it is

---

[25]Harry Emerson Fosdick, "What Is the Matter with Preaching?" *Harpers Magazine* (July 1928), 135.
[26]Ibid.
[27]Ibid.
[28]Ibid., 136.

totally out of place among Christians who profess to believe that Scripture is the inspired Word of God.

One recent best-selling evangelical book warns readers to be on guard against preachers whose emphasis is on *interpreting* Scripture rather than *applying* it. Wait a minute. Is that wise counsel? No, it is not. There is no danger of irrelevant doctrine; the real threat is an undoctrinal attempt at relevance. The nucleus of all that is truly practical is found in the teaching of Scripture. We don't *make* the Bible relevant; it is inherently so, simply because it is God's Word. And after all, how can *anything* God says be irrelevant (2 Tim. 3:16–17)?

THE CHURCH AS A PUB

The radical pragmatism of the "user-friendly" school of thought robs the church of its prophetic role. It makes the church a populist organization, recruiting members by providing them a warm and friendly atmosphere in which to eat, drink, and be entertained. The church becomes more like a saloon than a house of worship.

That is no overstatement. One recent best-selling book advocating pragmatic church-growth ideas included this suggestion:

> Remember how the corner tavern used to be the place where the men of the neighborhood would congregate to watch major sports events, like the World Series or championship boxing matches? While times have changed, that same concept can still be used to great impact by the Church. Most churches have a large hall or auditorium which could be used for special gatherings built around major media events— sports, political debates, entertainment specials and the like.[29]

In recent years, lots of church leaders, eager to be innovative, have applied that suggestion in the most literal sense. Men's meetings in some churches feature poker and cigars. Church-sponsored men's fraternal gatherings over pub drinks ("Grab a Brew, Share Your View") are likewise very stylish now.

That entire scenario is built on a set of presuppositions that are patently unbiblical. The church is not a lodge recruiting members. It is not a pub for the neighborhood. It is not a frat house enlisting pledges. It is not a community center where parties are held. It is not a country club for the masses. It is not a city precinct meeting where the community's problems

---

[29]George Barna, *The Frog in the Kettle* (Ventura, CA: Regal, 1990), 94–95.

are addressed. It is not a court to rectify society's injustices. It is not an open forum or a political convention or even an evangelistic rally.

The church is the body of Christ (1 Cor. 12:27), and church meetings are for corporate worship and instruction. The church's only legitimate goal is to "equip the saints for the work of ministry, for building up the body of Christ" (Eph. 4:12)—vital growth, not mere numerical expansion.

The notion that church meetings should be used to tantalize or attract non-Christians is a relatively recent development. Nothing like it is found in Scripture; in fact, the apostle Paul spoke of unbelievers entering the assembly as an exceptional event (1 Cor. 14:23). Hebrews 10:24–25 indicates that church services are for the benefit of believers, not unbelievers: "And let us consider how to stir up one another to love and good works, not neglecting to meet together."

Acts 2:42 shows us the pattern the early church followed when they met: "And they devoted themselves to the apostles' teaching and the fellowship, to the breaking of bread and the prayers." Note that the early church's priorities clearly were to worship God and uplift the brethren. The church came together for worship and edification; it scattered to evangelize the world.

Our Lord commissioned His disciples for evangelism in this way: "Go therefore and make disciples of all nations" (Matt. 28:19). Christ makes it clear that the church is not to wait for or invite the world to come to its meetings, but to *go* to the world. That is every believer's responsibility. I fear that an approach emphasizing a palatable gospel presentation within the walls of the church absolves the individual believer from his personal obligation to be a light in the world (Matt. 5:16).

Again we emphasize that the preaching of God's Word is to be central in the church (1 Cor. 1:23; 9:16; 2 Cor. 4:5; 1 Tim. 6:2; 2 Tim. 4:2). "In season and out of season," it is the task of God's ministers to "reprove, rebuke, and exhort, with complete patience and teaching" (2 Tim. 4:2). The pastor who sets entertainment above forceful preaching abdicates the primary responsibility of an elder: "hold[ing] firm to the trustworthy word as taught, so that he may be able to give instruction in sound doctrine and also to rebuke those who contradict it" (Titus 1:9).

The church's strategy has never been to appeal to the world on the world's terms. Churches aren't supposed to compete for the consumer on the same level as Miller Lite or MTV. We can't stimulate genuine growth by clever persuasion or inventive techniques. It is the Lord who adds to the church (Acts 2:47). Human methodologies cannot accelerate or supersede the divine process. Any additional growth they produce is a barren imitation.

Artificial or unnatural growth in the biological realm can cause disfigurement—or worse, cancer. Synthetic growth in the spiritual realm is every bit as unhealthy.

GOOD TECHNIQUE? NO, BAD THEOLOGY

The philosophy that marries marketing technique with church growth theory is the result of bad theology. It assumes that if you package the gospel right, people will get saved. It is rooted in Arminianism, which views conversion as nothing more than an act of the human will. Its goal is an instantaneous human decision, rather than a radical transformation of the heart wrought by almighty God through the Holy Spirit's convicting work and the truth of His Word. An honest belief in the sovereignty of God in salvation would bring an end to a lot of the nonsense that is going on in the church.

Moreover, this whole ad-agency approach to the church corrupts Christianity and caters to the fleshly lusts that are woven into the very fabric of this world's system (1 John 2:16). We have a society filled with people who want what they want when they want it. They are into their own lifestyle, recreation, and entertainment. When churches appeal to those selfish desires, they only fuel fires that hinder true godliness.

The church has accommodated our culture by devising a brand of Christianity where taking up one's cross is optional—or even unseemly. Indeed, many members of the church in the Western world suppose they can best serve God by being as non-confrontive to their world as possible.

Having absorbed the world's values, Christianity in our society is now dying. Subtly but surely, worldliness and self-indulgence are eating away the heart of the church. The gospel usually proclaimed today is so convoluted that it offers believing in Christ as nothing more than a means to contentment and prosperity. The offense of the cross (cf. Gal. 5:11) has been systematically removed so that the message might be made more acceptable to unbelievers. The church somehow got the idea it could declare peace with the enemies of God.

When on top of that punk rockers, ventriloquists' dummies, clowns, knife-throwers, professional wrestlers, weight lifters, bodybuilders, comedians, dancers, jugglers, ringmasters, rap artists, actors, and show-business celebrities take the place of the preacher, the gospel message is dealt a catastrophic blow. "How are they to hear without someone preaching?" (Rom. 10:14).

I do believe we can be innovative and creative in how we present the gospel, but we have to be careful to harmonize our methods with the profound spiritual truth we are trying to convey. It is too easy to trivialize the sacred message. And we must make the message, not the medium, the heart of what we want to convey to the audience.

Don't be quick to embrace the trends of the high-tech megachurches. And don't sneer at conventional worship and preaching. We don't need clever approaches to get people saved (1 Cor. 1:21). We simply need to get back to preaching the truth and planting the seed. If we're faithful in that, the soil God has prepared will bear fruit.

But if the church in America does not get back to biblical Christianity, we will soon see the end of our influence for Christ. Everyone is astonished to see how rapidly the face of the modern world is changing. What few Christians seem to realize is how frighteningly fast the church is coasting along the down-grade at the same time. We may be witnessing the last days of biblical evangelicalism in our nation. It is not really far-fetched to imagine that one day soon, missionaries from Africa, Asia, or Eastern Europe might be evangelizing America. (As a matter of fact, that is already beginning to happen.)

Portions of Europe that were once spiritually vibrant in the wake of the Protestant Reformation are now almost totally barren of spiritual life. That realization greatly alarms me, because I see the same thing occurring rapidly in the United Kingdom, America, and other parts of the world where the gospel is in decline and shallow religious entertainments are taking its rightful place in the church. We who know and love the truth must be the prophetic voice of our God and affirm the holiness of His name. We must demand that any effort in the name of our Lord manifest the integrity of His nature. He is "holy, holy, holy" (Isa. 6:3) and must be so represented. Anything less is not worthy of our Lord's majestic name.

THE BREAKING FORTH OF A LEPROSY

Spurgeon saw this tendency to import amusements into the church at the end of the nineteenth century, too. As the Down-Grade Controversy was raging in 1889, Spurgeon's health was waning badly, and he missed many Sundays in the pulpit. But on a Thursday evening in April, he brought a message at the Tabernacle in which he said,

I trust I am not given to finding fault where fault there is not; but I cannot open my eyes without seeing things done in our churches which, thirty years ago, were not so much as dreamed of. In the matter of amusements, professors have gone far in the way of laxity. What is worse, the churches have now conceived the idea that it is their duty to amuse the people. Dissenters who used to protest against going to the theatre, now cause the theatre to come to them. Ought not many [church buildings] to be licensed for stage-plays? If some one were to see to the rigid carrying out of the law, would they not be required to take out a license for theatricals?

I dare not touch upon what has been done at bazaars and fancy fairs. If these had been arranged by decent worldly people, could they have gone further? What folly has been left untried? What absurdity has been too great for the consciences of those who profess to be the children of God, who are not of the world, but called to walk with God in a separated life?

The world regards the high pretensions of such men as hypocrisy; and truly I do not know another name for them. Think of those who enjoy communion with God playing the fool in costume! They talk of wrestling with the Lord in secret prayer, but they juggle with the world in unconcealed gambling. Can this be right? Have right and wrong shifted places? Surely there is a sobriety of behaviour which is consistent with a work of grace in the heart, and there is a levity which betokens that the spirit of evil is supreme.

Ah, sirs! there may have been a time when Christians were too precise, but it has not been in my day. There may have been such a dreadful thing as Puritanic rigidity, but I have never seen it. We are quite free from that evil now, if it ever existed. We have gone from liberty to libertinism. We have passed beyond the dubious into the dangerous, and none can prophesy where we shall stop. Where is the holiness of the church of God to-day? . . . Now she is dim as smoking flax, and rather the object of ridicule than of reverence.

May not the measure of the influence of a church be estimated by its holiness? If the great host of professing Christians were, in domestic life and in business life, sanctified by the Spirit, the church would become a great power in the world. God's saints may well mourn with Jerusalem when they see spirituality and holiness at so low an ebb! Others may regard this as a matter of no consequence; but we view it as the breaking forth of a leprosy.[30]

The challenge for Christ's church is this: "Let us cleanse ourselves from

---

[30]"A Dirge for the Down-Grade, and A Song for Faith," *The Metropolitan Tabernacle Pulpit*, Vol. 35 (London: Passmore and Alabaster, 1889), 267–268.

every defilement of body and spirit, bringing holiness to completion in the fear of God" (2 Cor. 7:1). It isn't the cleverness of our methods, the techniques of our ministry, or the wit of our sermons that puts power in our testimony. It is obedience to a holy God and faithfulness to His righteous standard in our daily lives.

We must wake up. The down-grade is a dangerous place to be. We cannot afford to be indifferent. We cannot continue our mad pursuit of pleasure and self-gratification. We are called to fight a spiritual battle, and we cannot win by appeasing the enemy. A needy world must be confronted with the message of salvation, and there may be little time left. As Paul wrote to the church at Rome, "The hour has come for you to wake from sleep. For salvation is nearer to us now than when we first believed. The night is far gone; the day is at hand. So then let us cast off the works of darkness and put on the armor of light" (Rom. 13:11–12).

4

ALL THINGS TO ALL MEN

The extent to which sheer frivolity and utterly inane amusement have been carried in connection with some places of worship would almost exceed belief. . . . There can be no doubt that all sorts of entertainments, as nearly as possible approximating to stage-plays, have been carried on in connection with places of worship, and are, at this present time in high favour. Can these things promote holiness, or help in communion with God? Can men come away from such things and plead with God for the salvation of sinners and the sanctification of believers? We loathe to touch the unhallowed subject; it seems so far removed from the walk of faith and the way of heavenly fellowship. In some cases the follies complained of are even beneath the dignity of manhood, and fitter for the region of the imbecile than for thoughtful men.

CHARLES HADDON SPURGEON[1]

I doubt there has ever been anyone like Sister Paula in the entire history of Christianity. She describes herself as "an open transsexual Christian, preaching the gospel . . . Tammy Faye with a 5 o'clock shadow."[2] Sister Paula was born Larry Nielsen and supposedly became a Christian "in 1950, as a 12-year-old innately effeminate boy." After Larry became Paula in a sex-change operation a few years ago, a female Pentecostal televangelist friend urged Larry/Paula to start a television ministry. A 1992 issue of *People* magazine described Sister Paula as fifty-three years old, six feet one and a half inches tall, "built like a linebacker."[3] To this day, Sister Paula maintains her "ministry" on the Internet. She describes herself as "a true pioneer."

---

[1]"Restoration of Truth and Revival," *The Sword and the Trowel* (December 1887), 606.
[2]*People* (March 16, 1992), 68.
[3]Ibid.

Can you imagine anything more incongruous or more profane than a transsexual evangelist? Yet Sister Paula believes she can have a more effective ministry to people in our generation than the typical "straight" Christian using nothing but the gospel. Sister Paula's ministry philosophy is fundamentally the same strategy the church marketing experts advocate. Sadly, more and more people in the church are willing to see pragmatism taken even to such an extreme—and further yet.

The notion that the church must become like the world to win the world is hardly even controversial in the evangelical world anymore. Virtually every modern worldly attraction has a "Christian" counterpart. We have Christian motorcycle gangs, Christian bodybuilding teams, Christian dance clubs, Christian amusement parks, and even Christian nudist colonies.

Where did Christians ever get the idea we could win the world by imitating it? Is there a shred of biblical justification for that kind of thinking? Many church marketing specialists affirm that there is, and they have convinced a myriad of pastors. Ironically, they usually cite the apostle Paul as someone who advocated adapting the gospel to the tastes and lifestyle of the audience. One of the earliest evangelical authors who helped pave the way for the market-driven philosophy wrote, "Paul provided what I feel is perhaps the single most insightful perspective on marketing communications, the principle we call *contextualization* (1 Corinthians 9:19–23). Paul . . . was willing to shape his communications according to their needs in order to receive the response he sought."[4] Another expert in the genre echoed the same idea: "The first marketeer was Paul."[5]

After all, the apostle *did* write, "I have become all things to all people, that by all means I might save some. I do it all for the sake of the gospel, that I may share with them in its blessings" (1 Cor. 9:22–23). Is that a mandate for pragmatism in ministry? Was the apostle Paul suggesting the gospel message can be made to appeal to people by accommodating their relish for certain amusements or by pampering their pet vices? How far do you suppose he would have been willing to go with the principle of "contextualization"?

THE GREAT NON-NEGOTIABLE

One thing is clear: the apostle Paul was no men-pleaser. He wrote, "For am I now seeking the approval of man, or of God? Or am I trying to please man? If I were still trying to please man, I would not be a servant of Christ"

---

[4]George Barna, *Marketing the Church* (Colorado Springs: NavPress, 1988), 33.
[5]Cited in Mike McIntyre, "Marketing the Maker," *The San Diego Union* (November 6, 1988), D8.

(Gal. 1:10). Paul did not amend or abridge his message to make people happy. He was utterly unwilling to try to remove the offense from the gospel (Gal. 5:11). He did not use methodology that catered to the lusts of his listeners. He certainly did not follow the pragmatic philosophy of modern market-driven ministers.

What made Paul effective was not marketing savvy, but a stubborn devotion to the truth. He was Christ's ambassador, not His press secretary. Truth was something to be declared, not negotiated. Paul was not ashamed of the gospel (Rom. 1:16). He willingly suffered for the truth's sake (2 Cor. 11:23–28). He did not back down in the face of opposition or rejection. He did not compromise with unbelievers or make friends with the enemies of God.

Paul's message was *always* non-negotiable. In the same chapter where he spoke of becoming all things to all men, Paul wrote, "Necessity is laid upon me. Woe to me if I do not preach the gospel!" (1 Cor. 9:16). His ministry was in response to a divine mandate. God had called him and commissioned him. Paul preached the gospel exactly as he had received it directly from the Lord, and he always delivered that message "as of first importance" (1 Cor. 15:3). He was not a salesman or marketer, but a divine emissary. He certainly was *not* "willing to shape his communications" to accommodate his listeners or produce a desirable response. The fact that he was stoned and left for dead (Acts 14:19), beaten, imprisoned, and finally killed for the truth's sake ought to demonstrate that he didn't adapt the message to make it pleasing to his hearers! And the personal suffering he bore because of his ministry did *not* indicate that something was wrong with his approach, but that everything had been right!

So what did Paul mean when he wrote, "I have become all things to all people, that by all means I might save some. I do it all for the sake of the gospel"? As always, the context makes his meaning clear.

GIVING UP TO GAIN

Look again at what Paul is actually saying in these verses:

> For though I am free from all, I have made myself a servant to all, that I might win more of them. To the Jews I became as a Jew, in order to win Jews. To those under the law I became as one under the law (though not being myself under the law) that I might win those under the law. To those outside the law I became as one outside the law (not being outside the law of God but under the law of Christ) that I might win

those outside the law. To the weak I became weak, that I might win the weak. I have become all things to all people, that by all means I might save some. I do it all for the sake of the gospel, that I may share with them in its blessings. (1 Cor. 9:19–23)

The first sentence in that brief excerpt shows clearly what Paul was talking about. He was describing not his willingness to sacrifice the message, but his willingness to sacrifice himself to win people to Christ. He would give up everything—even become "a servant to all"—if that would promote the spread of the unadulterated gospel. His desire to win souls is the heart of this text, and he repeats it several times: "that I might win more of them" (v. 19); "in order to win Jews"; "that I might win those under the law" (v. 20); "that I might win those outside the law" (v. 21); "that I might win the weak"; and "that by all means I might save some" (v. 22). So winning people to Christ was his one objective. In order to do that, Paul was willing to give up all his rights and privileges, his position, his rank, his livelihood, his freedom—ultimately even his life. If it would further the spread of the gospel, Paul would claim no rights, make no demands, insist on no privileges.

And that is precisely how Paul lived and ministered. Not that he would modify the message to suit the world, but that he would behave so that he personally would never be an obstacle to anyone's hearing and understanding the message of Christ. He was describing an attitude of personal sacrifice, not compromise. He would never alter the clear and confrontive call to repentance and faith.

To put it another way, Paul was saying that Christian liberty must be circumscribed by love. That is the whole theme of 1 Corinthians 8–10. It is the context in which these verses are found. The Corinthians were evidently debating about Christian freedom. Some wanted to use their liberty to do whatever they desired. Others leaned toward legalism, begrudging those who enjoyed their liberty in Christ. Paul was reminding both groups that Christian freedom is to be used to glorify God and serve others, not for selfish reasons.

Some of the Corinthians had apparently asked Paul whether they were free to eat meat offered to idols (8:1). Such meat often was collected from the pagan temples and sold in the marketplace at bargain prices. Paul told them it is not inherently wrong to eat such food, but if doing so places a stumbling block in someone else's way, such an offense against another person is wrong. Paul summarized his reply with these words: "So, whether you eat or drink, or whatever you do, do all to the glory of God. Give no offense to Jews or to Greeks or to the church of God, just as I try to please everyone in everything I do, not seeking my own advantage, but that of many, that they may be saved" (10:31–33).

How did Paul use his own liberty in Christ? "Though I am free from all, I have made myself a servant to all, that I might win more of them" (9:19). He saw his personal liberty and human rights as something to be used for God's glory, not his own enjoyment. If he could trade his own liberty for an opportunity to proclaim the gospel and thus liberate others, he would do it gladly.

LIBERTY IN CHRIST

It is crucial that we understand the nature of Christian liberty. We are not under law, but under grace (Rom. 6:14). Freedom from the law certainly does not mean that the principles of righteousness revealed in the law are now nullified. It does not mean that the Ten Commandments have no application to our present lives. It does not mean that we can subjugate God's holy standards to personal preference. It certainly does not mean we are free from any moral requirements.

What does it mean? It means that Christians are not bound to observe Old Testament ritual. We don't have to sacrifice animals, observe the laws of ceremonial cleanness, and celebrate all the new moons and feasts and sacrifices. We don't have to follow the dietary laws given to Israel through Moses. We are free from all that.

Likewise, obviously, we are free from all Gentile religious ceremony and superstition. Whatever our religious background or heritage, in Christ we are free from all the trappings of it. We now live by God's grace, which has the principle of true righteousness built in.

In other words, our spiritual lives are governed not by an external code but by God's grace, which operates in us to fulfill the righteous requirements of the law (Rom. 8:4). Grace teaches us to deny ungodliness and worldly desires and to live sensibly, righteously, and godly (Titus 2:12). And grace empowers us to live holy lives.

This tremendous liberty is one of the most remarkable aspects of the Christian life. We have no need to yield to custom or ceremony or human opinion. There are no earthly priests to intercede between us and God: "There is one God, and there is one mediator between God and men, the man Christ Jesus" (1 Tim. 2:5). We don't need to make a pilgrimage to a temple somewhere to worship; our very bodies are temples of the Holy Spirit (1 Cor. 6:19). We can worship God in spirit and in truth anytime, anyplace (John 4:23–24). Whatever we ask in Jesus' name He will do (John 14:13–14). The Holy Spirit is given to us as our advocate and comforter (vv. 16, 26). All things belong to us, and we are Christ's, and Christ is God's (1 Cor. 3:21–23).

SERVANTS OF A NEW COVENANT

Yet there is a paradox that balances that truth. Though free, all Christians are slaves. It is a new kind of bondage: we are "ministers of a new covenant, not of the letter but of the Spirit. For the letter kills, but the Spirit gives life" (2 Cor. 3:6). As willing slaves, we must voluntarily restrict our own liberty for others' sakes. Isn't that what Jesus Himself taught? "If anyone would be first, he must be last of all and servant of all" (Mark 9:35). Paul applied the principle of voluntary servitude to evangelism. He made himself a slave to all—including the roughest, most contemptible, loathsome pagan. Being free, he nevertheless joyfully entered into slavery for the gospel's sake.

This principle of voluntary slavery was pictured graphically in the Old Testament law. Exodus 21:5–6 describes the process by which one could choose to make himself another's servant: "If the slave plainly says, 'I love my master, my wife, and my children; I will not go out free,' then his master shall bring him to God, and he shall bring him to the door or the doorpost. And his master shall bore his ear through with an awl, and he shall be his slave forever." The Israelites were permitted to keep fellow Jews as slaves only for six years. On the seventh year they were to be set free. But if one voluntarily chose to continue serving as a slave, his master would literally put his ear against the doorpost, take an awl, and drive it through the ear. The hole in the slave's ear was a sign to all that he was serving out of love, not because he had to. Paul was saying he had voluntarily relinquished his freedom in order to serve all men. In a spiritual sense, Paul had perforated his ear on behalf of the unsaved. "Though I am free from all, I have made myself a servant to all, that I might win more of them" (1 Cor. 9:19).

The word translated "made . . . a servant" is the Greek verb *douloō*, "to enslave." This is a strong expression. It is the same word used in 1 Corinthians 7:15 in relation to the marriage bond. And the same word is used in Romans 6:18, 22 to speak of our union with Christ. It describes an exceedingly secure bond. Paul had denied himself in the truest sense by placing himself under such a bond to everyone else.

The phrase "that I might win more of them" is not talking about winning earthly or heavenly rewards. Paul was speaking of winning the lost to Christ. Such was Paul's concern for lost souls that, though he was free in Christ, he was willing to enslave himself to people if it would give him an opportunity to proclaim the gospel. He expressed a similar commitment in 2 Timothy 2:10: "I endure everything for the sake of the elect, that they also may obtain the salvation that is in Christ Jesus with eternal glory."

Consider all that Paul suffered for the gospel's sake. He became a prisoner. He went to jail. He was beaten, whipped, shipwrecked, and stoned. He continually set his own life aside. Ultimately he was killed for the testimony of the gospel. He would have gone even further if it were possible. In Romans 9:2–3 he wrote these shocking words: "I have great sorrow and unceasing anguish in my heart. For I could wish that I myself were accursed and cut off from Christ for the sake of my brothers, my kinsmen according to the flesh." In other words, he felt as if he would have given up his own salvation if he could, so that his Jewish brethren could be saved.

In contrast, the Corinthians were demanding their rights. They were misusing their freedom at others' expense. Weaker brothers were stumbling, and it is very likely that unbelievers were repelled by the selfishness and strife that dominated the Corinthian fellowship, so carefully chronicled in Paul's first letter to them.

Paul wanted them to follow his example. "Be imitators of me, as I am of Christ" (11:1). And what was his example? Go back one verse, to the end of 1 Corinthians 10: "Just as I try to please everyone in everything I do, not seeking my own advantage, but that of many, that they may be saved" (v. 33).

That's the point Paul was making here. He was not advocating a marketing plan. He was not making a plea for "contextualization." He was not suggesting that the message be made more acceptable or that the role of preaching be replaced by psychology, skits, and worldly entertainment. He was calling for self-denial and sacrifice for the sake of those who do not know Christ.

FOR THE JEWS I BECOME JEWISH

How did Paul apply this principle? In 1 Corinthians 9:20, he describes the practical outworking of self-denial: "To the Jews I became as a Jew . . . to those under the law I became as one under the law." This describes a selfless sacrifice of Paul's personal liberty: "though not being . . . under the law," Paul willingly subjected himself to the law's ritual requirements, in order to win those who were under the law. In other words, he adopted their customs. Whatever their ceremonial law dictated, he was willing to do. If it was important to them to abstain from eating pork, he abstained. If their sensibilities demanded that a certain feast be observed, he observed it. Why? Not to appease their pride or win their favor, but in order to open a door of opportunity for him to preach the uncompromised truth, so that he might win them to Jesus Christ.

John Calvin understood this passage:

> [Paul] adopted the Jewish way of life in the company of Jews, but not before all of them; for many of them were obstinate, and under the influence of Pharisaism, pride, or ill-will they would have liked to see Christian freedom suppressed altogether. *Paul would never have deferred to the same extent to people like that, for Christ does not want us to trouble ourselves about them.* Our Lord says, "Let them alone; they are blind guides" (Matt. 15:14). Therefore we must adapt ourselves to the weak, but not to the stubborn. *His purpose was to bring them to Christ, not to further his own interests, or to retain their goodwill.*
>
> . . . Those people are in the wrong, whose main concern is to keep their lives free from trouble, and who, for that reason, take care not to give offence to people, to the wicked that is, rather than to the weak. Moreover, those who do not distinguish between things which are neutral, and things which are forbidden, are doubly in the wrong. Because they do not make that distinction they have no hesitation about undertaking things, which God has forbidden, in order to please men. *But their crowning sin is their making wrong use of this sentence of Paul's, in order to make excuses for their own wicked hypocrisy.*[6]

Paul would stoop to no compromise. He simply sacrificed personal freedoms and preferences, removing any unnecessary diversion or excuse, so that he would have an opportunity to declare the powerful, saving gospel plainly to them.

Paul was not suggesting that the gospel can be made more powerful by adapting it to a certain cultural context. He was not speaking about accommodating the *message*. He was simply saying he would not jeopardize his ability to preach the message by unnecessarily offending people. If the message was an offense, so be it: "We preach Christ crucified, a stumbling

---

[6]John Calvin, *The First Epistle of Paul to the Corinthians*, trans. John W. Fraser (Grand Rapids, MI: Eerdmans, 1960), 196, emphasis added.

block to Jews and folly to Gentiles" (1 Cor. 1:23). But Paul would not make *himself* a stumbling block to unbelievers: "Give no offense to Jews or to Greeks or to the church of God" (10:32).

Several illustrations of this may be adduced from the New Testament. In Acts 15 the Jerusalem Council, the first church council, met to determine how they should assimilate the Gentile converts. Many of the Jewish believers were so steeped in Jewish tradition that they were skeptical about the Gentiles who were turning to Christ. Then some men came down from Judea and began teaching the Christians, "Unless you are circumcised according to the custom of Moses, you cannot be saved" (v. 1). In other words, they were claiming the Gentiles couldn't become Christians unless they became Jewish first. The church was thrown into confusion.

So the Jerusalem Council was assembled to discuss the issue (v. 6). Scripture says there was "much debate" (v. 7). At one point Peter testified that he had been present when Gentiles first received the Holy Spirit, and all the evidence demonstrated that God was in it (vv. 7–11). Finally James, the leader, handed down this ruling: "My judgment is that we should not trouble those of the Gentiles who turn to God" (v. 19).

That settled the question. The church would accept Gentiles as they were, without placing them under the Jewish ceremonial law.

But then notice verse 20. James went on to add this: "[We will] write to them to abstain from the things polluted by idols, and from sexual immorality, and from what has been strangled, and from blood." He listed four things the Gentiles were to stay away from. First, "things polluted by idols" meant food offered to idols. That was precisely the issue that troubled the Corinthians. Eating food offered to pagan idols was grossly offensive to Jewish people. They despised pagan idolatry. But as Paul suggested, there is nothing inherently wrong with eating food that had been offered to idols. What is an idol anyway? "We know that 'an idol has no real existence,' and that 'there is no God but one'" (1 Cor. 8:4). Nevertheless, the Jerusalem Council added this warning to stay away from things contaminated by idols, so as not to needlessly offend the Jews.

Second, the Gentiles were to stay away from fornication. This does not mean simply that they were not to *commit* fornication. That is obvious. It is not a gray area. There was much in the apostolic teaching that prohibited every form of fornication, or sexual sin. So "abstain . . . from sexual immorality" is much more than a command against acts of fornication. Since the Gentile religions all revolved around sex rites, temple prostitutes, and orgiastic ritual, James was saying the Gentile believers should have nothing to do with their former ways of worship. They should not attend any activities where these things were going on. They were to sever the tie completely with pagan activity or Gentile styles of worship so repulsive to Jews.

Third, they were to abstain from the meat of strangled animals; and fourth, they were to stay away from blood. Strangled meat retains a lot of blood. Jewish law demanded that any animals to be eaten must have the blood completely drained from them. To the Jews, the eating of blood was one of the most offensive of all Gentile practices. And some pagan religious rites involved the drinking of pure animal blood. The Jerusalem Council therefore commanded Gentile believers to abstain from all such practices.

Understand the significance of this. The Jerusalem Council's decision was an explicit condemnation of legalism. The council refused to put the Gentiles under the Mosaic law. So why did they lay these four prohibitions on them? The reason is made clear in Acts 15:21 (NASB): "For Moses from ancient generations has in every city those who preach him, since he is read in the synagogues every Sabbath."

In other words, they were to abstain from those four things so they would not offend the Jewish unbelievers. If Christians had practiced these most offensive of all Gentile rituals, unbelieving Jews might turn away from the gospel before hearing it.

Acts 16 includes a similar illustration. It is the first time in Scripture we meet Timothy. Luke records that he was "the son of a Jewish woman who was a believer, but his father was a Greek" (v. 1). Jews would have considered him a Gentile because his father was a Gentile. Moreover, Timothy's mother would have been considered a virtual traitor for marrying a Gentile.

Yet Timothy was "well spoken of by the brothers at Lystra and Iconium. Paul wanted Timothy to accompany him, and he took him and circumcised him" (vv. 2–3).

Wait a minute. Why did he do that? Paul certainly didn't believe Gentiles needed to be circumcised to be saved. In fact, Paul refused to have Titus circumcised when the Jerusalem legalists demanded it (Gal. 2:1–5). Furthermore, Paul once opposed Peter to his face because Peter had compromised with the legalists (Gal. 2:11–14). He asked Peter, "If you, though a Jew, live like a Gentile and not like a Jew, how can you force the Gentiles to live like Jews?" (v. 14). So why did Paul have Timothy circumcised? Was he compromising the issue, demonstrating inconsistency?

No. Timothy wasn't doing it to be saved. He obviously did *not* undergo circumcision when he was saved. And he wasn't doing it to make hardened legalists happy or to tone down the offense of the gospel. He simply became like a Jew so that he might have an opportunity to preach the gospel to them. Paul and Timothy were not hoping to pacify pseudo-Christian legalists, act the part of hypocrites, or mitigate the gospel in any way. They simply wanted to keep open lines of communication to the Jews to whom they were going to preach. This was not an act of compromise or men-pleasing. It was loving, and very painful, self-sacrifice for the sake of the lost.

Wherever he could acknowledge the strong religious tradition of a people and not offend their sensitivities, he was glad to do so—when it did not violate God's Word or impinge on the gospel. But the apostle never adapted his ministry to pander to worldly lusts or sinful selfishness.

FOR THE GENTILES I BECOME A GENTILE

Going back to 1 Corinthians 9, we read in verse 21, "To those outside the law I became as one outside the law (not being outside the law of God but under the law of Christ) that I might win those outside the law." "Those outside the law" are the Gentiles. Note the qualifier Paul inserted. He specifically stated that he is "*not . . . outside the law of God but under the law of Christ.*" He clearly was not saying he became morally lawless to please despisers of true righteousness.

Though he became as "outside the law" in the ceremonial sense, he was not living licentiously or behaving unrighteously. He would have no sympathy with *antinomians*—people who believe all law is abolished for Christians. "Outside the law" is not a reference to the moral law. Paul is not implying that he lived it up just to make the Gentiles admire him. He did not encourage people to think they could become Christians and hang on to a worldly lifestyle. Again, he was talking about the Old Testament ceremonial law. When he ministered to Gentiles, he dropped all his non-moral Jewish traditions. When Paul was with the Gentiles, he followed Gentile customs and culture insofar as it did not conflict with the law of Christ. He avoided needlessly offending the Gentiles.

When Paul was in Jerusalem, for example, he followed Jewish religious customs. He observed the feasts and Sabbaths, and he followed Jewish dietary laws. When he went to Antioch, however, he ate with the Gentiles, even though that violated his own tradition and upbringing. Peter came to Antioch and also ate with the Gentiles, until some Judaizers showed up. Then Peter and some others withdrew and held themselves aloof (Gal. 2:12). Paul says, "Even Barnabas was led astray by their hypocrisy" (v. 13). That was when Paul rebuked Peter to his face in front of others.

Notice why Paul confronted Peter: "I saw that their conduct was not in step with the truth of the gospel" (v. 14). Paul's reason for becoming all things to all men was not so he could slip the gospel in covertly. On the contrary, it was so he could proclaim the truth of the gospel more straightforwardly than ever. He wanted to remove any personal offense, so the offense of the gospel would be the only one. Paul saw Peter's compromise as something that undermined the clarity and the force of the gospel, and that is why he confronted him.

FOR THE WEAK I BECOME WEAK

Again returning to 1 Corinthians 9, we note that Paul mentions a third group: "To the weak I became weak, that I might win the weak." Who are the weak? In Pauline theology this expression refers to overscrupulous Christians—immature believers who don't understand their liberty. In the Jewish community, for example, some new Christians still wanted to observe the Sabbaths, attend the synagogues, follow the dietary laws, and maintain all the feasts and ceremonies of the Old Testament law. There was nothing morally wrong with any of that, but some in the Christian community had weak consciences and still felt such things were obligatory. They were just emerging out of Judaism and still holding on, feeling the pangs of conscience to do those things that had become habit and were associated with the true God and the Old Testament Scriptures.

Among the Gentiles, on the other hand, there were those saved out of idolatry who now feared having anything to do with meat offered to idols. Perhaps some clung to old superstitions and feared demonic idols or simply wanted nothing to do with anything reminiscent of the former paganism.

Paul, of course, was free from such fears and superstitions. And he was free from the ceremonial law of the Old Testament. The law of Christ governed him. Although he felt free to do things that other people's consciences wouldn't allow them to do, when Paul was with weaker brethren he was careful not to violate their sensibilities. He adapted his behavior so as not to offend them. He yielded in love rather than offend a weaker brother.

How did he do that? At one point he took a Nazirite vow to quell a false rumor among the believing Jews in Jerusalem that he was preaching against Moses and urging Jewish people not to circumcise their children (Acts 21:17–26). Ironically, it was the carrying out of that vow that ultimately led to his arrest and imprisonment. The unbelieving Jews hated the message of the gospel, so they undertook to destroy the messenger. But they had no legitimate complaint against Paul personally, for he had gone out of his way to be a Jew for the Jews, a Gentile for the Gentiles, and a weak brother for the weak brethren.

Again the question comes, why did Paul subject himself to all that? First Corinthians 9:22–23 says, "that by all means I might save some. I do it all for the sake of the gospel." "By all means" may sound at first like an echo of pragmatism, but don't forget, Paul is speaking here of condescension, not compromise. What is the difference? To condescend is to remove needless offenses to people's religious consciences by setting aside some personal, optional liberty. To compromise is to set aside an essential truth and thereby alter or weaken the gospel message.

Paul set himself in contrast with the compromisers and marketeers in 2 Corinthians 2:17: "For we are not, like so many, peddlers of God's word, but as men of sincerity, as commissioned by God, in the sight of God we speak in Christ." The compromiser sells a cheap gospel and tries to make it appealing by stripping away the offense of Christ. Paul simply wanted to keep himself from being an obstacle or a stumbling block so that the unadulterated message could penetrate hearts and do its work. If people were offended by the message, Paul did not try to remove the offense of the gospel or abolish the stumbling block of the cross, and he would not tolerate those who tried (cf. Gal. 5:11). But he was willing to practice self-denial and deference if that opened opportunities for him to preach.

"CONTEXTUALIZATION" AND THE CORRUPTION OF THE CHURCH

It should be clear that modern church marketers cannot look to the apostle Paul for approval of their methodology or claim him as the father of their philosophy. Although Paul ministered to the vilest pagans throughout the Roman world, he never adapted the church to secular society's tastes. He would not think of altering either the message or the nature of the church. Each of the churches he founded had its own unique personality and set of problems, but Paul's teaching, his strategy, and above all his message remained the same throughout his ministry. His means of ministry, as we shall note in Chapter 5, was always preaching—the straightforward proclamation of biblical truth.

By contrast, the "contextualization" of the gospel today has infected the church with the spirit of the age. It has opened the church's doors wide for worldliness, shallowness, and in some cases a crass, party atmosphere. The world now sets the agenda for the church.

This is demonstrated clearly in a book by James Davison Hunter, a sociology professor at the University of Virginia. Hunter surveyed students in evangelical colleges and seminaries and concluded that evangelical Christianity changed dramatically in three decades' time. He found that by the end of the 1980s, young evangelicals had become significantly more tolerant of activities once viewed as worldly or immoral—including smoking, using marijuana, attending R-rated movies, and premarital sex. Hunter wrote,

> The symbolic boundaries which previously defined moral propriety for conservative Protestantism have lost a measure of clarity. Many of the distinctions separating Christian conduct from "worldly conduct" have been challenged if not altogether undermined. Even the words *worldly* and *worldliness* have, within a generation, lost most of their traditional meaning. . . . The traditional meaning of worldliness has indeed lost its relevance for the coming generation of Evangelicals.[7]

What Hunter noted among evangelical students is a reflection of what has happened to the entire evangelical church. In recent years, the situation has worsened considerably. There is no worldly preoccupation (up to and including sexual immorality, even perversions like homosexuality) that professing Christian students have not in some measure or another embraced and affirmed. Many evangelical young people appear to care far more about the world's opinion than they do for God's. Churches are so engrossed in trying to please non-Christians that many have forgotten their first duty is to please God (2 Cor. 5:9). The church has been so over-contextualized that it has become corrupted by the world.

BY ALL MEANS SAVE SOME

Paul's one aim in making himself the slave of all was in order that they might be saved. He was not trying to win a popularity contest. He was not seeking to make himself or the gospel appealing to them. His whole purpose was evangelistic. C. H. Spurgeon, preaching on this passage, said,

> I fear there are some who preach with the view of *amusing* men, and as long as people can be gathered in crowds, and their ears can be tickled, and they can retire pleased with what they have heard, the orator is content, and folds his hands, and goes back self-satisfied. But Paul did

---

[7]James Davison Hunter, *Evangelicalism: The Coming Generation* (Chicago: University of Chicago, 1987), 63.

not lay himself out to please the public and collect the crowd. If he did not save them he felt that it was of no avail to interest them. Unless the truth had pierced their hearts, affected their lives, and made new men of them, Paul would have gone home crying, "Who hath believed our report, and to whom is the arm of the Lord revealed?" . . .

Now observe, brethren, if I, or you, or any of us, or all of us, shall have spent our lives merely in amusing men, or educating men, or moralizing men, when we shall come to give our account at the last great day we shall be in a very sorry condition, and we shall have but a very sorry record to render; for of what avail will it be to a man to be educated when he comes to be damned? Of what service will it be to him to have been amused when the trumpet sounds, and heaven and earth are shaking, and the pit opens wide her jaws of fire and swallows up the soul unsaved? Of what avail even to have moralized a man if still he is on the left hand of the judge, and if still, "Depart, ye cursed," shall be his portion?[8]

That is precisely my concern about today's pragmatic church growth strategies. The design is to attract the unchurched. For what? To entertain them? To get them to attend church meetings regularly? Merely "churching" the unchurched accomplishes nothing of eternal value. Too often, however, that is where the strategy stalls. Or else it is combined with a watered-down gospel that wrongly assures sinners that a positive "decision" for Christ is as good as true conversion. Multitudes who are not authentic Christians now identify themselves with the church. The church has thus been invaded with the world's values, the world's interests, and the world's citizens.

By all means we are to seek the salvation of the lost. We must be servants to all, deferential to every kind of person. For Jews we should become Jewish, for Gentiles we should be like Gentiles, for children we should be childlike, and so on for every facet of humanity. But the primary means of evangelism we dare not overlook: the straightforward proclamation of the unadulterated Word of God. Those who trade the Word for amusements or gimmicks will find they have no effective means to reach people with the truth of Christ.

---

[8]"Soul Saving Our One Business," *The Metropolitan Tabernacle Pulpit*, Vol. 25 (London: Passmore & Alabaster, 1879), 674–676.

5

THE FOOLISHNESS OF GOD

Pray without ceasing, and preach the faithful Word in clearer terms than ever. Such a course of conduct may seem to some to be a sort of standing still and doing nothing, but in very truth it is bringing God into the battle; and when he comes to avenge the quarrel of his covenant he will make short work of it. "Arise, O Lord, plead thine own cause!"

CHARLES HADDON SPURGEON[1]

Down-grade tendencies have been continuous, not intermittent, throughout church history. There has never been a time when biblical Christianity was not threatened with worldliness and false doctrine. Contemporary evangelicalism provides a particularly poignant example of this. The history of the evangelical movement over the past century and a half has been one long and frustrating struggle against the influences of liberal theology and worldly compromise. Beginning with Spurgeon and the Down-Grade Controversy, evangelicalism has been torn and disrupted again and again by the very same issues that troubled Spurgeon.

Spurgeon's early warnings against modernism and the down-grade went largely unheeded. But by the first decade of the twentieth century, it was evident that orthodox Protestantism was losing the battle against liberalism. Beginning in 1909, an international group of Christian leaders committed to biblical truth began to write and publish a series of articles known as *The Fundamentals*. A. C. Dixon, pastor of Moody Memorial Church, Chicago, was chief editor of the series, assisted by R. A. Torrey and Louis Meyer. In 1911 Dixon was called to pastor The Metropolitan Tabernacle, London—Spurgeon's famous church. So the headquarters in the battle against the down-grade at last moved back to where it had begun.

---

[1] "Restoration of Truth and Revival," *The Sword and the Trowel* (December 1887), 607.

The Fundamentals articles were compiled into twelve books, and the series was completed by 1915. Financed by two Christian businessmen from California, nearly three million of the books were supplied free of charge to Christian workers around the world. They provided a sound biblical defense for every one of the essential doctrines then under attack by liberals. The articles condemned "higher criticism" (which imposed humanistic assumptions on biblical scholarship and often resulted in rank unbelief). They defended biblical inerrancy and authority, the historicity of Scripture, verbal inspiration, the deity of Christ, the doctrine of substitutionary atonement, and several other crucial biblical distinctives. Well-known contributors included B. B. Warfield, J. C. Ryle, G. Campbell Morgan, C. I. Scofield, James M. Gray (president of Moody Bible Institute), A. T. Pierson (another of Spurgeon's successors at the Tabernacle), and Thomas Spurgeon, Charles's son.

Those books gave rise to the movement known as *fundamentalism*. By 1919, the movement was a force to be reckoned with. In May of that year The World Conference on Christian Fundamentals was held in Philadelphia, attended by more than six thousand Christians from a variety of denominational backgrounds. Fundamentalism seemed to have a bright future. But the Philadelphia gathering proved to be the high-water mark of the fundamentalist movement. Before the end of the century *fundamentalist* would become a derogatory word, applied more often to ruthless Islamic Ayatollahs than to men of God. The fundamentalist movement is now fragmented and subdivided into tiny factions. And as we have seen, a new kind of modernism is pushing Christians onto the down-grade.

What happened? Why is it that biblical Christianity in modern times has been so vulnerable to doctrinal compromise and worldly influence?

A fascinating historical account of the fundamentalist/evangelical movement in microcosm is found in *Reforming Fundamentalism: Fuller Seminary and the New Evangelicalism* by George Marsden.[2] Tracing the history of one influential institution, Marsden recounts in detail how Fuller Seminary compromised and ultimately abandoned its commitment to biblical inerrancy. The school was originally founded to provide a conservative, biblical training ground after denominational seminaries had embraced liberalism or otherwise abandoned the faith. But within a few decades, Fuller Seminary itself capitulated on the issue of biblical inerrancy. Why? Marsden's account reveals that many of Fuller's founders and early faculty were obsessed with the notion of intellectual and academic respectability.

---

[2] Grand Rapids, MI: Eerdmans, 1987.

They wanted Fuller Seminary to be viewed in the elite academic community with the same esteem as the liberal denominational schools. Unfortunately, the intellectual climate of the age was almost unanimously sympathetic to skepticism, liberalism, humanism, and sub-Christian rationalism. The very community from which the Fuller men sought to win acceptance was at war with the theology that Fuller Seminary was founded to uphold. In order to gain the stature they sought, the Fuller men were forced to compromise. The history of the school is therefore a sad chronicle of controversy and doctrinal decline.

WHEN FOOLISHNESS IS WISE

Is intellectual and academic respectability a worthy goal? Not if the world sets the standards that determine what is acceptable and what is not. "Let no one deceive himself. If anyone among you thinks that he is wise in this age, let him become a fool that he may become wise. *For the wisdom of this world is folly with God*" (1 Cor. 3:18–19, emphasis added). It is folly to seek the approval of human wisdom; the goal itself is incompatible with biblical integrity.

The apostle Paul addressed this very issue at length in his first epistle to the Corinthians. Realizing that biblical truth is often viewed by the world as utter foolishness, Paul wrote, "The foolishness of God is wiser than men, and the weakness of God is stronger than men" (1:25). Even to speak of "the foolishness of God" is shocking, but Paul was using the expression to bring into clear focus the conflict between human philosophy and biblical truth. Divine wisdom may not always *appear* wise under human evaluation. In a pragmatic age like ours, what is true may be at odds with what "works." And what is right may be profoundly different from what is acceptable in the world's judgment. In fact, this is often the case. But that does not demonstrate any defect in the gospel. Rather, it underscores the deficiency of human wisdom.

Paul defended the gospel against the charge that it is inferior to this world's wisdom. He did not attempt to argue that the message of Christ is intellectually erudite, nor did he seek appreciation and esteem from the world's so-called scholars. Instead, he conceded that the gospel is utter foolishness in the eyes of human wisdom. He wrote:

> For Christ did not send me to baptize but to preach the gospel, and not with words of eloquent wisdom, lest the cross of Christ be emptied of its power. For the word of the cross is folly to those who are perishing,

but to us who are being saved it is the power of God. For it is written, "I will destroy the wisdom of the wise, and the discernment of the discerning I will thwart." Where is the one who is wise? Where is the scribe? Where is the debater of this age? Has not God made foolish the wisdom of the world? For since, in the wisdom of God, the world did not know God through wisdom, it pleased God through the folly of what we preach to save those who believe. For Jews demand signs and Greeks seek wisdom, but we preach Christ crucified, a stumbling block to Jews and folly to Gentiles, but to those who are called, both Jews and Greeks, Christ the power of God and the wisdom of God. For the foolishness of God is wiser than men, and the weakness of God is stronger than men.

For consider your calling, brothers: not many of you were wise according to worldly standards, not many were powerful, not many were of noble birth. But God chose what is foolish in the world to shame the wise; God chose what is weak in the world to shame the strong; God chose what is low and despised in the world, even things that are not, to bring to nothing things that are, so that no human being might boast in the presence of God. And because of him you are in Christ Jesus, who became to us wisdom from God, righteousness and sanctification and redemption, so that, as it is written, "Let the one who boasts, boast in the Lord."

And I, when I came to you, brothers, did not come proclaiming to you the testimony of God with lofty speech or wisdom. For I decided to know nothing among you except Jesus Christ and him crucified. And I was with you in weakness and in fear and much trembling, and my speech and my message were not in plausible words of wisdom, but in demonstration of the Spirit and of power, that your faith might not rest in the wisdom of men but in the power of God. (1 Cor. 1:17—2:5)

THE INFERIORITY OF HUMAN WISDOM

Remember that Paul was ministering in a civilization that had been brought to the pinnacle of glory under the Greek empire and was now enjoying a revival of high culture under the Roman government. The ancient Greeks viewed philosophy as the highest of human attainments, and they built their whole society around it. Educated Greeks took their philosophy very seriously. There were at least four dozen distinct philosophical systems that competed with each other for influence and acceptance. Many of them were overtly religious, explaining human origin, morality, social relationships, and human destiny in terms of a pantheon of pagan gods. These Greek philosophies were very sophisticated and were the basis of all social, economic, political, and educational relations. Most if not all of them were totally at odds with the revealed truth of Scripture.

In short, Greek society worshiped human wisdom. The very word *philosophy* means "love of wisdom." Unfortunately, some of the Corinthian converts held onto their love of human wisdom and tried to import it into the church. Evidently they thought human wisdom could enhance divine revelation or add to what they had in Christ. Paul set out in this passage to correct them.

Paul included a similar admonition in his epistle to the Colossians: "See to it that no one takes you captive by philosophy and empty deceit, according to human tradition, according to the elemental spirits of the world, and not according to Christ" (2:8). His point was that Christians have no business pursuing human wisdom. It does no good spiritually for the unsaved, and it can add nothing to the believer. In fact, human wisdom has nothing to offer but confusion and division.

It is important to note that Paul's argument was not against natural facts or rational truth. He was not taking a mindless, anti-intellectual stance. On the contrary, Paul himself usually appealed to the *minds* of his disciples: "Be transformed by the renewal of your *mind*" (Rom. 12:2); "Be renewed in the spirit of your *minds*" (Eph. 4:23); "Set your *minds* on things that are above" (Col. 3:2); "Be filled with the *knowledge* of his will in all *spiritual wisdom* and *understanding*" (Col. 1:9, emphasis added). He was no anti-intellectual. For Paul, all truth was objective, fixed, revealed infallibly by God through His Word. Knowing the truth required study, diligence (2 Tim. 2:15). It was a matter of understanding, not feeling (1 Cor. 14:14–20). Truth, he emphasized, is something to be understood rationally, not discerned by mystical intuition (cf. Job 38:36; Luke 24:45). Don't get the idea Paul depreciated the importance of the mind.

Nor was Paul on the offensive against technology and science. Medicine, architecture, engineering, mathematics, and other sciences had made great advances in Paul's day, just as they have in ours. Paul was not condemning any of these fields of knowledge per se. He was not opposed to learning and applying the God-given benefits of the scientific disciplines. Nor would he have objected to new areas of learning such as electronics or automotive mechanics. Christians can and should thank God for the blessings we enjoy from these fields. As long as they are used properly—that is, as long as they don't become a basis for speculation about God, right and wrong, good and evil, or the meaning of life—the true sciences pose no threat to the truth of the gospel.

What Paul opposed was the human wisdom behind worldly philosophy: "Has not God made foolish the wisdom of the world?" (1 Cor. 1:20). In another place Paul wrote, "Our boast is this, the testimony of our conscience, that we behaved in the world with simplicity and godly sincerity, *not by earthly wisdom but by the grace of God*, and supremely so toward you" (2 Cor. 1:12, emphasis added).

In contrast to Paul, contemporary evangelicalism has elevated human opinion and worldly, fleshly wisdom to an undue level. For most of the past century, evangelical theology has bowed at the shrine of academia, attempting to assimilate secular theology, philosophy, politics, psychology, moral relativism, evolutionary theory, and every other academic fad. Finding those things incompatible with the Bible and the simplicity of the gospel, Christians have too often been willing to twist and shape divine truth to try to make it fit. Multitudes have thus been drawn away from singular devotion to biblical truth to embrace human wisdom.

The desire for intellectual acceptability has undoubtedly steered more Christian leaders and institutions onto the down-grade than any other single force. In pursuit of that misguided goal, the worldly church has dutifully stayed one or two steps behind the world in its fashions and thinking. Bible-believing evangelicals have therefore had to wage a continual war against current human opinion.

The will to carry on that battle may be waning as more and more churches conform to the world. It is now standard practice among core evangelicals to borrow psychology and methodology from the world. Some think they can simply add human insights to Scripture and thus baptize worldly wisdom to make it "Christian."

Paul, on the other hand, was completely unwilling to incorporate human wisdom into the church. Instead he attacked it head-on as a despised enemy: "Christ did not send me to baptize but to preach the gospel, and not with words of eloquent wisdom, lest the cross of Christ be emptied of its power" (1 Cor. 1:17). "Eloquent wisdom" is from the Greek expression *sophia logou*—literally "wisdom of words." Paul's task was to preach God's Word, not man's wisdom.

It might be fair at this point to ask if it is *always* wrong to appeal to human wisdom, even in evangelistic contexts. After all, if our task is to reach the world with the gospel, why not try to express it in a way that appeals to the human mind? Paul answers that question by saying such an approach makes the cross of Christ void. Why? Two reasons. First of all, the message of the cross "is folly to those who are perishing" (v. 18). There is no way to make it otherwise and be faithful to the message. And second, it is impossible to elevate human wisdom without lowering God's truth. Human wisdom caters to self-will, human pride, fleshly lusts, and the desire for independence from God. Human wisdom and the gospel are therefore constitutionally incompatible. Try to combine the two, and Paul says you render the gospel null and void.

The very reason people love sophisticated religion and highbrow morality is that those things appeal to the human ego. At the same time, worldly wisdom scoffs at the gospel precisely because it confronts human conceit. The gospel demands that people acknowledge their sin and spiritual impotence. It humiliates them, convicts them, and calls them sinners. Moreover, it offers salvation as a gracious work of God—not something people can accomplish on their own. In every way the cross crushes human pride.

THE SUPERIORITY OF GOD'S WISDOM

Human wisdom dismisses the truth of God as "folly" (v. 18). Those who are wise according to this world often employ epithets like "simplistic," "irrelevant," "naive," "unsophisticated," and even "foolish" to describe the gospel—and so it seems to them. After all, how could Jesus' being nailed to a piece of lumber on a remote hill in a barren part of the world ages ago have any possible relevance to modern humanity or eternal destiny? Is there really no place for personal accomplishment, human goodness, natural benevolence, or religious merit? Is God really so harsh that He would punish sinners? Are we really such vile sinners after all? Thus reasons the fallen mind.

And so "the word of the cross is foolishness to those who are perishing" (v. 18).

When Paul speaks of "the word of the cross," he has in mind, of course, the gospel message. The cross is central to all we believe and proclaim. But remember that before people began to fashion crosses into pieces of jewelry and wear them as ornaments, the cross was a despised tool of execution. It was a place where the lowest of criminals were tortured and killed. What could be more contemptible than that? But the gist of Paul's argument embraces not just the part of the message that deals with the cross, but all of God's saving truth. The cross, being at the heart of God's revelation, is the central target of human contempt, but divinely revealed truth as a whole is deemed "foolishness" by the world and is subject to the scorn of this world's wisdom.

Paul had confronted human wisdom on Mars' Hill in Athens just before he arrived in Corinth (Acts 17:18–21). The Athenian intellectuals sneered at him over the resurrection (v. 32). He knew he would face more of the same in Corinth, a city known for its devotion to worldly philosophy, earthly pleasure, and fleshly appetites. A marketing expert might have suggested to Paul that he change his approach, adapt the message, soft-pedal the bits that he knew would offend people, speak to them about things that seemed more immediately relevant to their lives and interests. But Paul "decided to know nothing among [them] except Jesus Christ and him crucified" (1 Cor. 2:2). He was not going to change his message to suit the Corinthians. They had enough human opinion and earthly philosophy without Paul adding his own. What they needed was the profoundly simple yet simply profound message of the cross.

HUMAN WISDOM VS. THE FOOLISHNESS OF GOD

Although the natural mind finds the cross offensive and foolish, "to us who are being saved it is the power of God" (1 Cor. 1:18). The cross is the apex of divine wisdom and the demonstration of its superiority. God's wisdom overthrows human wisdom in several ways.

Human Wisdom Is Temporary; Divine Wisdom Is Eternal

"I will destroy the wisdom of the wise, and the discernment of the discerning I will thwart" (v. 19) is a quotation from Isaiah 29:14. Paul adds a series of questions that mock human wisdom: "Where is the one who is wise? Where is the scribe? Where is the debater of this age? Has not God made foolish the wisdom of the world?" (v. 20). In essence, he is asking, "Where are the people who have refined human wisdom to such a degree that they can claim superiority over God?" Has human wisdom eliminated war or hunger or crime or poverty or immorality? Where have all the clever arguments and impressive rhetoric brought humanity? Is mankind better off because of them—or simply more self-satisfied and complacent? Human wisdom has changed nothing. Life is filled with the same problems and the same dilemmas that have always troubled the human race.

Human opinions are often contradictory, always changing, sometimes falling out of vogue only to appear again in another generation. Having rejected divine authority, this world's wisdom has no anchor to hold it steady.

Human Wisdom Is Impotent; Divine Wisdom Is Powerful

Paul points out in verses 21–25 that worldly wisdom is spiritually ineffective. It cannot improve human nature or bring people closer to God.

The contemporary church desperately needs to see this truth. All the philosophers, intellectuals, sociologists, anthropologists, psychologists, politicians, and other wise men put together have never found any solution to the problem of sin or brought humanity one step closer to God. In fact, mankind is spiritually worse off today than ever before, with higher suicide rates, the threat of nuclear war, and epidemic levels of frustration, confusion, depression, and debauchery. Human wisdom in our age is as bankrupt as all the philosophies in ancient Corinth—maybe more so.

The truth is, human wisdom and human philosophy tend to make the state of humanity worse, not better. Contemporary problems such as war, racism, drunkenness, crime, divorce, drug problems, and poverty all attest to this. Those things are universally diagnosed as evil, but they continually grow more widespread and more serious as no cure is found. And the more the world depends on human wisdom, the worse these problems will become.

Is there a solution? There certainly is: "it pleased God through the folly of what we preach to save those who believe" (v. 21). "What we preach" is one word in the Greek text: *kērugma*. It emphasizes both the *message* and the *method* through which God chose to be the primary means of saving people: plainly proclaiming the gospel. The King James Version says, "It pleased God by the foolishness of preaching to save them that believe." Those who want to replace preaching with drama, music, and subtler means would do well to consider this: God *purposefully* chose a message and a methodology that the world's wisdom counts as foolishness. The Greek word for "foolishness" is *mōria*, from which we get the word *moronic*. God's means of salvation is literally moronic in the eyes of human wisdom. But it is God's only strategy for getting the message out.

"To us who are being saved it is the power of God" (v. 18). Those who give up human wisdom for divine foolishness receive eternal life. This "foolishness" is every person's only hope. The simple gospel thus provides all that complex human wisdom has ever sought. "If anyone among you thinks that he is wise in this age, let him become a fool that he may become wise" (3:18).

Note that God does not *expect* people to come to a knowledge of the truth through human ingenuity. *He* chose the foolishness of preaching.

People cannot reason their way to God. But God is "pleased . . . through the folly of what we preach to save those who believe" (v. 21). That is His plan, ordained "in the wisdom of God."

Paul was not advocating foolish preaching. He was simply pointing out that preaching the gospel is foolish *according to worldly wisdom*. Those who promote marketing principles in church ministry suggest that if people don't want preaching, we should give them what they want. What was Paul's perspective on that?

Paul was unequivocal: "For Jews demand signs and Greeks seek wisdom, but *we preach Christ crucified*, a stumbling block to Jews and folly to Gentiles" (vv. 22–23, emphasis added). The Jews want a sign; why not give them one? The Greeks love philosophy; why not frame the message in a philosophical dialogue? After all, isn't this the same apostle who said, "I have made myself a servant to all"? But here again we see that although Paul was willing to become a servant to all, he was *not* willing to modify the gospel or alter God's design for preaching it. He would not cater to the preferences of human wisdom, performing signs on demand for those who wanted something sensational or fashioning the message in philosophical terms for those whose tastes were more cerebral. Instead Paul preached Christ crucified, a stumbling block to unbelieving Jews and foolishness to the philosophical Greeks.

The Jews wanted to see power; the Greeks wanted to hear wisdom. Only those who responded to the foolishness of the preached message found both: "to those who are called, both Jews and Greeks, Christ the *power* of God and the *wisdom* of God" (v. 24, emphasis added). Ironically—and tragically—the very thing human wisdom deems foolish and weak is the clearest possible expression of God's power and wisdom. "The [so-called] foolishness of God is wiser than men, and the [so-called] weakness of God is stronger than men" (v. 25).

Human Wisdom Is for the Elite; Divine Wisdom Is for All

Paul knew very well the members of the Corinthian church. And so he reminded them that very few of them had attained stature in the world: "For consider your calling, brothers: not many of you were wise according to worldly standards, not many were powerful, not many were of noble birth. But God chose what is foolish in the world to shame the wise; God chose what is weak in the world to shame the strong" (vv. 26–27). Carrying on with the dual contrast of foolish/wise and weak/strong, Paul pointed out that very few Christians in Corinth were highly educated, powerful, rich, or famous. And of course those who were would have lost much of their status when they became Christians.

God's strength is made perfect in human weakness (2 Cor. 12:9). His wisdom appears foolish by human standards. Yet he uses the foolishness of this world to shame those who are wise, the weak things to shame those who are powerful, the lowly things to shame those who are proud, the despised things to shame those who are eminent (1 Cor. 1:27–28). We tend to think God must use intellectuals to win other intellectuals. But the fact is, no one is won to Christ by intellectual prowess. Those seeking to be impressed intellectually will find the message foolish. On the other hand, those who have plumbed the depths of worldly wisdom and found it empty do not need an impressive argument to convince them of the gospel. I know doctors and college professors who were won to Christ by janitors and day laborers. The Lord designed the gospel that way so "that no human being might boast in the presence of God" (v. 29).

Human Wisdom Exalts Man; Divine Wisdom Glorifies God

"Because of him you are in Christ Jesus, who became to us wisdom from God, righteousness and sanctification and redemption, so that, as it is written, 'Let the one who boasts, boast in the Lord'" (1:30–31). Salvation is entirely God's doing. "For by grace you have been saved through faith. And this is not your own doing; it is the gift of God, not a result of works, so that no one may boast. For we are his workmanship" (Eph. 2:8–10). "Then what becomes of our boasting? It is excluded. By what kind of law? By a law of works? No, but by the law of faith. For we hold that one is justified by faith apart from works of the law" (Rom. 3:27–28). "Let the one who boasts, let him boast in the Lord" (2 Cor. 10:17).

Human wisdom wants to devise a way of salvation where people get the credit. If they can't have all the credit, they will settle for some of it. But in God's design no one who is saved has anything to boast about. That's because God accomplishes everything on behalf of those He saves. They contribute nothing. He chooses them, calls them, draws them, and enables them to believe. His sovereign will—not human resolve or a human decision—even determines *who* will be saved. Everything is by *His* doing. No aspect of salvation hinges on anything good in the believer. But "because of him you are in Christ Jesus, who became to us wisdom from God, righteousness and sanctification and redemption" (1 Cor. 1:30).

We will examine more closely in subsequent chapters God's sovereign role in salvation. Note here, however, that the essence of God's saving work is seen in our union with Christ. God doesn't simply *give* us wisdom, righteousness, sanctification, and redemption. Rather, He places us "*in* Christ Jesus, who *became to us* wisdom . . . righteousness and sanctification and redemption" (v. 30). God sovereignly unites us with Christ, so that all that He is becomes ours.

Note the perfect sufficiency of God's saving work. Wisdom, righteousness, sanctification, and redemption—is there more that we need beyond what is given to us in Christ? Certainly not. In fact, any attempt to augment what God has done on our behalf only nullifies His grace (cf. Gal. 2:21). Any effort to add to His perfect gift only diminishes it (Jas. 1:17). Any bid to amplify divine wisdom with earthly insights only defaces its utter perfection. How could we ever improve on Christ and His Word?

Unlike human wisdom, which exalts the sinner, divine wisdom glorifies God. "Just as it is written, 'Let the one who boasts, boast in the Lord'" (1 Cor. 1:31). Elsewhere Paul wrote, "Far be it from me to boast except in the cross of our Lord Jesus Christ, by which the world has been crucified to me, and I to the world" (Gal. 6:14).

No wonder Paul was determined to know nothing except Jesus Christ crucified (1 Cor. 2:2). Why should he discuss philosophy or human insight? Those things have nothing to offer. But Jesus Christ—the crucified, risen, and redeeming Savior—offers the only true hope for the world. The faithful preacher—indeed, every true disciple—must uphold Jesus Christ to an unbelieving world as the only way, the only truth, and the only true life (cf. John 14:6). If we try to win them with entertainment or clever arguments or scholastic credentials or worldly wisdom, we will fail, and we will ultimately mislead them.

Paul told the Corinthians, "My speech and my message were not in plausible words of wisdom, but in demonstration of the Spirit and of power, that your faith might not rest in the wisdom of men but in the power of God" (1 Cor. 2:4–5). If he had won them through erudition or clever language or a dynamic speech, their confidence would have been misplaced.

Remember, Paul came to Corinth after being beaten and imprisoned in Philippi, run out of Thessalonica and Berea, and sneered at in Athens (Acts 16:22–24; 17:10, 13–14, 32). He knew that Corinth was a morally corrupt city—a center of loose living and prostitution. The city epitomized the pagan lifestyle. Paul might have been tempted to be less confrontive, perhaps packaged his ministry differently, maybe softened the offense of the cross. But he explicitly says that he consciously determined not to do any of those things. His "speech and . . . message were not in plausible words of wisdom" (v. 4). He was not interested in changing people's minds; he wanted God to change their lives. He did not have a message of his own to preach; he was called to proclaim the gospel. And that was what made his ministry so powerful.

In an 1871 sermon, Charles Spurgeon said,

> Jesus Christ is made of God unto us wisdom. We look no more for wisdom from the thoughts that spring of human mind, but to Christ himself; we do not expect wisdom to come to us through the culture that is of man, but we expect to be made wise through sitting at our Master's feet and accepting him as wisdom from God himself.

Spurgeon added this wry observation, which foreshadowed his stance years later in the Down-Grade Controversy:

> Now, as it was in the apostle's day, so is it very much at this present. There are those who will have it that the gospel—the simple gospel—such as might have been preached by John Bunyan or Whitefield, or Wesley, and others, was very well for the many, and for the dark times in which they lived—the great mass of mankind would be helped and improved by it; but there is wanted, according to the wiseacres of this intensely luminous century, a more progressive theology, far in advance of the evangelism now so generally ridiculed. Men of mind, gentlemen of profound thought, are to teach us doctrines that were unknown to our fathers; we are to go on improving in our knowledge of divine truth till we leave Peter and Paul, and those other old dogmatists far behind. Nobody knows how wise we are to become.
>
> Brethren, our thoughts loathe this; we hate this cant about progress and deep thought; we only wish we could know as much of Christ as the olden preachers did. We are afraid that instead of getting into greater light through the thinkings of men, the speculations and contemplations of the scribes, ancient and modern, and the discoveries of the intellectual and eclectic, we have made darkness worse, and have quenched some of the light that was in the world. Again has it been fulfilled: "I will destroy the wisdom of the wise, and will bring to nothing the understanding of the prudent. Where is the wise? where is the scribe? where is the disputer of this world? hath not God made foolish the wisdom of this world?"[3]

---

[3]"The Fourfold Treasure," *The Metropolitan Tabernacle Pulpit*, Vol. 17 (London: Passmore and Alabaster, 1871), 281.

God has again and again made foolish the wisdom of the world. Yet the church has again and again been romanced by the notion that worldly wisdom has something of value or something useful that we must master in order to minister effectively. Paul knew otherwise. Men of God throughout the ages have always known otherwise. Our faith cannot rest in the wisdom of men but in the power of God (1 Cor. 2:5).

6

THE POWER OF GOD UNTO SALVATION

Where the gospel is fully and powerfully preached, with the Holy Ghost sent down from heaven, our churches do not only hold their own, but win converts; but when that which constitutes their strength is gone—we mean when the gospel is concealed, and the life of prayer is slighted—the whole thing becomes a mere form and fiction. For this thing our heart is sore grieved.

CHARLES HADDON SPURGEON[1]

One book in the "user-friendly" genre includes a section entitled "Different Times Require Different Messages." That title caught my eye, so I began reading. This author—who pastors a large, user-friendly church—says modern times have ravaged people's self-esteem so badly that people today actually need to hear a different message from what was appropriate a hundred years ago. He writes,

In times past the human spirit was far more sturdy than it is now. Modernity has taken a high toll of the human spirit, as has the high cost of the American dream. The stress of modern life has had a greatly negative impact on the self-esteem of modern man.

Consequently, there is a high level of fragility in the modern human ego. [Baby] boomers particularly have been fragmented and shattered by the fast pace of modern-day development. That's why our baby boomers today are in a very fragile state.

Have you ever taken the time to read messages by some of the great nineteenth-century preachers . . . ? If you have, you will probably have noted that [men of that era] addressed quite a different crowd than we do today and they addressed them in a very different manner. And because of those differences, I disagree with those who say that such messages are appropriate for our time.

You see, people in our culture are truly broken and deeply wounded. They need desperately to be healed and put back together. But the process of healing, I believe, is different for every era and every generation, including this one.

Yes, different times do require different messages.[2]

That author is unusually frank in stating his perspective. He candidly admits he believes preaching should accommodate the spirit of the age. (His book also carries unqualified endorsements from several of the top names in the user-friendly, church marketing, and church growth movements.) How does this pastor think we should determine what is the appropriate message for our time? He gives this list of suggestions for preachers:

1. Visit those how-to sections in your local bookstores.

2. Regularly have a small group submit a list of their greatest challenges at home and on the job.

3. Similarly, acquire inventories of needs from several secular people in your community.

4. Periodically, examine issues of *Time*, *Newsweek* and *USA Today*, as these publications tend to be on the cutting edge of the felt needs and fears that people are facing.

5. Apply practical aims to every study, message or program in your church.

6. Practice composing practical, catchy titles for your messages (sermons) from various biblical texts.

7. Limit your preaching to roughly 20 minutes, because boomers don't have too much time to spare. And don't forget to keep your messages light and informal, liberally sprinkling them with humor and personal anecdotes.[3]

That list is a recipe for weak and insipid preaching. It is also diametrically opposed to biblical ministry.

In a superb critique of the church marketing movement, Douglas D. Webster compares biblical preaching to user-friendly methods:

Biblical preaching was God-centered, sin-exposing, self-convicting and life-challenging—the direct opposite of today's light, informal sermons that Christianize self-help and entertain better than they convict.

---

[2]Doug Murren, *The Baby Boomerang* (Ventura, CA: Regal, 1990), 217–218.
[3]Ibid., 102–103.

There are so many illustrations in today's market-sensitive sermons that the hearer forgets the biblical truth that is being illustrated; so many personal anecdotes that the hearer knows the pastor better than she knows Christ; so many human-interest stories that listening to the sermon is easier than reading the Sunday paper; so practical that there is hardly anything to practice.

No wonder nominal Christians leave church feeling upbeat. Their self-esteem is safely intact. Their minds and hearts have been sparked and soothed with sound-bite theology, Christian maxims and a few practical pointers dealing with self-esteem, kids or work. But the question remains: has the Word of God been effectively and faithfully proclaimed, penetrating comfort zones and the veneer of self-satisfaction with the truth of Jesus Christ?[4]

The simple reality is that one *cannot* follow a market-driven strategy and remain faithful to Scripture. Preachers who concern themselves with user-friendliness cannot fearlessly proclaim the whole counsel of God. Those who aspire to preach a timely message will find themselves at odds with the timeless truth of the Bible. Ministers who take their cues from *USA Today* rather than from God's Word will quickly discover the message that seemed so relevant last week is now yesterday's news. Preaching that conceals the unchanging gospel behind the fleeting issues of our time cloaks the very force that makes good preaching truly powerful. After all, it is not our anecdotes, applications, how-tos, jokes, catchy titles, clever outlines, or other contrivances but *the gospel* that is "the power of God unto salvation" (Rom. 1:16, KJV).

I AM SET APART FOR THE GOSPEL

Paul's epistle to the Romans is a thorough exposition of the gospel in almost point-by point fashion. In the first verse of the epistle, Paul describes himself as one "set apart for the *gospel*." The gospel was the foundation of Paul's ministry, and in Romans he gives a clear and thorough presentation of it. He writes about God's wrath and human sin (chapters 1–3), justification and imputed righteousness (3–5), sanctification and practical righteousness (6–8), election and Israel's rejection of Christ (9–11), and then makes practical applications of various gospel truths in chapters 12 through the end of the epistle. The gospel is his theme throughout, and one of Paul's reasons for writing Romans seems to be to demonstrate the centrality of the gospel to all Christian life and ministry.

---

[4]*Selling Jesus: What's Wrong with Marketing the Church* (Downers Grove, IL: InterVarsity, 1992), 83–84.

When we speak of "the gospel" we tend to think of an evangelistic message—and surely the gospel is that. But it is not only a four- or five-point outline of salvation truths. The *gospel*—in the sense Paul and the apostles employed the word—includes all the truth about Christ (cf. Rom. 1:1–6). It does not stop at the point of conversion and justification by faith but embraces every other aspect of salvation, from sanctification to ultimate glorification. The gospel's significance therefore does not end the moment the new birth occurs; it applies to the entire Christian experience. And when Paul and the other New Testament writers spoke of "preaching the gospel," they were not talking about preaching only to unbelievers (cf. v. 15).

All ministry in the early church revolved around the gospel. No one would have suggested a debate about secular politics, a weight-loss program, a comedy act, a stage show, or a seminar on time management for businessmen as means to boost church attendance. The church and all its ministries were single-mindedly committed to the one task of strengthening believers for the furthering of the gospel in the world.

Paul's personal commitment to the gospel as the heart of all ministry is seen clearly in the opening chapter of Romans, where Paul expresses his desire to come to Rome and minister to the saints there. He desperately wanted to get to Rome. Not to renew old personal relationships, though he had many good friends who were part of the church there. Not so he could minister in one of his own churches, for Paul did not plant the church at Rome. Not to escape persecution elsewhere, for he was certain to become a target in a city that was militantly opposed to Christianity. But Paul's passion was to preach the gospel, and he couldn't wait to do it in Rome, the center of the civilized world.

I SERVE GOD BY PREACHING THE GOSPEL

Paul writes, "I thank my God through Jesus Christ for all of you, because your faith is proclaimed in all the world. For God is my witness, whom I serve with my spirit in the gospel of his Son, that without ceasing I mention you always in my prayers, asking that somehow by God's will I may now at last succeed in coming to you" (Rom. 1:8–10). There's a wealth of spiritual truth about biblical ministry in those brief verses, and I have commented on them in depth elsewhere.[5] Here I want to begin by focusing on one brief phrase in verse 9: "I serve [God] with my spirit in the [preaching of the] gospel of his Son."

---

[5]*Romans 1–8* (Chicago: Moody, 1991).

For Paul, preaching the gospel was an act of spiritual worship. The Greek word translated "serve" is *latreuō*, the same word translated "worship" in Philippians 3:3: "We are the circumcision, who worship by the Spirit of God and glory in Christ Jesus and put no confidence in the flesh." Paul "served" (worshiped) God in his spirit by preaching the gospel. In other words, Paul viewed his ministry like that of a priest before God rendering high and holy duty: "If I preach the gospel, that gives me no ground for boasting. For necessity is laid upon me. Woe to me if I do not preach the gospel!" (1 Cor. 9:16). Yet it was not only a duty; it was an immense privilege as well. "I am eager to preach the gospel to you" (Rom. 1:15).

Paul's eagerness to serve God emanated from his spirit from the moment of his salvation. His first question as a Christian was, "What shall I do, Lord?" (Acts 22:10). His heart and energies were fixed on preaching, and he did it with his whole soul.

Notice that Paul's concern was for the *spiritual* welfare of those to whom he ministered: "I long to see you, that I may impart some spiritual gift to strengthen you" (Rom. 1:11). He was not wanting to visit Rome as a tourist. He was not interested in merely entertaining the Roman believers or seeing how many unbelievers he could draw to their meetings. He wasn't thinking of his own rewards or reputation or remuneration. He wanted to give of himself for their spiritual benefit.

What "spiritual gift" did Paul want to impart to the Romans? He was not, of course, speaking about spiritual gifts such as those listed in 1 Corinthians 12 and Romans 12. Those gifts are imparted by the Holy Spirit to every believer (1 Cor. 12:7–11), not handed out from person to person. Paul was speaking of a gift of spiritual value, something that would help them "be established" (NASB). What he had in mind involved preaching to them (cf. Rom. 1:15). He wanted to encourage them with the full riches of gospel truth and be encouraged in return by their faith in that truth: "that is, that we may be mutually encouraged by each other's faith, both yours and mine" (v. 12).

So Paul's burden for the church at Rome was bound up in his desire to serve them through the preaching and ministry of the gospel. Ultimately Paul did make it to Rome, but at a very dear price. He was brought there in chains, bound to Roman guards. Had he known when he wrote this epistle what it would finally cost him to get to Rome, Paul's desire to preach the gospel in Rome would not have been diminished in the least. After all, he went to Jerusalem even though he knew he would be imprisoned there (cf. Acts 21:10–15). When the brethren tried desperately to talk him out of going to Jerusalem, he replied, "What are you doing, weeping and breaking my heart? For I am ready not only to be imprisoned but even to die in Jerusalem for the name of the Lord Jesus" (Acts 21:13). Paul would have willingly gone to Rome under the same circumstances—and ultimately he did. He wrote to the Philippians from Rome, "All the saints greet you, especially those of Caesar's household" (Phil. 4:22). Paul was under house arrest when he wrote that, waiting for the verdict of the imperial court. Even under those trying circumstances Paul was faithfully preaching the gospel. Evidently he had even been used to lead people from Caesar's own household to a saving knowledge of Christ.

Obviously, proclaiming the gospel was a compulsion for Paul. That's why he spoke of himself as "set apart for the gospel" (Rom. 1:1). He knew of no other kind of ministry.

I AM DEBTOR TO ALL THE LOST

Paul wrote, "I am under obligation both to Greeks and to barbarians, both to the wise and to the foolish" (Rom. 1:14). The King James Version renders that verse, "*I am debtor* both to the Greeks, and to the Barbarians; both to the wise, and to the unwise" (emphasis added). Paul did not preach the gospel for personal reasons or because the calling seemed attractive. He considered himself under obligation.

At the time of Paul's conversion, he was the church's most determined opponent. He hated Christ and all Christians. When Stephen, the first martyr, was killed, Paul was there, "in hearty agreement with putting him to death" (Acts 8:1, NASB). After his salvation, Paul's zeal for Christ was even greater than his zeal to persecute Christians had been before. This verse gives us an insight as to why. Paul's perspective was that since God had chosen and called an enemy like him, "the foremost" of all sinners (1 Tim. 1:15), Paul was then obligated to other sinners to preach the gospel to them. He knew he had been sovereignly appointed to this role, and he was obliged to carry it out.

All of us who have believed the gospel are under the same kind of obligation. First, as we noted earlier, Christ Himself commands us to preach the gospel (Mark 16:15). And second, we who know the way of eternal life are obligated to unbelievers in the same sense we would be responsible to warn someone whose house is on fire or morally constrained to give water to someone dying of thirst.

Paul was equally obligated to Jews and Gentiles, educated people and barbarians. He didn't target the young, upwardly mobile, cultured people and ignore the slaves and dregs of society. He preached the gospel to them all, because he was obligated to them all. "There is no respect of persons with God" (Rom. 2:11, KJV); so Paul was no respecter of persons.

In stark contrast, "target marketing" is a key concept in the user-friendly church movement. George Barna has written,

> To successfully market your product, you have to identify its prospective market. The key to market identification—sometimes referred to as "target marketing"—is to be as specific as possible in selecting the audience to whom you will market the product. By matching the appeal of your product to the interests and needs of specific population segments, you can concentrate on getting your product to your best prospects without wasting resources on people who have no need or interest in your product. . . . By knowing the product's market, the product itself can be developed to address the special needs of that segment, and the entire marketing effort can be designed with maximum efficiency.[6]

In other words, decide to whom you're going to minister, fashion the "product" to suit that audience, and don't "waste resources" on people outside that targeted group.

Why do you suppose nearly all the user-friendly churches identify their "target market" as young suburban professionals and other moneyed groups? Why are so few of these churches ministering to poor and inner-city congregations or mixtures of all classes and types of people? The answer may be obvious. One leading pastor in the movement says, "A pastor can define his appropriate target audience by determining with whom he would like to spend a vacation or an afternoon of recreation." It would be hard to imagine a ministry philosophy more at odds with the Word of God than that. Doesn't Scripture say, "My brothers, show no partiality as you hold the faith in our Lord Jesus Christ, the Lord of glory" (Jas. 2:1)? And, "has not God chosen those who are poor in the world to be rich in faith and heirs of the kingdom, which he has promised to those who love him?" (v. 5). "But if you show partiality, you are committing sin and are convicted by the law as transgressors" (v. 9).

Those who narrow their ministry to a select "target audience" certainly are not ministering in the spirit of Paul, who considered himself debtor to all and ministered to all alike.

---

[6]George Barna, *Marketing the Church* (Colorado Springs: NavPress, 1988), 42–43.

I AM EAGER TO PREACH THE GOSPEL

But by saying he was "under obligation" to preach the gospel, Paul was in no way implying that he was a grudging witness for Christ. He makes this clear to the Romans: "I am eager to preach the gospel to you also who are in Rome" (Rom. 1:14–15). He was not only willing but also eager, even *determined* to preach the gospel.

The King James Version translates verse 15, "So, as much as in me is, I am ready to preach the gospel." That captures even more of Paul's eagerness. With every fiber of his being, he desired to preach the gospel at Rome. Paul would not have been able to understand preachers who, given the privilege of preaching the gospel, choose instead to entertain people, tell anecdotes, or give speeches on self-esteem. He was ready to suffer persecution, be beaten, go to prison, or even be killed for the privilege of preaching the gospel.

C. H. Spurgeon said,

> The apostle was ready to go anywhere with the gospel, but he was not ready to preach another gospel; no one could make him ready to do that. He was not ready to hide the gospel, he was not ready to tone it down, he was not ready to abridge it or to extend it. He said, "I am not ashamed of the gospel of Christ: for it is the power of God unto salvation to everyone that believeth; to the Jew first, and also to the Greek." As to the matter of preaching the gospel, Paul was always ready for that; he kept not back any one of its truths, nor any part of its teaching. Even if it should bring upon him ridicule and contempt, though it should be to the Jews a stumbling block, and to the Greeks foolishness, Paul would say, "As much as in me is, I am ready to preach the gospel" to them all. He did not always feel alike fit for the work; he did not always find the same openings, or the same freedom in speech; but he was always ready to preach wherever the Lord gave him the opportunity.[7]

At the end of his life, Paul was able to say, "I have fought the good fight, I have finished the race, I have kept the faith" (2 Tim. 4:7). That's because he never allowed himself to be deterred from his calling. He never gave in to the temptation to seek popularity. He never compromised with the enemies of the gospel. He never allowed his ministry to be conformed to the world. He never tickled the ears of the crowds.

---

[7] "Paul the Ready," *The Metropolitan Tabernacle Pulpit*, Vol. 38 (London: Passmore and Alabaster, 1892), 578.

Externally, it may have seemed to the world that Paul was a failure. He was arrested, imprisoned for years, and finally killed by the Roman officials. Yet even in those dark hours Paul kept preaching. When he couldn't preach to crowds, he preached to the soldiers assigned to guard him. When he couldn't minister in the churches, he ministered in the prisons. He was always ready to preach—but never to compromise.

I AM NOT ASHAMED OF THE GOSPEL

Paul's next statement could be called the thesis statement of the epistle: "I am not ashamed of the gospel, for it is the power of God for salvation to everyone who believes" (Rom. 1:16). That is one of the most potent, penetrating statements in all the New Testament. Paul equates the gospel itself with God's almighty power! No wonder he says he is not ashamed of the gospel.

The rest of the epistle is an exposition of this one statement, unfolding in brilliant detail the truth of the gospel and showing why it is so powerful. No wonder Romans takes such a prominent place among the Pauline epistles. Paul was so committed to the gospel that occasionally he referred to it as "my gospel" (Rom. 2:16; 16:25; 2 Tim. 2:8). Far from being ashamed of it, he spoke of it as if it were his own prized possession!

But as Paul well knew, the cost of standing up for the gospel could be great. Consequently, too many Christians *did* behave as if they were ashamed of the gospel.

Mockery was a key weapon used by the earliest enemies of Christianity. The Romans especially tended to look upon Christianity as a crude and uncultured religion. Rumors circulated among Roman society that Christians were cannibals, because they partook of the Lord's Supper. Christians were accused of sedition, murder, and other treacherous crimes. Some enemies of the gospel claimed the Christians were having orgies. Pagans even attacked believers as atheists because they rejected all the mythological gods. The price for following Christ could be extremely high.

As we have noted repeatedly, the gospel itself is disagreeable, unattractive, repulsive, and alarming to the world. It exposes sin, condemns pride, convicts the unbelieving heart, and shows human righteousness—even the best, most appealing aspects of human nature—to be worthless, defiled, filthy rags (cf. Isa. 64:6, KJV). It affirms that the real problems in life are not because of anyone but ourselves. We are fallen sinners, with deceitful hearts, evil motives, pervasive pride. We cannot blame anyone else for our failure and misery. That is not a popular view, particularly in today's psychological climate. It comes as bad news to those who love sin, and many who hear it for the first time react with disdain against the messenger.

It is not easy to take a bold stand for the gospel and not be ashamed. Most of us must confess that we have a lot in common with the weakness of Peter, who on the night of Jesus' crucifixion denied the Lord three times, cowering in fear before a servant girl who recognized him as a follower of Christ (Luke 22:56–62).

There is no record of any incident like that in Paul's life, however. From the moment of his conversion, Paul was a man with a mission, and he never wavered from his one purpose: to preach the gospel. He knew the gospel's remarkable power to transform lives, and he longed to be the herald to proclaim it. How could he ever be ashamed of the gospel? Having received the gospel directly from the risen Jesus Himself (Acts 20:24; 1 Cor. 11:23; 15:23), Paul was eager to proclaim it to everyone, without fear or shame.

The Gospel Is the Power of God

It is hard to imagine that anyone who truly understands the power of the gospel can possibly be ashamed to proclaim it. "It is the power of God" (1:16). *Dunamis* is the Greek word translated "power." We derive the word *dynamite* from the same Greek word, and *dynamite* is not too strong a word to express what Paul is saying here.

Inherent in the gospel message is the power of an omnipotent God. That power alone is sufficient to save the vilest sinner and transform the hardest heart—apart from any human arguments, illustrations, or ingenuity.

The prophet Jeremiah wrote, "Can the Ethiopian change his skin or the leopard his spots? Then also you can do good who are accustomed to do evil" (Jer. 13:23). The truth is, people are utterly powerless to overcome their own sin. Sin is part of our nature, like a leopard's spots. We cannot change ourselves. Self-help techniques and recovery programs might temporarily help people feel better about themselves, but they have no power to remove sin or change the human heart.

That only the gospel can do. "It is the power of God for salvation." In other words, the objective truth of the gospel is inherently powerful for transforming lives when divinely applied. Peter spoke of the Word of God as the seed that generates new life and a new birth: "You have been born again, not of perishable seed but of imperishable, through the living and abiding word of God" (1 Pet. 1:23). Both apostles were saying essentially the same thing:

God's Word—the message of the gospel—is the vehicle through which God's transforming power invades a life and brings about the new birth.

We noted in a previous chapter Paul's similar words to the Corinthian believers: "the word of the cross is folly to those who are perishing, but *to us who are being saved it is the power of God*" (1 Cor. 1:18, emphasis added). And, "we preach Christ crucified, a stumbling block to Jews and folly to Gentiles, but to those who are called, both Jews and Greeks, *Christ the power of God and the wisdom of God*" (vv. 23–24, emphasis added). The gospel is the *only* message God uses for salvation. There is a place for persuasion, graphic illustration, and relevant application. Certainly every worthy preacher or evangelist will seek ways to stimulate people's interest—but only to capture a hearing for the gospel. If the plain truth of the gospel doesn't penetrate the heart, no amount of cajoling or salesmanship on the part of the evangelist is going to bring a person to salvation.

Note that the gospel "is the power of God for salvation *to everyone who believes*" (Rom. 1:16, emphasis added). Some people remain unaffected by the gospel. As powerful as the message is, it has no positive effect on those who turn away disbelieving. Paul, of course, experienced much rejection and mocking from those who rejected the gospel. Nevertheless he refused to change his methods or adapt the message to their tastes. He did not assume unbelievers' rejection was due to any lack of power in the gospel. He knew too well the unrivaled power of the gospel to transform "everyone who believes."

In referring to the gospel as "the power of God for salvation," Paul was also affirming that the gospel reveals the *only way* of salvation. Jesus said, "I am the way, and the truth, and the life. No one comes to the Father except through me" (John 14:6). Acts 4:12 says, "There is salvation in no one else, for there is no other name under heaven given among men by which we must be saved." Biblical preaching means preaching Jesus Christ (2 Cor. 4:5)—His person and work. Perhaps the most serious indictment of contemporary market-conscious preaching is the absence of Christ. His name or some fact about Him may be thrown in at the end, but He is rarely central in the trendy preaching of today.

The Gospel Reveals God's Righteousness

The term *the gospel* is much abused these days. Elsewhere I have addressed in detail some of the contemporary fallacies regarding the gospel.[8] Here

---

[8] *The Gospel According to Jesus*, second edition (Grand Rapids, MI: Zondervan, 1994); *Faith Works: The Gospel According to the Apostles* (Dallas: Word, 1993).

it is sufficient to note that many evangelicals have redefined the gospel in man-centered terms. Instead of declaring Christ crucified and focusing on God's righteousness, they talk about human needs. But the gospel is first of all a message about God's righteousness: "For in it the righteousness of God is revealed from faith for faith; as it is written, 'The righteous shall live by faith'" (1:17).

The word *righteousness* and its derivatives appear at least thirty-five times in Romans. Divine righteousness is the starting point and the theme of the gospel message. God's righteousness, defied by sinning humanity, was perfectly fulfilled by Christ incarnate, is imputed to the sinner who repents and believes in the Lord Jesus, and will be manifested in practical ways in the life of the Christian. That is a summary of the gospel as Paul unfolds it in Romans.

"The righteousness of God" carries two connotations. In one sense it speaks of God's holy hatred of sin. In the early 1500s, Martin Luther sat in the tower of the Black Cloister, Wittenberg, reading this verse. "That expression 'righteousness of God' was like a thunderbolt in my heart," Luther said years later. "I hated Paul with all my heart when I read that the righteousness of God is revealed in the gospel."[9] Luther saw God's righteousness as an unassailable obstacle to eternal life. Luther was deeply aware of his own sinfulness, and he knew because of it he was unacceptable to a righteous God. Therefore as he read this verse he was seized with despair.

But there is a second connotation of righteousness in verse 17: "As it is written, 'The righteous shall live by faith.'" This speaks of Christ's perfect righteousness, which is imputed to the account of the believing sinner (Rom. 4:24). When Luther finally understood this sense of the word *righteousness*, he knew the true meaning of the gospel, and that discovery resulted in the Protestant Reformation.

The doctrine is known as *justification*. It means that God freely reckons all of Christ's perfect righteousness to the assets side of the believer's ledger, and he cancels out all the sin on the debit side. When God looks at the believing one, he sees that person as if he or she were as fully righteous as Christ Himself. That's how God "justifies the ungodly" (Rom. 4:5). Because Christ made full atonement for sin by His death and resurrection, God can justify sinners without compromising His own righteousness— "that he might be just and the justifier of the one who has faith in Jesus"

---

[9]*Table Talk*, ed. Theodore G. Tappert, in Helmut T. Lehmann, gen. ed. *Luther's Works*, 55 vols. (Philadelphia: Fortress, 1967), 54:308–309.

(Rom. 3:26). This is the very heart of the gospel. It is why the message is *good news*.

The Gospel Reveals God's Wrath

But the gospel is not *all* good news. In fact, it is not good news at all for those who turn away from Christ. Note that the starting point for Paul's gospel is God's wrath against sin: "For the wrath of God is revealed from heaven against all ungodliness and unrighteousness of men" (v. 18). Paul then spends more than two full chapters systematically proving that all humanity is sinful and under the wrath of God.

God's wrath is almost entirely missing from modern presentations of the gospel. It is not fashionable to speak of God's wrath against sin or to tell people they should fear God. The typical presentation today starts exactly opposite where Paul started. He wrote of "the wrath of God . . . against all ungodliness and unrighteousness of men." But modern evangelism begins with, "God loves you and wants to make you happy."

Read the literature of the user-friendly movement and you'll notice a preoccupation with conveying every message in a positive tone. One leading pastor in the movement writes,

> Though unchurched [baby] boomers may privately acknowledge they are flawed—and maybe even sinful—they are hardly going to sit in a public place and listen to themselves being described as worms, wretches, fallen creatures and other totally depraved types. . . .
>
> As a pastor to boomers, I'm convinced that they need to hear even negative messages presented in positive terms. It's the grid through which we filter things. So if we can't be positive—even when talking about negative topics—boomers will probably not listen.
>
> We need to be very careful, therefore, about the tone we take in our services. . . . I've made a deliberate practice of making sure that the messages I direct to my age-group always strike a positive note.[10]

Comments like that in recent church growth writings almost always come with disclaimers assuring readers that what the author has in mind is not compromise—and this one is no exception. He goes on to say, "Now, I'm not backing down on the biblical premise that we are all fallen sinners and desperately need to be saved. Admittedly, we are depraved; yet the gospel also presents the premise that because we were created in God's image,

---

[10]Murren, *The Baby Boomerang*, 215–217.

God considered us of high enough value to send His Son to redeem us."[11]
He goes on to say again that those who want to minister effectively in this
generation must remember to keep their tone "optimistic."

Let me say first of all that I minister to a rather large group from the
baby-boom generation, and I disagree with that writer's unwarranted gen-
eralization that they automatically tune out negative truth. Furthermore,
it is one thing to say that "we are all fallen sinners and desperately need
to be saved" and quite another to say, as Paul does, that "the wrath of
God is revealed from heaven against all ungodliness and unrighteousness
of men." Both statements are true, of course. The gospel is not complete
without both sides, however. It is Paul's starting point—the wrath of God,
not a statement about human need—that is frequently left out by preachers today.

As we noted in an earlier chapter, there is no way to synthesize the truth
about God's wrath with a positive-only presentation of the gospel. There
is no way to declare the truth about God's wrath to an unbelieving sinner
in an "optimistic" tone. As a result, the gospel preached in these churches
is often truncated, and the point that is most deliberately censored is the
very place Paul began his gospel presentation—the reality of divine wrath!

Those who feel they must be forever optimistic are forced to ignore
crucial sections of Scripture, including most of Romans 1, Luke 16, all the
Hebrews warning passages, much of the core of Old Testament truth, and
about half of Jesus' teaching. And so the philosophy shapes the message.

Don't get the impression I am in favor of preaching that is dour, always
negative, oppressive, and grim. Of course I am not. But as we have noted
repeatedly, there must be a biblical balance of negative *and* positive or we're
not ministering according to the will of God. And the strategy currently in
fashion is to try to style the gospel so that it is entirely positive. That can't
be the biblical message. It is certainly not the gospel that is the power of
God unto salvation.

For Paul, the threat of God's eternal wrath was the *first* point to be
taken up. He was determined that people understand the awful reality of
God's holy wrath and the desperate heinousness of human depravity. It was
not an upbeat way to introduce the subject. But that is how Paul, under the
inspiration of the Holy Spirit, dealt with it.

God's wrath is crucial to who He is. All his attributes are balanced
in divine perfection. If He had no righteous anger, He would not be God.
Apart from His wrath, the concept of His love is rendered meaning-

---

[11]Ibid.

less: "You have loved righteousness and hated wickedness" (Ps. 45:7). Furthermore, God hates sin just as perfectly and as thoroughly as He loves fallen sinners. One side without the other is utterly hollow.

Often the twin emphases of wrath and mercy are side by side. "Whoever believes in the Son has eternal life; whoever does not obey the Son shall not see life, but the wrath of God remains on him" (John 3:36). That verse appears in the same chapter as the more familiar words of John 3:16. Without an understanding of the severity of God's wrath against sin, even the phrase "should not perish" in John 3:16 loses its significance.

God's wrath is not a secondary theme in Scripture. It is emphasized throughout both the Old and New Testaments. Psalm 7:11–12 says, "God is a righteous judge, and a God who has indignation every day. If a man does not repent, God will whet his sword; he has bent and readied his bow." The phrase "The anger of the LORD was kindled against Israel" is found repeatedly in the Old Testament (e.g. Judg. 2:14, 20; 3:8; 10:7; 2 Sam. 6:7; 24:1; 2 Kings 13:3; Ps. 106:40). The New Testament is replete with warnings about God's wrath (e.g. Rom. 2:5; 3:5; 9:22; Eph. 5:6; Col. 3:6; Rev. 14:10). The writer to the Hebrews says simply, "Our God is a consuming fire" (Heb. 12:29; cf. Deut. 4:24; 9:3).

Those truths are not *supposed* to make us feel comfortable or self-confident. They are supposed to fill us with severe anxiety and fear. After all, "The fear of the LORD is the beginning of wisdom" (Prov. 9:10). Only when the gospel provokes a holy dread of God can it be appreciated for the truly good news it is. "In the fear of the LORD one has strong confidence" (Prov. 14:26); "The fear of the LORD is a fountain of life" (14:27); "The fear of the LORD is instruction in wisdom" (15:33); and "The fear of the LORD leads to life, and whoever has it rests satisfied; he will not be visited by harm" (19:23).

A DIFFERENT MESSAGE FOR A DIFFERENT TIME?

The gospel that should be preached today is the same message Paul committed his life to preach. He solemnly warned the church not to tamper with that gospel or alter it in any way (Gal. 1:6–9). Church history is strewn with examples of those who thought they could mold the message for their own time—but ended up corrupting the truth and damning themselves. Most of those seeking to make the church "user-friendly" have no intention of perverting the gospel in such a way. But they need to recognize that their desire for a pleasing, attractive message is utterly incompatible with the true gospel. As their movement gathers momentum, it is becoming more and more clear that they are heading down the same road traveled by the modernists of a hundred years ago.

If church history teaches us anything, it is that different times do *not* require different messages. Those who preach anything other than the unadulterated gospel forfeit the power of God in their ministries.

Charles Spurgeon said the modernists of his day were trying to devise "a faith fashioned for the present century—perhaps we ought rather to say, for the present month."[12] He wrote,

> The idea of a progressive gospel seems to have fascinated many. To us that notion is a sort of cross-breed between nonsense and blasphemy. After the gospel has been found effectual in the eternal salvation of untold multitudes, it seems rather late in the day to alter it; and, since it is the revelation of the all-wise and unchanging God, it appears somewhat audacious to attempt its improvement. When we call up before our mind's eye the gentlemen who have set themselves this pre-sumptuous task, we feel half inclined to laugh; the case is so much like the proposal of moles to improve the light of the sun. . . .
>
> Do men really believe that there is a gospel for each century? Or a religion for each fifty years?[13]

Spurgeon clearly understood that those who desired to be embraced as "relevant" by a changing world could not and would not long remain faithful to the unchanging Word of God. He quoted approvingly from a let-ter written by Henry Varley to the editor of *Word and Work*. Varley wrote, "Revelation, which is unchanging, is not fast enough for an age of which it may be said, 'Change is its fashion.' All the more necessary, therefore, does it become to 'hold fast the form of sound words,' and contend earnestly . . . 'for the faith once for all delivered to the saints.'"[14]

If change was the fashion of the nineteenth century, how much more true is that today? More than any preceding generation of Christians we must be careful to guard the treasure that has been entrusted to us (2 Tim. 1:14). Let's not exchange it for the fads and fancies of a vacillating world.

The gospel is to be preached persuasively, earnestly, and clearly. There

---

[12]"Attempts at the Impossible," *The Sword and the Trowel* (December 1888), 619.

[13]"Progressive Theology," *The Sword and the Trowel* (April 1888), 157–158.

[14]Quoted in "Notes," *The Sword and the Trowel* (August 1888), 445. Years before, Varley, a butcher turned lay evangelist, had been one of the key men responsible for encouraging D. L. Moody on his first visit to England. Being Plymouth Brethren, Varley and Spurgeon were by no means close theological allies. Over the years Spurgeon had been outspoken in his criticism of the Plymouth Brethren and their hyper-exclusive tendencies. But Varley's defense of Spurgeon in this lengthy and eloquent letter to the editor was one of the high points of the Down-Grade Controversy.

certainly is a crucial need for preachers and witnesses for Christ with unique intellectual and creative gifts to apply their communication abilities to the careful presentation of the gospel. It is certainly not wrong to want to be fresh, resourceful, persuasive, and interesting. Any preacher who is truly excited about and committed to the gospel will naturally display those attributes. But keep the focus on the message, not the style. We must make the gospel our one message to the world. After all, it is the gospel— not human inventiveness, not "user-friendliness," not clever techniques or modern methodology—that is the power of God unto salvation to all who believe.

7

PAUL ON MARS' HILL

In days gone by, [preachers on the down-grade] aimed at being thought respectable, judicious, moderate, and learned, and, in consequence, they abandoned the Puritanic teaching with which they started, and toned down their doctrines. The spiritual life which had been the impelling cause of their dissent declined almost to death's door. . . . Alas! Many are returning to the poisoned cups which drugged that declining generation.

CHARLES HADDON SPURGEON[1]

Those who believe "cultural relevance" is the secret to powerful preaching often point to Paul's ministry in Athens as a prime example of how Paul accommodated his message and his methodology to the culture in which he ministered. They suggest that Paul's sermon on Mars' Hill is a paradigm for market-driven ministry.

And at first sight it may seem they have a case. Paul was preaching among the city's intellectual elite. He spoke to them in their own language, quoted extemporaneously from their own poets and philosophers, and used their method of discourse—public debate—as the vehicle through which he communicated to them. Is this not a fitting prototype for "contextualization" and market-driven methodology?

Acts 17:16–33 thus becomes a key text in addressing the contemporary church-marketing movement:

> Now while Paul was waiting for them at Athens, his spirit was provoked within him as he saw that the city was full of idols. So he reasoned in the synagogue with the Jews and the devout persons, and in the marketplace every day with those who happened to be there. Some of the Epicurean and Stoic philosophers also conversed with him. And

---

[1]"Another Word Concerning the Down-Grade," *The Sword and the Trowel* (August 1887), 398.

some said, "What does this babbler wish to say?" Others said, "He seems to be a preacher of foreign divinities"—because he was preaching Jesus and the resurrection. And they took him and brought him to the Areopagus, saying, "May we know what this new teaching is that you are presenting? For you bring some strange things to our ears. We wish to know therefore what these things mean." Now all the Athenians and the foreigners who lived there would spend their time in nothing except telling or hearing something new. So Paul, standing in the midst of the Areopagus, said: "Men of Athens, I perceive that in every way you are very religious. For as I passed along and observed the objects of your worship, I found also an altar with this inscription, 'To the unknown god.' What therefore you worship as unknown, this I proclaim to you. The God who made the world and everything in it, being Lord of heaven and earth, does not live in temples made by man, nor is he served by human hands, as though he needed anything, since he himself gives to all mankind life and breath and everything. And he made from one man every nation of mankind to live on all the face of the earth, having determined allotted periods and the boundaries of their dwelling place, that they should seek God, in the hope that they might feel their way toward him and find him. Yet he is actually not far from each one of us, for 'In him we live and move and have our being'; as even some of your own poets have said, 'For we are indeed his offspring.' Being then God's offspring, we ought not to think that the divine being is like gold or silver or stone, an image formed by the art and imagination of man. The times of ignorance God overlooked, but now he commands all people everywhere to repent, because he has fixed a day on which he will judge the world in righteousness by a man whom he has appointed; and of this he has given assurance to all by raising him from the dead."

Now when they heard of the resurrection of the dead, some mocked. But others said, "We will hear you again about this." So Paul went out from their midst.

The early part of Acts 17 describes how Paul had been run out of Thessalonica and Berea. Some of the Christians at Berea had smuggled Paul out of the city by sea, and they took him as far as Athens (v. 15). Silas and Timothy had been left in Berea, and Paul sent word for them to join him at Athens.

So Paul was in Athens alone, waiting for Timothy and Silas. This could very well have been a low point for Paul. He felt the sense of aloneness at other times in his life (cf. 2 Tim. 4:9–22). The ministry that had brought him to this point was one long chronicle of persecution and rejection. Now he was by himself in a vast, highly cultured, but extremely pagan city.

Scripture says nothing about Paul's feelings at this point, but don't get the idea he was spiritually discouraged. His epistles give a wonderful insight into how he handled situations like this. He wrote to the Corinthians, "We are afflicted in every way, but not crushed; perplexed, but not driven to despair; persecuted, but not forsaken; struck down, but not destroyed" (2 Cor. 4:8–9). In the same epistle, he wrote, "For the sake of Christ, then, I am content with weaknesses, insults, hardships, persecutions, and calamities. For when I am weak, then I am strong" (12:10). Paul, from a position of weakness, was about to be a channel for the power of God to be unleashed in Athens.

ONE MAN AGAINST A CITY

Remember that Paul was brought up under the strictest pharisaical discipline. "I am a Jew, born in Tarsus in Cilicia, but brought up in this city, educated at the feet of Gamaliel according to the strict manner of the law of our fathers, being zealous for God" (Acts 22:3); "circumcised on the eighth day, of the people of Israel, of the tribe of Benjamin, a Hebrew of Hebrews; as to the law, a Pharisee . . . as to righteousness under the law, blameless" (Phil. 3:5–6). He was also a Roman citizen, with knowledge of the military and of politics. Tarsus, where Paul grew up and was trained, was very cosmopolitan; so Paul's rich education equipped him and acclimated him for almost any culture in the Roman Empire. Even Athens, for several centuries the very heart of the intellectual and art world, was no exception. Paul was thoroughly familiar with Greek culture, manners, religion, art, and philosophy. He was a scholar, well read and well traveled. All Paul's life had equipped him for situations precisely like this one.

In the fourth and fifth centuries B.C. Athens was considered by many to be the greatest city in the world. Some aspects of Athenian culture have never been equaled. Athens reached the pinnacle in art, literature, architecture, and philosophy. Never in history has any one city achieved the height of glory in those fields that was seen in Athens during the golden age of the Greek empire. Athens was in the province of Achaia, where Corinth, not far away, was the capital city. But Athens was still the center of the cultural and intellectual world, just as Rome was the political center. Athens was sometimes referred to as the university of the world. All the great minds of the world congregated there.

Athens also offered a home to the pantheon of gods in Greek mythology. Every civic building in Athens was a shrine to a god. The place where
public records were kept, for example, was dedicated to the mother of the
gods. The centerpiece of the city council building was an idol of Apollo. A
popular saying was, "It is easier to find a god in Athens than a man." The
city was pagan to the core; although they had gods for everything, they did
not know the one true God.

It is interesting to note how Athens affected Paul. You might think
that with his cultural and educational background, Paul would have been
fascinated to see Athens. The city was filled with ancient temples, glorious
artwork, magnificent buildings, sublime sculptures, engaging orators, inge-
nious philosophers, and spectacular sights to interest a scholar like Paul.
And in Paul's day the marble and gold still glittered.

What *was* Paul's response to Athens? "His spirit was provoked within
him as he saw that the city was full of idols" (v. 16). Instead of being awed
by all the marvelous sites, Paul saw only a city full of idols, and it grieved
him greatly.

A nineteenth-century Bible dictionary says,

> Paul had at his feet the Theseion [a spectacular marble temple near the
> marketplace], and on his right hand the Akropolis, with its splendid
> temples intact. Such surroundings would fill with enthusiasm every
> cultured Christian of to-day. Wherever St. Paul turned, his glance must
> have fallen on the severe and lovely works of art which still adorned
> the decadent city. Thus a table was spread before him of which nine-
> teenth century humanists are laboriously but thankfully gathering up
> the scattered crumbs. To St. Paul's Semitic imagination nothing of all
> this appealed. It was to him just gold or silver or stone, graven by art
> and man's device, the work of a period of ignorance at which God had
> mercifully winked.[2]

One writer who lived in Paul's time visited Athens and wrote six volumes
describing the glories of the city. If Paul had been writing a travelogue, he
would have said simply, "It's full of idols." Period. Obviously Paul was not
obtuse or insensible. It wasn't that he lacked the knowledge to appreciate
Athenian culture; on the contrary, here was a man who was ideally suited
for such a city. But he had a higher calling and more serious business than
tourism or curiosity or even academic research. He saw deeper than the

---

[2]F. C. Conybeare, "Areopagus," *A Dictionary of the Bible*, ed. James Hastings (New York: Scribner's, 1898), 1:144.

city's glittering facade or the well-dressed, well-bred Athenian intellectuals. And what he saw were people doomed to a Christless eternity.

Athens stirred Paul's emotions. The phrase "his spirit was provoked within him" employs a Greek word, *paroxunō* ("provoked"), which speaks of intense agitation. Our word *paroxysm* comes from this root. Paul was saddened, grieved, indignant, and outraged at the widespread idolatry he saw. He knew these people were giving stone idols glory that rightfully belonged to God alone.

PAUL IN THE MARKETPLACE

Paul's response was to do what he had done in virtually every city where he had ever ministered. He went to the synagogue and the marketplace and preached Christ. Verse 17 says, "So he reasoned in the synagogue with the Jews and the devout persons, and in the marketplace every day with those who happened to be there." His approach was direct, confrontive evangelism. He did not do a community survey. He did not conduct any special research. He didn't try to put together an evangelization committee. He just went to the synagogue and the marketplace and preached to whoever was there.

"God-fearing Gentiles" refers to Gentiles who were associated with the synagogue—people who knew about Jehovah God and believed enough about Him to fear Him. So Paul was ministering to Jews, God-fearing Gentiles, and rank pagans. There was no marketing focus or target group. Paul proclaimed the truth everywhere, just as he had done all over Asia Minor.

The marketplace in Athens was called the Agora. It was the hub of all activity for Athens. Situated at the southern edge of the ancient city, it stood in the shadow of the hill called Areopagus. Looming to the southeast was the great Acropolis, the geographical high point of Athens, where the most spectacular temples were situated—including the massive Parthenon, a magnificent marble structure that was already five hundred years old by the time Paul saw it.

The Agora was a large courtyard in the midst of all the civic buildings. There, under a large colonnade, people would set up little shops and booths. Vendors would peddle their wares. Farmers would bring produce and cattle to sell. Tradesmen would be there to ply their services. It was always a busy place. A modern equivalent might be a town square or the central area of a city mall. In the middle of the marketplace, philosophers would congregate and vie with one another for people's attention. Peripatetic teachers in the tradition of Aristotle, specialists in the healing arts, magicians, hucksters, and street performers of all kinds had a forum where they could work the crowds.

Paul saw it as an ideal place in which to preach. Scripture says he reasoned there "every day with those who happened to be there." What form did his discourse take? He preached the gospel. Verse 18 says so explicitly. He was preaching about "Jesus and the resurrection"—classic Pauline ministry.

How could one man hope to have an effect on a city like Athens? From a human perspective Paul stood literally alone against centuries of traditional paganism—and intellectual paganism at that. What could he hope to accomplish by standing in the marketplace and preaching about Jesus and the resurrection?

Those are questions a marketing specialist might have asked, but not Paul. He didn't see himself as one man alone against a city. He saw himself as a voice through which the power of God—the gospel—could be turned loose on the largest and most influential metropolis in that part of the world. He believed that by standing there in the Agora proclaiming Christ he was unleashing God's own power on the city of Athens. The impact of it was in God's hands.

THE APOSTLE VERSUS THE PHILOSOPHERS

It didn't take Paul long to be noticed. "Some of the Epicurean and Stoic philosophers also conversed with him." Far from being impressed with his speaking savvy and relevance, some were saying, "What would this babbler wish to say?" (v. 18). The word translated "idle babbler" (NASB) is the Greek word *spermologos*, literally "seed-picker." It referred to the birds that picked seeds out of the gutter. It was a mockery of Paul and his message. Clearly, the Athenian intellectuals were not swept away by Paul's erudition or cleverness!

Nonetheless, Paul had attracted the attention and piqued the interest of these two groups of philosophers. The Epicureans dated back four centuries to their founder, Epicurus. They believed that everything happens by chance. They had no god in their system who was sovereign. Therefore they believed the outcome of everything is questionable. They also believed death is the end of human existence. And so they taught that pleasure is the natural aim and highest good in life (though they emphasized that true pleasure is found only in right living, so they were highly moral). A corrupted form of Epicureanism is echoed in the beer ads once popular on television: "You only go around once, so grab all the gusto you can get." Modern existentialism is also nothing more than a dissipated variety of Epicureanism.

The other group that took notice of Paul were the Stoics. Their philosophy was in many ways antithetical to the Epicureans. They were pantheistic fatalists. They believed everything is god, and everything happens because god wills it. In contrast to the Epicureans, they were strongly humanitarian. Because of their extreme pantheism, they treated everyone as a god. Their philosophy was therefore very altruistic, charitable, and magnanimous. We use the word *stoic*, of course, to refer to someone who is able to bear suffering unemotionally. That's because the Stoics' fatalism caused them to be resigned to the notion that whatever happened was the will of god.

As we noted, some of these pagan philosophers were overtly mocking Paul, calling him a seed-picker. But others were intrigued by his message: "'He seems to be a proclaimer of strange deities,'—because he was preaching Jesus and the resurrection" (v. 18, NASB). It is certainly curious that they used the plural "deities," but it seems they may have misunderstood the word for "resurrection," *anastasis*. They were so used to personifying everything as a deity, perhaps they thought he was speaking of a goddess named Anastasia. They had gods of piety, mercy, and modesty, for example—why not a goddess of resurrection? Perhaps they mistakenly thought that was what Paul was saying.

Whatever their assumption, they wanted to hear more.

THE PREACHER AND THE SCHOLARS

"And they took him and brought him to the Areopagus, saying, 'May we know what this new teaching is that you are presenting? For you bring some strange things to our ears. We wish to know therefore what these things mean'" (vv. 19–20). It was not at all that they were under conviction. To them Paul was a philosophical oddity, someone with something novel to say. This was a pastime with them: "Now all the Athenians and the foreigners who lived there would spend their time in nothing except telling or hearing something new" (v. 21). Something about Paul caught their fancy, so they took him off to the Areopagus.

The Areopagus was the Athenian court of philosophers. The Greek word *areopagus* means "hill of Aries." The Roman name for Aries was

Mars; so the Latinized name of the place where this court met is Mars' Hill. So when Scripture says Paul stood "in the midst of the Areopagus" (v. 22), it has reference primarily to the court of philosophers, not the hill. But this meeting probably took place either on the hill or in the very near vicinity. The Areopagus court included at least thirty men who were the supreme judges of Athens. They ruled on criminal and civil cases, just like a court of appeals. But more than that, they were the guardians of Athenian philosophy. They listened to new teachings to determine if they should be outlawed as blasphemy. Evidently the philosophers wanted the judges to hear Paul's teaching and try to decide whether the "strange deities" he was proclaiming could be added to all the ones already in the pantheon.

What an opportunity! These men actually hauled Paul before the highest court in the city and asked him to explain what he was preaching about! This was the kind of situation Paul lived for, and he made the most of it.

This, of course, was by no means Paul's only sermon in Athens, nor was it the first. The text does not say how many days he had been preaching in the synagogue and marketplace. Nor are any of those sermons recorded for us in Scripture. But this message before the Areopagus is a fascinating insight into the way Paul preached. Several remarkable features make it a unique model of gospel preaching.

Paul Was Polite but Confrontive

"Paul, standing in the midst of the Areopagus, said: 'Men of Athens, I perceive that in every way you are very religious'" (v. 22). The King James Version translates that last phrase, "I perceive that in all things ye are too superstitious." About that translation, Spurgeon said,

> He did not say, "Too superstitious," as our version has it, that would have needlessly provoked them at the outset. He went on to say, "... What, therefore, ye worship without knowing it, that I announce unto you." He did not say, "Whom ye ignorantly worship." He was far too prudent to use such an expression. They were a collection of thoughtful men, of cultured minds, and he aimed at winning them by courteously declaring to them the gospel.[3]

As we have noted, there *is* a legitimate sense in which the apostle matched his style to the people he was trying to win. To the Jews he became Jewish. In Athens he became Greek. He spoke to these men with great respect for

---

[3]"By All Means Save Some," *The Metropolitan Tabernacle Pulpit*, Vol. 20 (London: Passmore and Alabaster, 1874), 248.

their position. He addressed them as deferentially as if he were a citizen of the city they presided over.

"As I passed along and observed the objects of your worship, I found also an altar with this inscription, 'To the unknown god.' What therefore you worship as unknown, this I proclaim to you" (v. 23). Note the tact with which Paul confronts them. Having noticed the altar to an unknown god, Paul used that to make the very powerful point that their religion was unable to give them certain knowledge of *any* god, much less the true God. He gently implied that the existence of such an altar was a plain admission that they did not know the truth about God at all. He clearly regarded the inscription on the altar as their own testimony of spiritual ignorance.

Paul framed his message in terminology that was diplomatic, courteous, friendly ("I perceive that in every way you are very religious")—yet he got right to the point ("What therefore you worship as unknown, this I proclaim to you"). Boldly, he immediately established that he was going to declare the truth about God they did not know. No careful posturing, no guarded rhetoric—he just came out with it. That dogmatic approach was no more typical in the Areopagus court than it is today. In fact, it may have been something of a shock to these men who represented the most elite minds of Athens. But Paul did not ease off, lose confidence, or try to soften the authority of the gospel. He spoke with as much boldness as he would have anywhere.

What was this altar to an unknown god? Actually, there were many of these in Athens. Six hundred years before Paul's time, Athens had been stricken with a terrible plague. Hundreds were ill and dying, and the city grew desperate. A famous poet from Crete named Epimenides devised a plan to pacify whatever gods were causing the plague. He went to the Areopagus and turned loose a flock of sheep. The plan was to let the sheep roam the city freely. When the sheep lay down, they were to be sacrificed to the god of the nearest temple. The assumption was that the angry gods would draw the sheep to themselves. When the sheep were turned loose, however, many of them lay down in places with no temples nearby. Epimenides decided to sacrifice the sheep anyway and erect altars wherever they lay down, just to make sure no unfamiliar deities were overlooked. Since these were nameless gods, the people simply erected altars and shrines "TO AN UNKNOWN GOD." It was undoubtedly one of these altars Paul spotted.

Paul boldly said, "I know this unknown God. Let me tell you who He is." He then began with great authority to tell them very clearly and very thoroughly who God is.

He Related to Them without Compromising the Message

Paul launched right into his message, beginning with creation: "The God who made the world and everything in it, being Lord of heaven and earth, does not live in temples made by man, nor is he served by human hands, as though he needed anything, since he himself gives to all mankind life and breath and everything" (vv. 24–25). There's a wealth of truth about God in those words, and it directly contradicted Greek religious belief. Paul was not stepping around their sensitivities or trying to avoid truth they might not want to hear.

All their gods dwelt in man-made temples, and they were manlike entities, not at all like the transcendent Supreme Being Paul was describing. These men were well-educated and undoubtedly familiar with the Hebrew God. They knew about His exclusivity ("The LORD our God, the LORD is one. You shall love the LORD your God with all your heart and with all your soul and with all your might"—Deut. 6:4–5). They knew His first commandment was, "You shall have no other gods before me" (Exod. 20:3; Deut. 5:7). Surely as soon as Paul began speaking, these men understood that he was declaring the same God the Hebrews worshiped, and they would have understood the ramifications of that.

Paul identified God as the *Creator*: He "made the world and everything in it" (Acts 17:24). He is the *sustainer* of all life: "He himself gives to all mankind life and breath and everything" (v. 25). He is *sovereign*: He is "Lord of heaven and earth" (v. 24). "He made from one man every nation of mankind to live on all the face of the earth, having determined allotted periods and the boundaries of their dwelling place" (v. 26). And He is *omnipresent*: "He is actually not far from each one of us" (v. 27).

Moreover, Paul told them, God desires that people "should seek God, in the hope that they might feel their way toward him and find him" (v. 27). Paul was telling these philosophers that seeking God is a moral obligation. If He is indeed the sovereign, omnipotent Creator who desires that we seek Him, then *not* to seek Him is sin. That truth would not have escaped these philosophers. They knew that Paul was laying before them a clear imperative that they seek and worship the one true God he represented. In other words, Paul said in essence, "The God I declare to you is supreme over every other being, and He is worthy of your exclusive loyalty and worship. You had better seek Him until you find Him." This struck a blow directly at their syncretism and polytheism. There could have been no question in their minds about *adding* Paul's God to their own pantheon. Paul was urging them to abandon their religion and to worship the eternal Creator of all things, the God who made all other gods petty and obsolete.

Notice the unusual way Paul buttresses his defense of the true God: he quotes Greek poetry. "'In him we live and move and have our being'; as even some of your own poets have said, 'For we are indeed his offspring'" (v. 28). (The punctuation in the *New American Standard Bible* is misleading at this point. Both the first and the closing phrases of that verse are quotations from Greek poets.) Epimenides—the *same* poet who erected altars to the unknown god—said, "In him we live and move and have our being." Aratus was the poet who said, "We are his offspring."

Oddly enough, when Epimenides said, "In *thee* we live and move and have our being," and when Aratus wrote, "We are indeed *his* offspring," they were both talking about Zeus.[4] Why would Paul quote paeans to an idol and apply those statements to God? Because he was making a defense of the faith. His point may be paraphrased like this: "Your own poets, with no knowledge of the true God whatsoever, nevertheless gave testimony to the inescapable fact that there had to be a sovereign, life-giving, all-powerful creator. Zeus does not fit that description. But the God I declare to you, whom you don't know yet, is that Almighty One." Paul's use of ancient poets simply underscored the truth of Romans 1:19–20: "What can be known about God is plain to them, because God has shown it to them. For his invisible attributes, namely, his eternal power and divine nature, have been clearly perceived, ever since the creation of the world, in the things that have been made." The rational mind demands an eternal cause for the effect of creation. Therefore many attributes of God are so obvious that even pagan poets understand them—although they attached them to the wrong god.

It was a powerful point. Paul was making the most of the situation, declaring that the true God whom they didn't know is Creator, Sustainer, and Sovereign of the universe, then quoting their own poets as proof that such a sovereign Creator must exist. Spurgeon said, "It was most adroit on his part to refer to that inscription upon the altar, and equally so to quote from one of their own poets. If he had been addressing Jews, he would neither have quoted from a Greek poet nor referred to a heathen altar: his intense love for his hearers taught him to merge his own peculiarities in order to secure their attention."[5]

---

[4]The line from Epimenides is taken from the poem "Cretica" (and is part of the same verse Paul quotes in Titus 1:12). The quotation from Aratus is the fifth line in that poet's "Phaenomena."
[5]"By All Means Save Some."

But Paul was not content with *merely* securing their attention. He was not trying to impress them with his intellect or obtain their approval of him personally. He was not trying to win the world's respect or to gain acceptance as a philosopher. His sole aim was to convert these people to Christ, and he was just coming to the heart of his message.

He Was Both Bold and Direct

Paul's next words were a fatal shot at Athenian paganism. "Being then God's offspring, we ought not to think that the divine being is like gold or silver or stone, an image formed by the art and imagination of man" (v. 29). In other words, "If God made us (as your own poets have indicated), God Himself must be greater than any man-made image." This is a very important point. It was as if Paul took one enormous philosophical sledgehammer and smashed all their idols. If God is really the sovereign, infinite being even the poets acknowledged He must be, we can't know Him by means of an idol, a shrine, or any other graven image.

Paul now went directly to the heart of the matter: "The times of ignorance God overlooked, but now he commands all people everywhere to repent, because he has fixed a day on which he will judge the world in righteousness by a man whom he has appointed; and of this he has given assurance to all by raising him from the dead" (vv. 30–31). Note that Paul preached repentance, as always. He didn't try to accommodate the Epicureans by promising them a wonderful and pleasure-filled life. And he didn't attempt to win the Stoics by trying to make the gospel sound as much like their philosophy as possible. He called both groups to repentance, referring to the golden age of Greek philosophy as "times of ignorance."

The word "ignorance" comes from the same Greek root as "unknown" in verse 23. And the word "overlooked" comes from a word that means "not interfere." It doesn't mean God disregarded or was indifferent to sinful idolatry. It means He didn't intervene in judgment.

As Paul told them, however, God has appointed a day in which He *will* judge the world in righteousness. The agent of that judgment will be a Man whom He has ordained and given testimony to by raising Him from the dead. We know who that Man is, of course. It is Jesus Christ, to whom God has given all judgment (John 5:22).

But at this point Paul was interrupted, and he evidently never even got to name the name of Christ. "Now when they heard of the resurrection of the dead, some mocked. But others said, 'We will hear you again about this.' So Paul went out from their midst" (Acts 17:32–33). The Epicureans did not believe in a resurrection at all, while the Stoics believed in a spiritual resurrection but not the resurrection of the body. Perhaps stung by his call for repentance, they responded collectively by mocking Paul. In fact, as soon as he mentioned the resurrection, the skeptics began to scoff. Evidently some had heard enough to reject Paul's message without even hearing him out. Others said they would hear more later. So Paul simply went out of their midst.

Not everyone doubted or delayed, however. "Some men joined him and believed, among whom also were Dionysius the Areopagite and a woman named Damaris and others with them" (v. 34). Enough of the truth had penetrated their hearts so that these people followed Paul to find out more. Obviously, Paul continued his sermon for those who wanted to hear, and some of them were converted. One of the converts was Dionysius, a member of the Areopagus court. Another was a woman named Damaris. Since she is given no title, we can assume she was a common woman. So this sermon reached people at both ends of the social spectrum—philosophers and housewives, men and women, intellectuals and ordinary people. This little band of converts joined Paul and became the first Christians in Athens.

THE CHRISTIAN IN SECULAR SOCIETY

It may seem to some that Paul did not have much impact on Athens. That handful of converts in Athens somehow looks less spectacular than the revivals Paul saw in Antioch or Thessalonica. But Paul had a dramatic affect on a city at the top level. He exposed the highest court in the city to the knowledge of the true God. This event planted a church in Athens and launched Paul's ministry in nearby Corinth. Paul also opened up more opportunities to preach ("We will hear you again about this"). Although the response of the Areopagus court may not have been as sensational as Paul's preaching had provoked elsewhere, we can be certain that God's purposes were accomplished and the Word did not return void. The three-fold response of that day—contempt, curiosity, and conversion—is typical whenever the gospel is faithfully preached.

It was immediately after the Areopagus incident that Paul went to Corinth. Years later he wrote, "I, when I came to you, brothers, did not come proclaiming to you the testimony of God with lofty speech or wisdom. For I decided to know nothing among you except Jesus Christ and him crucified" (1 Cor. 2:1–2). Some interpreters believe Paul was renouncing the approach he had employed at the Areopagus. That view undoubt-edly reads too much into 1 Corinthians 2. Paul nowhere indicates he viewed his Athens ministry as a failure. I reject the notion that his sermon at the Areopagus miscarried. From all we are told in Scripture, it was totally consistent with Paul's approach to ministry everywhere else. Nevertheless, this much is clear from 1 Corinthians 2, as well as from the rest of Paul's pastoral epistles: Paul did not believe the secret to his powerful ministry lay in his ability to quote Greek poets. You don't see him counseling Timothy or Titus to bone up on secular culture, learn to quote the classics, or study philosophy so they could engage in debates with the intellectual elite. He simply commanded them to preach the Word, in season and out of sea-son—and to be prepared to face the world's hostility if they were faithful in that task.

Acts 17 proves that while Paul adjusted his style in speaking, he never adapted his message. Most significantly, he never adopted the spirit of his age. A few years ago Francis Schaeffer wrote, "To accommodate to the world spirit about us in our age is the most gross form of worldliness in the proper definition of the world."[6] That is precisely what many today are doing—but what Paul would not do. He never conformed himself—and more importantly he never tried to conform the God he declared—to the tastes and expectations of his audience. He was content—as we must be—to allow the power of the gospel to speak for itself.

---

[6]*The Great Evangelical Disaster* (Wheaton, IL: Crossway Books, 1984), 142. Schaeffer added, "Unhappily, today we must say that in general the evangelical establishment has been accommodating to the forms of the world spirit as it finds expression in our day. I would say this with tears—and we must not in any way give up hoping and praying. We must with regret remember that many of those with whom we have a basic disagreement over these issues of accommodation are brothers and sisters in Christ. But in the most basic sense, the evangelical establishment has become deeply worldly" (ibid).

8

THE SOVEREIGNTY OF GOD
IN SALVATION

Children of God, whatever you have not got, you have a God in whom you may greatly glory. Having God you have more than all things, for all things come of him; and if all things were blotted out, he could restore all things simply by his will. He speaketh, and it is done; he commandeth, and it stands fast. Blessed is the man that hath the God of Jacob for his trust, and whose hope Jehovah is. In the Lord Jehovah we have righteousness and strength; let us trust in him for ever. Let the times roll on, they cannot affect our God.

CHARLES HADDON SPURGEON[1]

One of the lamest ideas I have seen in a long time is a "Jesus action figure" doll for children. The plastic character comes dressed in a robe and sandals. It is just one of a whole line of "Bible Greats Action Figures" manufactured by a Michigan-based company. Others in the series include John the Baptist, Peter, David and Goliath, and Daniel and the lions. For girls, the alternatives include Mary, Ruth, and Esther. Or resourceful parents may simply buy biblical costumes from the company and turn their child's Barbie doll into a "woman of faith."

Not to be outdone, a Florida dollmaker offers "Jesus The Doll," a $29.95 rag doll that is fully machine-washable. Designed primarily to "help children discover Jesus," the floppy toy supposedly also "can provide solace for the elderly and the infirm, for those in recovery programs, and those under emotional duress. In other words everybody." What kind of "solace" can a rag-doll Jesus provide that the real Jesus can't?

---

[1]"A Sermon for the Time Present," *The Metropolitan Tabernacle Pulpit*, Vol. 33 (London: Passmore and Alabaster, 1887), 605–606. This sermon was preached October 30, 1887.

According to the dollmaker, the actual Jesus isn't tangible enough: "It's hard to hug air."

More rag dolls are planned to complete the line, which the manufacturer calls "FIRSTFRUITS." The next two will be Mary and God. Asked what a rag-doll god might look like, the dollmaker brought out a prototype. It is two feet tall, white-haired and white-bearded, with a long, rainbow-colored robe—completely machine-washable, of course.

When I first read about Jesus The Doll and the Jesus action figure, they struck me as fitting metaphors of the way some professing Christians imagine our Lord. Too many think of Him as someone who can be manipulated any way they please, rather than the utterly sovereign Jehovah of the Bible. The truth is, the average person would actually prefer a benign, utterly passive, white-bearded, rag-doll image to the Almighty God revealed in Scripture.

GOD'S ABSOLUTE SOVEREIGNTY

No doctrine is more despised by the natural man than the truth that God is absolutely sovereign. Human pride loathes the suggestion that God orders everything, controls everything, rules over everything. The carnal mind, burning with enmity against God, abhors the biblical teaching that nothing comes to pass except according to His eternal decrees. Most of all, the flesh hates the notion that salvation is entirely God's work. If God chose who would be saved, and if His choice was settled before the foundation of the world, then believers deserve no credit for any aspect of their salvation.

But that is, after all, precisely what Scripture teaches. Even faith is God's gracious gift to His elect. Jesus said, "No one can come to me unless it is granted him by the Father" (John 6:65). "No one knows the Son except the Father, and no one knows the Father except the Son and anyone to whom the Son chooses to reveal him" (Matt. 11:27). Therefore no one who is saved has anything to boast about (cf. Eph. 2:8–9). "Salvation belongs to the LORD!" (Jon. 2:9).

The doctrine of divine election is explicitly taught throughout Scripture. For example, in the New Testament epistles alone, we learn that all believers are "chosen of God" (Titus 1:1, NASB). We were "predestined according to the purpose of him *who works all things according to the counsel of his will*" (Eph. 1:11, emphasis added). "He chose us in him before the foundation of the world. . . . He predestined us for adoption as sons through Jesus Christ, according to the purpose of his will" (vv. 4–5). We "are called according to his purpose. For those whom he foreknew he also predestined to be conformed to the image of his Son, in order that he might be the first-born among many brothers. And those whom he predestined he also called, and those whom he called he also justified, and those whom he justified he also glorified" (Rom. 8:28–30).

When Peter wrote that we are chosen "according to the foreknowledge of God the Father" (1 Pet. 1:1–2), he was not using the word "foreknowledge" to mean that God was aware beforehand who would believe and therefore chose them because of their foreseen faith. It means He determined before time began to know and love and save them; and He chose them without regard to anything good or bad they might do. We'll return to this point again, but for now note that those verses explicitly state that God's sovereign choice is made "according to the purpose of his will" and "according to the purpose of him who works all things according to the counsel of his will"—that is, not for any reason external to Himself. Certainly he did not choose certain sinners to be saved because of something praiseworthy in them or because he foresaw that they would choose Him. He chose them solely because it pleased Him to do so. God declares "the end from the beginning . . . saying, 'My counsel shall stand, and I will accomplish all my purpose'" (Isa. 46:10). He is not subject to others' decisions. His purposes for choosing some and rejecting others are hidden in the secret counsels of His own will.

Moreover, everything that exists in the universe exists because God allowed it, decreed it, and called it into existence. "Our God is in the heavens; he does all that he pleases" (Ps. 115:3). "Whatever the Lord pleases, he does, in heaven and on earth, in the seas and all deeps" (Ps. 135:6). He "works all things according to the counsel of his will" (Eph. 1:11). "From him and through him and to him are all things" (Rom. 11:36). "For us there is one God, the Father, from whom are all things and for whom we exist, and one Lord, Jesus Christ, through whom are all things and through whom we exist" (1 Cor. 8:6).

What about sin? God is not the author of sin, but He certainly allowed it; it is integral to His eternal decree. God has a purpose for allowing it. He cannot be blamed for evil or tainted by its existence (1 Sam 2:2: "There is none holy like the Lord"). But He certainly wasn't caught off-guard or standing helpless to stop it when sin entered the universe. We do not know His purposes for allowing sin. If nothing else, He permitted it in order to destroy evil forever. And God sometimes uses evil to accomplish good (Gen. 45:7–8; 50:20; Rom. 8:28). How can these things be? Scripture does not answer all the questions for us. But we know from His Word that God is utterly sovereign, He is perfectly holy, and He is absolutely just.

Admittedly, those truths are hard for the human mind to embrace, but Scripture is unequivocal. God controls all things, right down to choosing who will be saved. Paul states the doctrine in inescapable terms in Romans 9, by showing that God chose Jacob and rejected his twin brother Esau "though they were not yet born and had done nothing either good or bad—in order that God's purpose of election might continue, not because of works but because of him who calls" (v. 11). A few verses later, Paul adds this: "He says to Moses, 'I will have mercy on whom I have mercy, and I will have compassion on whom I have compassion.' So then it depends not on human will or exertion, but on God, who has mercy" (vv. 15–16).

Paul anticipated the argument against divine sovereignty: "You will say to me then, 'Why does he still find fault? For who can resist his will?'" (v. 19). In other words, doesn't God's sovereignty cancel out human responsibility? But rather than offering a philosophical answer or a deep metaphysical argument, Paul simply reprimanded the skeptic: "But who are you, O man, to answer back to God? Will what is molded say to its molder, 'Why have you made me like this?' Has the potter no right over the clay, to make out of the same lump one vessel for honorable use and another for dishonorable use?" (vv. 20–21).

Scripture affirms both divine sovereignty and human responsibility. We must accept both sides of the truth, though we may not understand how they correspond to one another. People are responsible for what they do with the gospel—or whatever light they have (Rom. 2:19–20), so that punishment is just if they reject the light. And those who reject the gospel do so voluntarily. Jesus lamented, "Yet you refuse to come to me that you may have life" (John 5:40). He told unbelievers, "Unless you believe that I am [God] you will die in your sins" (John 8:24). In John 6, our Lord combined both divine sovereignty and human responsibility when He said, "All that the Father gives me will come to me, and whoever comes to me I will never cast out" (v. 37); "For this is the will of my Father, that everyone who looks on the Son and believes in him should have eternal life" (v. 40); "No one can come to me unless the Father who sent me draws him" (v. 44); "Truly, truly, I say to you, whoever believes has eternal life" (v. 47); and, "No one can come to me unless it is granted him by the Father" (v. 65). How both of those two realities can be true simultaneously cannot be understood by the human mind—only by God.

Above all, we must not conclude that God is unjust because He chooses to bestow grace on some and not on everyone. God is never to be measured by what seems fair to human judgment. Are we so foolish as to assume that we who are fallen, sinful creatures have a higher standard of what is right than an unfallen and infinitely and eternally holy God? What kind of pride is that? And pride is the real problem. In Psalm 50:21 God says, "[You] thought that I was one like yourself." But God is *not* like us, nor can He be held to human standards. "For my thoughts are not your thoughts, neither are your ways my ways, declares the LORD. For as the heavens are higher than the earth, so are my ways higher than your ways and my thoughts than your thoughts" (Isa. 55:8–9).

We step out of bounds when we conclude that anything God does isn't fair. In Romans 11:33–34 the apostle writes, "Oh, the depth of the riches and wisdom and knowledge of God! How unsearchable are his judgments and how inscrutable his ways! For who has known the mind of the Lord, or who has been his counselor?"

DIVINE SOVEREIGNTY VERSUS PRAGMATISM

What does God's sovereignty have to do with the subject of this book? Everything. The very reason many contemporary churches embrace pragmatic methodology is that they lack any understanding of God's sovereignty in the salvation of the elect. They lose confidence in the power of the preached gospel to reach hardened unbelievers. That's why they approach evangelism as a marketing problem. Their methodology is shaped accordingly.

Several decades ago, J. I. Packer wrote,

> If we forget that it is God's prerogative to give results when the gospel is preached, we shall start to think that it is our responsibility to secure them. And if we forget that only God can give faith, we shall start to think that the making of converts depends, in the last analysis, not on God, but on us, and that the decisive factor is the way in which we evangelize. And this line of thought, consistently followed through, will lead us far astray.
>
> Let us work this out. If we regarded it as our job, not simply to present Christ, but actually to produce converts—to evangelize, not only faithfully, but also successfully—our approach to evangelism would become pragmatic and calculating. We should conclude that our basic equipment, both for personal dealing and for public preaching, must be twofold. We must have, not merely a clear grasp of the meaning and application of the gospel, but also an irresistible technique for

inducing a response. We should, therefore, make it our business to try and develop such a technique. And we should evaluate all evangelism, our own and other people's, by the criterion, not only of the message preached, but also of visible results. If our own efforts were not bearing fruit, we should conclude that our technique still needed improving. If they were bearing fruit, we should conclude that this justified the technique we had been using. We should regard evangelism as an activity involving a battle of wills between ourselves and those to whom we go, a battle in which victory depends on our firing off a heavy enough barrage of calculated effects.[2]

What Packer was warning against is exactly the kind of thinking that has given rise to the user-friendly church and its market-driven, pragmatic philosophy.

Actually, the pragmatic approach to ministry is nothing new. It has roots deep in American church history. The main contribution was not made by Harry Emerson Fosdick, Norman Vincent Peale, Robert Schuller, or any other contemporary advocate. They along with others have followed the influence of another man—the early nineteenth-century evangelist Charles G. Finney.

Charles Finney got off on the wrong foot when he dismissed the orthodox view of divine election as "an exercise of arbitrary sovereignty."[3] He rejected the doctrine that conversion is wholly a work of God. He taught instead that faith is fundamentally a human decision and that salvation is secured by the sinner's own movement toward God.

Although Finney's fundamental theological error was his rejection of God's sovereignty, that led inevitably to other errors in his teaching. He concluded that people are sinners by *choice*, not by nature. He believed the purpose of evangelism should therefore be to convince people to *choose* differently—or as many would say today, make a decision for Christ. The sinner's choice—not God's—therefore became the determinative issue in conversion. The means of moving out of darkness into light was in Finney's opinion nothing more than a simple act of the human will. The preacher's task was to secure a decision of faith, applying whatever means proved useful. Finney introduced "new measures" (unconventional methodology) into his ministry, often using techniques whose sole design was to shock and intrigue apathetic churchgoers. He was willing to implement virtually any means that would elicit the desired response from his audiences.

---

[2]J. I. Packer, *Evangelism and the Sovereignty of God* (Downers Grove, IL: InterVarsity, 1961), 27–28.
[3]Charles Finney, *Systematic Theology* (Whittier, CA: Colporter Kemp, 1944 reprint), 489.

Charles Finney's approach to ministry thus foreshadowed and laid the foundation for modern pragmatism. His teaching and his methods have colored much of American evangelism for the past century and a half. He could rightly be called the father of evangelical pragmatism. The modern market-driven ministry is simply a culmination of the movement Finney began (see Appendix 3). We would expect those who reject the biblical doctrine of God's sovereignty to follow Finney, but not those who say they affirm it. Their pragmatism becomes a denial of their theology—a kind of spiritual schizophrenia.

SALVATION IS OF THE LORD

Spurgeon fought the Down-Grade Controversy several years after Finney's heyday. But Finney's influence was still being felt—even in London.[4] Reformation theology was in serious decline. Pragmatic methodology was all the rage. Spurgeon was often a lone voice, particularly on the doctrine of God's sovereignty. One of Spurgeon's contemporaries, R. W. Dale, wrote in 1881 that "Mr. Spurgeon stands alone among the modern leaders of Evangelical Nonconformity in his fidelity to the older Calvinistic creed."[5] Virtually all the other influential evangelicals in England had abandoned their confidence in divine sovereignty.

Spurgeon saw very clearly how that disastrous loss of confidence could put churches on the down-grade. He was in full agreement with a published letter to the editor of *The Christian Age* written by Dr. David Brown, principal of the Free Church College, Aberdeen: "All our churches are honeycombed with the mischievous tendency to minimize all those features of the gospel which the natural man cannot receive. And no wonder, for their object seems to be to attract the natural mind. Wherever this is the case, the spirituality of the pulpit is done away, and the Spirit himself is not there."[6]

Spurgeon regarded divine sovereignty as "the clue to the truth of God."[7] He saw this doctrine at the heart of the gospel itself: "I have my own private opinion that there is no such thing as preaching Christ and Him crucified, unless we preach what nowadays is called Calvinism. . . . I do not believe we can preach the gospel, if we do not preach justification

---

[4]Finney held an extensive campaign in London in 1849–1851 and returned to minister throughout the British Isles in 1859–1860. He left a lasting mark on certain segments of English evangelicalism. His *Systematic Theology* was published in England in 1851. Editions of the book were still being printed as late as 1878—less than ten years before the Down-Grade Controversy erupted.
[5]Cited in Iain Murray, *The Forgotten Spurgeon* (Edinburgh: Banner of Truth, 1966), 176.
[6]Cited by Spurgeon in "The Case Proved," *The Sword and the Trowel* (October 1887), 512.
[7]*C. H. Spurgeon's Autobiography*, 4 vols. (London: Passmore and Alabaster, 1897), 1:167.

by faith, without works; nor unless we preach the sovereignty of God in
His dispensation of grace."[8]

Spurgeon quoted Jonah 2:9: "Salvation is of the LORD" (KJV), then
commented,

> That is just an epitome of Calvinism; it is the sum and substance of it. If
> anyone should ask me what I mean by a Calvinist, I should reply, "He
> is one who says, *Salvation is of the Lord.*" I cannot find in Scripture
> any other doctrine than this. It is the essence of the Bible. "He *only* is
> my rock and my salvation." Tell me anything contrary to this truth,
> and it will be a heresy; tell me a heresy, and I shall find its essence here,
> that it has departed from this great, this fundamental, this rock-truth,
> "God is my rock and my salvation." What is the heresy of Rome, but
> the addition of something to the perfect merits of Jesus Christ—the
> bringing in of the works of the flesh, to assist in our justification? And
> what is the heresy of Arminianism but the addition of something to
> the work of the Redeemer? Every heresy, if brought to the touchstone,
> will discover itself here.[9]

SCRIPTURE AND THE SOVEREIGNTY OF GOD

Is salvation wholly the Lord's work? Or has He already done all He can do
and now awaits the sinner's decision? Scripture is clear. If salvation were
dependent on the sinner's initiative, no one would ever be saved. "No one
understands; no one seeks for God" (Rom. 3:11). "No one can come to
me unless the Father who sent me draws him" (John 6:44). God Himself
prompts faith in those whom He has appointed to eternal life (Acts 13:48).
Then the seeking begins, as in Isaiah 55:6–7: "Seek the LORD while he may
be found; call upon him while he is near; let the wicked forsake his way, and
the unrighteous man his thoughts; let him return to the LORD, that he may
have compassion on him, and to our God, for he will abundantly pardon."
That text is followed by an affirmation of God's sovereignty in the classic
words of verse 11: "So shall my word be that goes out from my mouth; it
shall not return to me empty, but it shall accomplish that which I purpose,
and shall succeed in the thing for which I sent it." And if such a paradox is
confusing, verses 8–9 help explain it: "My thoughts are not your thoughts,
neither are your ways my ways, declares the LORD. For as the heavens
are higher than the earth, so are my ways higher than your ways and my
thoughts than your thoughts."

---

[8]Ibid., 1:172.
[9]Ibid.

God commands all men to repent (Acts 17:30)—but ultimately it is He himself who must grant repentance (Acts 5:31; 11:18; 2 Tim. 2:25). And although God demands the response of faith, *He* must graciously prompt and empower that response in the hearts of the elect (cf. Acts 18:27). The human heart is so depraved that left to ourselves, none of us would ever believe. If we could generate faith on our own, we would certainly have something to boast about. But Scripture says "For by grace you have been saved through faith. And this is not your own doing; it is the gift of God, not a result of works, so that no one may boast. For we are his workmanship, created in Christ Jesus for good works, which God prepared beforehand, that we should walk in them" (Eph. 2:8–10).

These truths are not hidden in isolated passages of Scripture, but as Spurgeon suggested, they are "the essence of the Bible," affirmed throughout the sacred text. I want to focus, however, on one brief passage that is particularly clear regarding God's sovereignty in salvation. So for the remainder of this chapter we turn our attention to 1 Peter 1:1–5:

> Peter, an apostle of Jesus Christ, To those who are elect exiles of the dispersion in Pontus, Galatia, Cappadocia, Asia, and Bithynia, according to the foreknowledge of God the Father, in the sanctification of the Spirit, for obedience to Jesus Christ and for sprinkling with his blood: May grace and peace be multiplied to you. Blessed be the God and Father of our Lord Jesus Christ! According to his great mercy, he has caused us to be born again to a living hope through the resurrection of Jesus Christ from the dead, to an inheritance that is imperishable, undefiled, and unfading, kept in heaven for you, who by God's power are being guarded through faith for a salvation ready to be revealed in the last time.

CHOSEN BY GOD

This, of course, is only the salutation of Peter's letter. He thus takes a theological plunge of profound proportions at the very outset. Many preachers—even some who would affirm the doctrine—avoid any mention of election in their public teaching, because the subject is so often misunderstood and abused. But Peter began his first epistle with a clear affirmation of the doctrine. He gets into the thick of the issue before he is out of the first verse.

Remember, Peter was writing to persecuted believers at all levels of maturity, scattered throughout Asia Minor. In the midst of their persecution—when they might be questioning God's sovereignty or His care for them—Peter was eager to remind them that they were the chosen of God. The Greek word translated "chosen" is *eklektos*, from the verb *kaleo* ("to call") and the preposition *ek* ("out"). Literally, it means "called-out ones." The term is often used in the New Testament as a synonym for Christians (e.g. Col. 3:12; 2 Tim. 2:10; Titus 1:1).

The expression "called-out ones" emphasizes that we who are saved are redeemed because of God's choice, not our own. Jesus told His disciples, "You did not choose me, but I chose you" (John 15:16). In other words, if you are a Christian, it is ultimately because you were chosen by God Himself, not because of anything you did to get yourself into the kingdom of God. As Spurgeon wrote,

> When I was coming to Christ, I thought I was doing it all myself, and though I sought the Lord earnestly, I had no idea the Lord was seeking me. . . . [Then] the thought struck me, *How did you come to be a Christian?* I sought the Lord. *But how did you come to seek the Lord?* The truth flashed across my mind in a moment—I should not have sought Him unless there had been some previous influence on my mind to *make me* seek Him. . . . I saw that God was at the bottom of it all, and that He was the Author of my faith, and so the whole doctrine of grace opened up to me. . . . I desire to make this constant confession, "I ascribe my change wholly to God."[10]

In 1 Peter 2:9, Peter restates the theme of God's sovereign election in these terms: "You are a chosen race, a royal priesthood, a holy nation, a people for his own possession, that you may proclaim the excellencies of him who called you out of darkness into his marvelous light." Is God attempting to save the whole world? No, He is calling out a people for His name (cf. Acts 15:14). In John 17:9, Jesus prays for the elect, "I am praying for them. I am not praying for the world but for those whom you have given me."

Before the world began, in the timelessness of eternity past, the Father chose a people for His name. Ephesians 1:4–5 says, "He chose us in him before the foundation of the world, that we should be holy and blameless before him. In love he predestined us for adoption as sons through Jesus Christ, according to the purpose of his will." We who are saved were in His mind before the beginning of time. Before the world began, we were chosen. We have always been chosen. That is an unfathomable yet intensely thrilling thought.

---

[10]Ibid., 1:168–169.

He "saved us and called us to a holy calling, not because of our works but because of his own purpose and grace, which he gave us in Christ Jesus *before the ages began*" (2 Tim. 1:9, emphasis added). That's how our names could be "written before the foundation of the world in the book of life of the Lamb who was slain" (Rev. 13:8). The apostle Paul clearly stated that he preached as "an apostle of Jesus Christ, for the sake of the faith of God's elect" (Titus 1:1). He knew when he preached the gospel that God would save the elect through the truth he preached (cf. Acts 18:9–11). His task was to preach saving truth so God's Spirit could use it to activate the faith of the elect.

If you struggle with these truths, you're not alone. They are difficult to receive, impossible to comprehend, even repugnant to our human sensibili ties. The fallen human mind tends to think it is unjust for God to choose some but not everyone—as if we had a right to demand His grace. *That's not fair!* is the typical response. But it's not supposed to be fair. We wouldn't want it to be fair. "Fair" would mean everyone is eternally condemned. God graciously saves many who deserve only His wrath. If he chooses to display His wrath on others, that in no way taints His righteousness (Rom. 9:21–23).

Nevertheless, it is not unusual for people to respond to the sovereignty of God by becoming angry. Luke 4 describes an incident when Jesus touched on the doctrine of election, and the crowd became hostile. He was teaching in the synagogue at Nazareth, just after He commenced His public ministry. At first, "All spoke well of him and marveled at the gracious words that were coming from his mouth" (v. 22). They had heard of His great miracles done in Capernaum and wanted to see similar miracles in Nazareth. They were astonished—and obviously a bit skeptical—that one from their own community would have the power to display such signs and wonders.

But it was not God's sovereign plan for Him to work miracles in Nazareth. Anticipating what the people wanted, Jesus told them,

> "Doubtless you will quote to me this proverb, 'Physician, heal yourself.' What we have heard you did at Capernaum, do here in your hometown as well." And he said, "Truly, I say to you, no prophet is acceptable in his hometown. But in truth, I tell you, there were many widows in Israel in the days of Elijah, when the heavens were shut up three years and six months, and a great famine came over all the land, and Elijah was sent to none of them but only to Zarephath, in the land of Sidon, to a woman who was a widow. And there were many lep-

ers in Israel in the time of the prophet Elisha, and none of them was cleansed, but only Naaman the Syrian." (vv. 23–27)

In other words, God is sovereign as to how, when, and where He displays His grace. Jesus would not perform a show of miracles on demand.

What was the crowd's response? These people who had seemed so appreciative moments before "were filled with wrath. And they rose up and drove him out of the town and brought him to the brow of the hill on which their town was built, so that they could throw him down the cliff" (Luke 4:28–29). They didn't want to hear the truth. They hated it. And they vented their hatred against Him. "But passing through their midst, he went away" (v. 30). The miracle they wanted to see happened without their realizing it. He simply walked through their midst and supernaturally escaped the mob.

Sovereign choice is one of those truths that proves the Bible is the inspired Word of God. It is not a truth human reason would or could invent. The only reason anyone believes it is that it is so clearly revealed in the Word of God. We cannot comprehend it with out limited facilities; we must simply receive it by faith. But receive it we must. Otherwise we are not giving God the glory He is due as the sovereign, all-wise, perfectly righteous Lord who chose us. And otherwise we will ultimately take credit ourselves for what is really God's work in us.

RESIDING AS ALIENS

Notice another phrase in 1 Peter 1:1 that Peter uses to describe his audience: "those who reside as aliens" (NASB). Peter was writing to Jewish believers who had been dispersed throughout Asia Minor in a series of terrible persecutions. But he had in mind far more than their alien status in an earthly nation. He was reminding them that as God's chosen ones they were "strangers and exiles on the earth" (Heb. 11:13)—aliens in this world.

As Christians, we belong to the kingdom of heaven, not to this world. We are not to love the world (1 John 2:15). We are not to be friends of the world (Jas. 4:4). We are here as ambassadors of Christ (2 Cor. 5:20). We are alien people who live by a higher standard. We are *in* the world, but not *of* the world (cf. John 17:11, 14, 16).

Peter wanted those scattered, persecuted believers to understand that although the world had rejected them, God Himself had chosen them. He knew it would encourage them and strengthen them to know that while they were foreigners and outcasts in this world, they were chosen citizens of the kingdom of God.

FOREKNOWN FROM ETERNITY

Let's examine the phrase "according to the foreknowledge of God the Father" (1 Pet. 1:2). That is similar to the language Paul used in Romans 8:29: "whom he foreknew he also predestined." God chose us according to His foreknowledge. As we noted earlier, this does not mean that God sat back in eternity and looked across time to see what we would do, then elected those whom He foresaw would choose to believe. That would make people sovereign and God subject to their choice. After all, the very point Peter is making is that God chose us, not that we chose Him.

The word "foreknowledge" is from the Greek word *prognōsis*. Peter uses a different form of the same word later in this chapter. Verse 20 says that Christ Himself "was foreknown before the foundation of the world." Could "foreknown" in that verse possibly refer simply to God's omniscient foresight? Obviously not. God did not look into the future to see what Christ would do. In this context it clearly means God the Father knew Christ Himself intimately and personally before the foundation of the world.

Peter also used the word "foreknowledge" in his Pentecost sermon. In Acts 2:23, speaking of Jesus, he said, "This Jesus, delivered up according to the definite plan and foreknowledge of God, you crucified and killed by the hands of lawless men." Peter was not suggesting that God foresaw the crucifixion and decided to make the best of it. No, this was His "predetermined plan" (NASB). He knew it ahead of time because He decreed it. He planned it. He predetermined it. The crucifixion was the focus of His eternal design for redemption. Here "foreknowledge" clearly carries the idea of deliberate foreordination.

(Notice, by the way, the corresponding truth: "*you* crucified . . . *by the hands of lawless men.*" These people who had cried, "Crucify Him" were not absolved of their horrible responsibility just because their actions were part of God's eternal plan. *You* did it, Peter told them. They were guilty. They were responsible for their actions, even though those actions accorded perfectly with God's eternal plan. Divine sovereignty does not negate human responsibility. The fact that God predetermined and foreknew Christ's death did not absolve those who actually murdered Him, nor did it spare them from damning guilt.)

How, then, are we to understand the term *foreknowledge*? We have seen that it can mean personal, intimate knowledge. And it can signify deliberate choice. Combine those two ideas and you have the sense of it.

This kind of foreknowledge was a familiar concept to Peter's Jewish readers. Similar expressions were employed in the Old Testament to speak of God's eternal love for His elect. For example, God told Jeremiah, "Before I formed you in the womb I knew you, and before you were born I consecrated you" (Jer. 1:5). In Amos 3:2 (KJV), God says to Israel, "You only have I known of all the families of the earth." He told Moses, "You have found favor in My sight, and I have known you by name" (Exod. 33:17, NASB). All those passages speak of an intimate relationship. The Hebrew word *yada* ("to know") carried this connotation so strongly that it was often employed as a euphemism for sexual relations: "Adam *knew* Eve his wife; and she conceived" (Gen. 4:1, KJV, emphasis added).

The New Testament also uses the word *know* to describe our Lord's close personal relationship with His elect. Jesus said, "My sheep hear my voice, and I know them" (John 10:27). Those who lack that relationship are damned. To them He will say in the judgment, "I never *knew* you; depart from me" (Matt. 7:23, emphasis added).

So when Scripture says God's election is according to His foreknowledge, it means He knew His chosen ones intimately from before the foundation of the earth. He predetermined in His eternal plan to set His love upon certain people, and those were the ones He chose. In other words, He established His loving relationship with them even before time began, and it is in that sense that He eternally foreknew them. The writer of Hebrews thus calls the plan "the eternal covenant" (13:20). Paul told Titus that this entire saving plan was promised by God "before the ages began"—a phrase meaning before time (1:2).

APPOINTED TO SANCTIFICATION

Election is not the same thing as salvation. Believers are *chosen* from eternity past. But at a specific point in time they pass from death unto life. All who are elect will certainly be saved, but God does not save them apart from the means he has chosen: the Word of God, conviction of sin, repentance, faith, and sanctification. God's chosen ones must believe to be saved. That is how the divine and eternal decree becomes a fact of history.

Peter stresses this truth by the phrase "elect . . . through sanctification of the Spirit" (1 Pet. 1:2, KJV). Here he uses the term *sanctification* not in the technical, doctrinal sense, but as a broad term to include every experiential aspect of salvation—repentance, faith, regeneration, obedience, sanctification, and all that the Holy Spirit produces in the elect.

Note that it is the "sanctification of the *Spirit.*" This is the Spirit's work, to set us apart from sin, consecrate us, make us holy. He is conforming us to the image of Christ. In 2 Thessalonians 2:13, the apostle Paul uses similar language: "God has chosen you from the beginning for salvation through sanctification by the Spirit and faith in the truth" (NASB). In other words, all three members of the Trinity are involved in the process. God planned our salvation. Christ purchased our salvation. The Holy Spirit effects our salvation.

Sanctification does not mean perfection. It means separation. It speaks of being set apart from sin and set apart unto God. Every Christian is sanctified. That's why Paul could write even to the troubled Corinthian church and say, "You were washed, you were sanctified, you were justified in the name of the Lord Jesus Christ and by the Spirit of our God" (1 Cor. 6:11). Separation from sin is now the *direction* of our lives, and someday it will be the *perfection* of our lives.

Sanctification is a lifelong process. We are constantly *being* separated from sin and conformed to Christ's likeness. We will not reach ultimate sanctification or perfection until death or the Second Coming brings us face-to-face with Him: "When he appears we shall be like him, because we shall see him as he is" (1 John 3:2). And no one falls out of that process (cf. John 6:39–40 and Rom. 8:30–39).

As Peter's language suggests, sanctification is so closely related to election that the two are inseparable. Thus he affirms that no one who is truly chosen of God can skirt the sanctification process. We are "predestined to be conformed to the image of his Son" (Rom. 8:29). It would be a contradiction to say that God chose a person to be in Christ but did not begin to make that person holy. Yet thousands today believe they are Christians but have never seen any change in their lives. Such people had better "be all the more diligent to make your calling and election sure" (2 Pet. 1:10).

God's sovereign election encompasses every aspect of our salvation from beginning to end. He is the author and the perfecter of our faith (Heb. 12:2, KJV). Saving us is all *His* work, including foreknowledge and election, regeneration (Jas. 1:18), repentance (Acts 11:18), faith (John 6:44; Rom. 12:3), justification (Rom. 3:24), sanctification (Heb. 2:11)—everything from our predestination to our final glorification (Rom. 8:30). Those who are elect are chosen by God not for heaven only, but for every phase of His saving work. We dare not view sanctification as something optional. "Without [holiness] no man shall see the Lord" (Heb. 12:14, KJV).

ORDAINED TO OBEDIENCE

Peter carries this thought a step further. You are chosen, he says, "for obedience to Jesus Christ." Again we return to Ephesians 2:10, which says, "We are his workmanship, created in Christ Jesus for good works, which God prepared beforehand, that we should walk in them." So even our good works were foreordained by a sovereign God.

Jesus said, "You did not choose me, but I chose you and appointed you *that you should go and bear fruit*" (John 15:16, emphasis added).

Good works are certainly not the *cause* of our election. They are not *grounds* for justification. They are not in any sense the *basis* for our salvation. But they are the inevitable *evidence* of it. If we are truly "his workmanship," if He chose us and sovereignly prepared good works that we should walk in them, then there is no way God's elect can live an earthly life devoid of obedience to Jesus Christ. To suppose such a possibility is to attack the sovereignty and omnipotence of the One who chose us so that we might obey Jesus Christ.

SPRINKLED WITH HIS BLOOD

Peter continues, "[You are chosen] for obedience to Jesus Christ and *for sprinkling with his blood*" (v. 2, emphasis added). To what does this refer?

In the Old Testament, blood from the sacrifices was often sprinkled on inanimate objects. At the Passover, it was sprinkled on the doorposts and lintel. In connection with some of the sin offerings it was sprinkled on the altar and around the Tabernacle. Hebrews 9:22 says, "Under the law almost everything is purified with blood."

But rarely in the Old Testament were *people* sprinkled with blood. In fact, blood was applied directly to people in only two cases of the Levitical law. One was in the symbolic cleansing of a leper (Lev. 14:7, 14). The other was when the Levites were consecrated to the priesthood (Exod. 29:20–21; Lev. 8:24, 30).

First Peter 1 is not talking about cleansing lepers or consecrating priests, however. So we turn to the only other incident in Scripture where people were sprinkled with blood. This was a one-time occurrence when Moses sprinkled the Israelites (Exod. 24:8).

The blood Moses sprinkled on the Israelites was called "the blood of the covenant." After Moses had proclaimed God's word to the people, they responded several times with a promise to obey it. That was the covenant. Blood sprinkled symbolized their obedience. It was the outward sign of their promise to obey. Moses built an altar and made a sacrifice of two oxen. Half of the blood of those sacrifices he sprinkled on the altar, symbolizing God's promise to save and bless. The rest he sprinkled on the people, saying, "Behold the blood of the covenant that the LORD has made with you in accordance with all these words" (Exod. 24:8), symbolizing the people's promise to obey. The blood was required to seal the covenant: "Therefore not even the first covenant was inaugurated without blood. For when every commandment of the law had been declared by Moses to all the people, he took the blood of calves and goats, with water and scarlet wool and hyssop, and sprinkled both the book itself and all the people" (Heb. 9:18–19).

It is this symbolic sprinkling of the blood of Jesus Christ upon believers that Peter has in mind in 1 Peter 1:2. "[Chosen for] obedience to Jesus Christ and for sprinkling with his blood" means that the elect upon their salvation pledged obedience to the Lord who had already provided salvation and blessing for them. Peter is saying that God brought us into this covenant when He chose us—before the foundation of the world.

Do you see how comprehensively God's sovereignty covers our salvation? *He* chose us before time began. *He* loved us with an everlasting love (Jer. 31:3). *He* saved us. *He* appointed us to sanctification. *He* ordained us to obedience. *He* established His covenant with us. We are truly *His* workmanship (Eph. 2:10).

APPLYING THE DOCTRINE OF DIVINE SOVEREIGNTY

The doctrine of God's sovereignty is often abused, misunderstood, and misapplied. Many Christians decide it is too deep, too confusing, too hard to understand, or too offensive. But we should not run from it; we should run to it. We should not be afraid of it; we should rejoice in it. This doctrine crushes human pride, exalts God, and strengthens the believer's faith. What could be more encouraging than to know that God is sovereignly in control of all His creation? The universe is not subject to chance. There is no possibility that God's plans will fail. "We *know* that for those who love God all things work together for good, for those who are called according to his purpose" (Rom. 8:28, emphasis added). That's the best-known and best-loved promise in all of Scripture, and it hinges on the doctrine of God's sovereignty.

Moreover, the doctrine of God's sovereignty should be a motivation for evangelism. We know when we witness or preach that God has His chosen ones who *will* respond positively, and that should encourage us to be faithful. Election is not an excuse for inactivity. Those who think they can remain idle and leave it to God to save the elect through some mystical means do not understand the Scriptures. The elect are not saved apart from evangelism. "How then will they call on him in whom they have not believed? And how are they to believe in him of whom they have never heard? And how are they to hear without someone preaching?" (Rom. 10:14).

That's why we are to proclaim the gospel to every person (Mark 16:15; Luke 24:47). And we can do it with the confidence that "*whoever* believes in him [will] not perish but have eternal life" (John 3:16).

Central to the theme of this book, our confidence in God's sovereignty will lead us in determining *how* we should preach. Our methods of ministry will be revolutionized if we are willing to examine them in light of God's sovereignty. In J. I. Packer's wonderful book *Evangelism and the Sovereignty of God*, he discusses these very issues with much insight and wisdom. Packer includes a valuable section entitled "By What Means and Methods Should Evangelism Be Practiced?" In it, he writes,

> There is only one *method* of evangelism: namely, the faithful explanation and application of the gospel message. From which it follows—and this is the key principle which we are seeking—that the test for any proposed strategy, or technique, or style, of evangelistic action must be this: will it in fact serve the word? Is it calculated to be a means of explaining the gospel truly and fully and applying it deeply and exactly? To the extent to which it is so calculated, it is lawful and right; to the extent to which it tends to overlay and obscure the realities of the message, and to blunt the edge of their application, it is ungodly and wrong.[11]

Packer suggests a number of questions we should ask about every new form of ministry: "Is this way of presenting Christ calculated to impress on people that the gospel is a *word from God*?" "Does this way of presenting Christ savor of human cleverness and showmanship? Does it tend thereby to exalt man?" "Is this way of presenting Christ calculated to promote, or impede, the work of the word in men's *minds*? Is it going to clarify the

---

[11]Packer, *Evangelism and the Sovereignty of God*, 86.

meaning of the message, or to leave it enigmatic and obscure?" "Is this way of presenting Christ calculated to convey to people the *doctrine* of the gospel, and not just part of it?" "Is this way of presenting Christ calculated to convey to people the *application* of the gospel? . . . Will it, for instance, leave people unaware that they have any immediate obligation to respond to Christ at all?" "Is this way of presenting Christ calculated to convey gospel truth in a manner that is appropriately *serious?* Is it calculated to make people feel that they are indeed facing a matter of life and death? . . . Will it help them to realize that it is a fearful thing to fall into His hands? Or is this way of presenting Christ so light and casual and cozy and jolly as to make it hard for the hearers to feel that the gospel is a matter of any consequence . . . ?"[12]

Faith in God's absolute sovereignty would deliver the church from the down-grade of pragmatism and worldliness. It would drive us back to biblical preaching. If preachers only had confidence in God's power and God's Word, they would not feel it necessary to trim and adjust and tone down the message. They would not feel they could use artificial means and thereby induce more people to be saved. They would not view evangelism as a marketing problem, but they would see it for what it is—the proclamation of divine revelation as the only means by which God calls the elect to Himself. They would rely more on the gospel, "the power of God for salvation." And they would abandon the worldly gimmicks that are propelling the church faster and further along the downhill slope.

Listen to the God-breathed Word:

> You have been born again, not of perishable seed but of imperishable, through the living and abiding word of God; for "All flesh is like grass and all its glory like the flower of grass. The grass withers, and the flower falls, but the word of the Lord remains forever." And *this word is the good news that was preached to you.*" (1 Pet. 1:23–25, emphasis added)

---

[12]Ibid., 87–90.

9

I WILL BUILD MY CHURCH

Let no man dream that a sudden crotchet has entered our head, and that we have written in hot haste: we have waited long, perhaps too long, and have been slow to speak. Neither let any one suppose that we build up our statements upon a few isolated facts. . . . We have had no motive but the general progress of the cause of truth, and the glory of God.

CHARLES HADDON SPURGEON[1]

Several years ago a journalist writing a feature on large churches came to interview me about Grace Community Church. At one point near the end of our conversation he asked, "Have you always been driven by a desire to build a large church?"

It was an unexpected question, but I answered immediately, "I have no desire to build the church. None."

He looked at me quizzically and said, "I don't understand that."

I said, "Jesus Christ said *He* would build his church, and I don't want to be in competition with Him."

I wasn't being funny. That is precisely my perspective on the church. Frequently at pastors' conferences and leadership seminars I am asked the secret to growing a large church. I have to confess that if one desires to be faithful to Christ and His Word, there is no technique or system that will guarantee a large church. Growth in the spiritual realm is like growth in the physical realm. It can be nourished and encouraged. We can do things to insure *healthy* growth. But we cannot *engineer* true growth. Nothing can make a miniature shrub grow as large as a giant redwood. If some genetic technology could be found to make it happen, the result would be a monstrosity. The same is true in the spiritual realm. "Unless the LORD builds the house, those who build it labor in vain" (Ps. 127:1).

---

[1]"Our Reply to Sundry Critics and Enquirers," *The Sword and the Trowel* (September 1887), 463.

I must ascribe our church's numerical and spiritual growth to the will of our sovereign God. There are no marketing techniques or modern methods that can explain it. Nor would we rely on such tactics. We don't want growth that is manufactured by human formulas, programs, and gimmicks. We are content to focus on aggressive biblical ministry and leave it to the Lord to add to His church (Acts 2:47). Our task is to be faithful in what He has designed for us to do.

Again we return to the principle of the omnipotent and sovereign God. We must not forget that building the church is *His* work. Ours is to "go into all the world and proclaim the gospel to the whole creation" (Mark 16:15). Once we begin to think of ourselves as the architects and builders of the church, we usurp God's rightful role, and we redefine our objective in terms of success, numbers, size, and other artificial standards. A church built merely on that philosophy may seem to flourish for a while, but it is doomed to ultimate spiritual failure.

The key biblical text for this truth, of course, is in Matthew 16:18–19. Jesus said to Peter: "I tell you, you are Peter, and on this rock I will build my church, and the gates of hell shall not prevail against it. I will give you the keys of the kingdom of heaven, and whatever you bind on earth shall be bound in heaven, and whatever you loose on earth shall be loosed in heaven."

That passage has been a source of controversy between the Roman Catholic Church and the Protestant church for centuries. It does pose some problems for the interpreter. But at its very heart, it contains simple, profound, rich, glorious truth about the church Christ is building. And it makes a fitting climax to our study.

THE FOUNDATION OF IT—"ON THIS ROCK"

Let's establish the context of the passage. Jesus spoke these words immediately after Peter's great confession, "You are the Christ, the Son of the living God" (Matt. 16:16). The Lord responded by saying, "Blessed are you, Simon Bar-Jonah! For flesh and blood has not revealed this to you, but my Father who is in heaven" (v. 17), thus underscoring God's sovereignty in bringing Peter to the truth and faith.

Jesus' next words raise the issue that has stirred so much controversy between Catholics and Protestants: "You are Peter, and on this rock I will build my church." On the basis of that statement, the Roman Catholic Church teaches that the church is built on Peter, thus making Peter the first

Pope, establishing papal succession, and making the papacy the very heart and soul of divine authority on earth.

Most Protestants, on the other hand, say the phrase "on this rock" is to be understood as a play on words. The name *Peter* (literally, "small stone") contrasts with "this rock" (literally, "large stone"). The "rock," they believe, refers to Peter's confession, not to Peter himself. They would paraphrase the meaning like this: "You are a little stone, but I will build my church on the solid rock of the truth you have confessed." They also point out that Scripture clearly teaches that Christ is the head of the church (Eph. 5:23; Col. 1:18), and nothing in the Bible speaks of an earthly surrogate who heads the church in Christ's place.

That view is more consistent with biblical truth than with the Catholic interpretation and is a viable interpretation of this text. Jesus was certainly not making Peter a pope (or establishing a line of papal succession) in this passage. After all, within a few verses we read that the Lord rebuked Peter and called him "Satan" (v. 23).

A more natural interpretation of this phrase, however, is that Jesus was addressing Peter as the leader and representative of the Twelve. Scripture *does* say that the church is "built on the foundation of the apostles and prophets, Christ Jesus himself being the cornerstone" (Eph. 2:20). So there is a biblical sense in which Peter and all the apostles constituted the foundation on which the church is built. The church that Christ is building is raised up on the sure foundation of apostolic doctrine and ministry. Luke records that the earliest church "devoted themselves to the apostles' teaching" (Acts 2:42), and building on that foundation, "the Lord added to their number day by day those who were being saved" (v. 47). Throughout the rest of the book of Acts, apostolic teaching and ministry continues to be the foundation on which every local congregation is built (cf. 4:31–32; 8:12, 35–40; 10:34–48; 12:24–25; 13:44–49).

The church is a building of "living stones . . . built up as a spiritual house, to be a holy priesthood, to offer spiritual sacrifices acceptable to God through Jesus Christ" (1 Pet. 2:5). In other words, every Christian is a stone in the structure. Peter and the apostles were the foundation stones. Christ Himself, not Peter, is the chief cornerstone.

THE CERTAINTY OF IT—"I *WILL* BUILD MY CHURCH"

Jesus' statement "I will build my church" is the heart of this passage. Everything else in these verses amplifies those words, which are most germane to our theme.

It was, first and foremost, a promise meant to encourage the disciples. They were walking along the dusty roads of Caesarea Philippi, far north of Jerusalem, at the top of Israel near the mountains of Lebanon. They were essentially in exile. Jesus had been rejected by Israel, both in Judea (the southern region) and in Galilee (the northern region). The Jewish religious and political leaders had targeted Jesus and were determined to have Him dead. The people were looking for a political, military, and economic Messiah to deliver them from Roman rule, but Jesus had already disappointed those hopes. The multitudes that once followed Him had turned away as soon as His teaching challenged them (John 6:66). And the messianic experts—the scribes and Pharisees—were the most venomous and hateful of all those who were against Him.

Who could blame the disciples if they were discouraged? The whole concept of the kingdom as the disciples had understood it seemed far out of reach. Their glorious messianic expectation—with Jesus on an earthly throne, His dominion centered in Israel, and His kingdom sweeping across the globe—did not appear to be happening. On the contrary, they were a little band of nobodies, ill-equipped, rejected, and seemingly going nowhere. They had retreated into an obscure place in a largely Gentile community to find rest, privacy, and safety. The disciples must have been wondering whether the program was still on schedule. Certainly it looked as if everything was turning out opposite to their plans.

As if all that weren't bad enough, "Jesus began to show his disciples that he must go to Jerusalem and suffer many things from the elders and chief priests and scribes, and be killed" (v. 21). Peter was so outraged at that suggestion that he "took [Jesus] aside and began to rebuke him, saying, 'Far be it from you, Lord! This shall never happen to you'" (v. 22).

Their confidence was shattered. Their hope was waning. Ominous signs were threatening them. And they must have been very confused and very concerned. It was in the context of all this that Jesus reassured them, "I *will* build my church." He wanted them to know that this was no variation from the original plan. Nothing was lost. The program had not changed.

We can derive comfort in our own time from those words. No matter how beleaguered, persecuted, martyred, rejected, maligned, poor, or ignoble the true church may seem, the Lord will not abandon His chosen ones. When the people of God seem weakest, look again. Jesus is *still* building His church. The original plan is still in operation. Modern times are no threat to His sovereign purposes. The circumstances of our troubled world do not alter His design. And no matter how corrupt and worldly the visible church has been or may become, Jesus Christ is still building *His* church on the original, sure foundation of apostolic teaching and ministry.

When Jesus said, "*I* will build my church," He gave the strongest possible guarantee of the church's ultimate success. If it were left only to the people of God, the building would have crumbled long ago. Church history is filled with the proof of human failure, worldly corruption, unfaithfulness, doctrinal deviation, compromise, and weakness. Yet the Lord still builds the church. No matter what the church appears to be on the outside, there is at the core of it a body that Christ Himself is building—made of God's elect—and it grows strong and faithful. Even in the bleakest times, there is always "a remnant, chosen by grace" (Rom. 11:5).

Paul, at the end of his life and ministry, wrote, "All who are in Asia turned away from me" (2 Tim. 1:15), and "At my first defense no one came to stand by me, but all deserted me" (4:16). The apostle John, near the end of his life, was in exile on the Isle of Patmos when the Lord gave him the task of recording the letters to the seven churches of Asia Minor (Rev. 2–3). Five of the seven had severe problems that threatened their very existence.

Yet Christ continues building *His* church, and He personally protects the purity of the believing remnant. Ephesians 5:25–27 says, "Christ loved the church and gave himself up for her, that he might sanctify her, having cleansed her by the washing of water with the word, so that he might present the church to himself in splendor, without spot or wrinkle or any such thing, that she might be holy and without blemish." The church that Christ is building will ultimately be holy and blameless. And He will present it to Himself a glorious church. In other words, the church is designed as a vehicle through which Christ can eternally manifest His own glory.

That's why we must oppose human wisdom. But that is also why worldliness, carnality, ineptitude, indifference, and apostasy cannot stop the church that Christ is building. They may stop a congregation, but the church will go on. Christ will *certainly* build His church. If He is for us, who can be against us?

THE INTIMACY OF IT—"I WILL BUILD *MY* CHURCH"

Jesus' words also speak of a sacred intimacy. Building the church is no impersonal enterprise with Him. The church is His own precious possession. Acts 20:28 speaks of "the church of God which He purchased with His own blood" (NASB).

Scripture even speaks of the church as His body (Col. 1:24). We are linked inseparably with Him in holy union. Remember when Saul of Tarsus was persecuting the church? Christ arrested him on the Damascus Road and asked, "Saul, Saul, why are you persecuting *me*?" (Acts 9:4, emphasis added). Those who attack the church attack Christ Himself. "He who is joined to the Lord becomes one spirit with him" (1 Cor. 6:17).

There is an Old Testament parallel to this truth. Zechariah told the nation of Israel, "He who touches you touches the apple of his [God's] eye" (Zech. 2:8). "The apple of his eye" refers to the pupil. God was saying those who persecute Israel are poking their finger in His eye. That is precisely the same kind of relationship Christ has with the church. He is seriously irritated when anyone offends his chosen ones (cf. Matt. 18:6, 10).

THE INVINCIBILITY OF IT—"THE GATES OF HADES SHALL NOT OVERPOWER IT"

The church that Christ builds is invincible. "The gates of hell [margin, Hades] shall not prevail against it" (v. 18). The imagery of this passage is often misunderstood. Jesus was not suggesting that the church would be impervious to attacks from Hades. The word "gates" does not suggest an offensive push. Gates are not weapons; they are barricades. Jesus was picturing Hades like a prison, suggesting that its gates would not be able to contain or imprison the church.

"Hades" is the abode of the dead. It is the Greek equivalent of the Hebrew word *Sheol* (cf. Ps. 6:5). Both the English Standard Version and the King James Version translate this phrase, "the gates of hell shall not prevail against it," but that is misleading. Jesus was not talking about the torment of eternal hell; He was saying that the grave cannot hold the elect. The gates of death could not hold Jesus Christ, and they cannot hold Christians captive. "O death, where is your victory? O death, where is your sting?" (1 Cor. 15:55).

Actually, "the gates of Hades shall not prevail against it" is a promise of resurrection. The language of death and resurrection were becoming common themes in Jesus' teaching. He knew His disciples were facing treacherous days and that all of them (except John) would ultimately give their earthly lives as martyrs for Him. He was about to tell them, "Whoever would save his life will lose it, but whoever loses his life for my sake will find it" (Matt. 16:25). But first he told them that the grave could never hold the elect.

This theme runs all through the New Testament. Since Christ conquered death, Christians have nothing to fear from it. "Christ, being raised from the dead, will never die again; death no longer has dominion over him" (Rom. 6:9), nor can it be master over those who are united to Him by faith. Jesus promised, "Because I live, you also will live" (John 14:19). In John's apocalyptic vision, Jesus told him, "Fear not, I am the first and the last, and the living one. I died, and behold I am alive forevermore, and I have the keys of Death and Hades" (Rev. 1:17–18). Jesus Christ destroyed "the one who has the power of death, that is, the devil, and deliver[ed] all those who through fear of death were subject to lifelong slavery" (Heb. 2:14–15). He took the keys to death and Hades, and now the grave cannot contain His elect.

These disciples would one day be in the heat of battle, and the Holy Spirit would call to their minds this promise. It must have brought them great comfort and new vigor. They were ultimately invincible. They would be persecuted—they would even die for their faith—but ultimately they were guaranteed to emerge victors. The gates of Hades could not prevail against them.

THE AUTHORITY OF IT—"I WILL GIVE YOU THE KEYS OF THE KINGDOM OF HEAVEN"

Then Jesus told Peter, "I will give you the keys of the kingdom of heaven, and whatever you bind on earth shall be bound in heaven, and whatever you loose on earth shall be loosed in heaven" (Matt. 16:19).

How to interpret that statement has also been a matter of disagreement between Protestants and Catholics over the years. Catholic theology teaches that Christ was instituting the rite of absolution in this promise.

Admittedly, Jesus *does* seem to be granting a tremendous amount of heavenly authority to Peter in this statement. But before we concede that this made Peter the Pope, note that after His resurrection, in John 20:23, Jesus gave similar authority to *all* the apostles. He told them all, "If you forgive the sins of any, they are forgiven them; if you withhold forgiveness from any, it is withheld." Again it seems that in Matthew 16 our Lord was speaking to Peter as a representative of them all.

But notice that Jesus made a similar statement about "binding and loosing" in the context of his instructions for church discipline (Matt. 18:15–20). We looked at it briefly in Chapter 2. You will recall that Jesus told the disciples if a sinning believer refuses to repent after a private confrontation, a second warning with one or two witnesses, and then public rebuke by the entire congregation, the person is to be treated "as a Gentile and a tax collector" (v. 17). Then Jesus told them, "Whatever you shall bind on earth shall be bound in heaven, and whatever you loose on earth shall be loosed in heaven" (v. 18).

Several truths must be noted from that passage. First, it applies not just to Peter. It is not even limited to the disciples. These are instructions to all believers.

Second, "binding and loosing" has nothing to do with how we handle evil spirits. And verse 19 ("if two of you agree . . . it will be done for them") is not an instruction about how to gain answers to prayer. Jesus was giving directions on how to deal with sin in the assembly of the redeemed. What is "bound" is the sin of the unrepentant person; what is "loosed" is that person's guilt when he or she repents. And any believer can affirm those conditions on the basis of how someone responds to the call to repentance. The issue on which "two of you agree" is how to handle the sinning member of the flock. Jesus was saying that the authority to deal with sin is granted to *any* assembly as small as "two or three . . . gathered in my name" (v. 20).

Third, the source of that authority is Christ, not an earthly vicar: "There am I among them" (v. 20). He personally mediates His rule through the fellowship of believers acting in accord with His principles.

And, fourth, none of this implies authority isolated from the Word of God. Jesus was not authorizing a ruler who could pass down *ex cathedra* edicts. He was not giving anyone authority for literally binding and loosing others. He was certainly not making Peter head of the church. The authority He spoke of belongs to every believer. And that authority lies in the fact that we have heaven's word on "all things that pertain to life and godliness, through the knowledge of him who called us to his own glory and excellence" (2 Pet. 1:3). Jesus was commissioning Peter and the other disciples to make the kingdom message—the Word of God—authoritative in the lives of people. Thus He gave them the keys to the kingdom.

The keys of the kingdom are a sacred trust from Christ to His church. Those keys symbolize custody of the very entrance to the kingdom. He has placed the church in the world and commanded us to preach the gospel so that we can stand as a beacon to point the way to that kingdom. If we compromise His Word or camouflage the gospel, we cease to be that beacon, and we forfeit the only authority we have to use the keys of the kingdom.

When the church is faithful to God and His Word, however, we actually enact heaven's decisions here on earth. We can speak with authority to an unbelieving world. When heaven is in agreement with us, the issue is settled in accord with the highest possible authority. But if we compromise God's Word, we forfeit the very source of our authority. That is why it is so crucial for the church to deal seriously with God, to handle His Word with integrity, and to stand apart from the world. And that is what we mean when we pray, "Your will be done, on earth as it is in heaven" (Matt. 6:10).

MARKS OF AN EFFECTIVE CHURCH

It should be clear that the church is a supernatural work. Christ himself—not marketing know-how, human cleverness, or church-growth techniques—adds to the church, causes its genuine growth, and blesses the church with health and vitality.

Numerical growth alone does not insure a healthy church. To be sure, growth is one of the signs of life, but as we have seen, size is no proof of God's blessing or of a church's spiritual health.

What are the signs of a healthy church? What are worthy goals for a church to pursue as we seek to let the Lord build his church His way? In closing, let me simply suggest a few marks of a healthy church. I have expanded on this list elsewhere,[2] but perhaps this brief summary will be helpful for those seeking something besides marketing principles that can help a struggling church get on target. These, I believe, are the basic biblical principles that provide a blueprint for the church that Christ builds.

Godly Leadership

Jesus' own earthly ministry was invested primarily in eleven men who would become the core of leadership for the early church. Leadership is primary, and the principal requirement for church leaders is that they must be skilled teachers of the Word of God who are above reproach.

I would venture to say that the chief deficiency in most churches today is in this area of leadership. Too many churches ignore the spiritual requirements for leaders and instead choose men because they seem like strong natural leaders or motivators, are successful in business, have money, or wield influence. But church leaders are supposed to be godly teachers, "hold[ing] firm to the trustworthy word as taught . . . able to give instruction in sound doctrine and also to rebuke those who contradict it" (Titus 1:9).

First Timothy 3:1–7 and Titus 1:5–8 contain Paul's profile of the kind of people who are to be leading the church. Putting those two passages together, we come up with a comprehensive list of spiritual qualities that

---

[2]See *The Master's Plan for the Church* (Chicago: Moody, 1991).

pastors and elders must possess. They are to be above reproach, devoted to their wives, temperate, prudent, gentle, respectable, just, devout, hospitable, lovers of good, able to teach, not self-centered or self-willed, not quick-tempered or pugnacious, not contentious, free from the love of money, good managers of their own households, men with a good reputation among unbelievers—and mature believers, not recent converts. From that platform of godly example, they teach the Scripture and lead their people to Christlikeness.

Do those seem like extremely high standards? Yet those are the qualifications that Scripture establishes. Churches that ignore those guidelines set themselves against God's design and forfeit His blessing. To compromise on the issue of leadership is, as Charles Spurgeon would say, "The most suicidal act that a church can commit."[3]

Surely one of the tragic disasters of American evangelicalism in our generation is the ease with which a man can be restored to leadership after scandalous moral failure. It is not at all uncommon for Christian leaders to scandalize the church though gross moral failure, then step back into leadership almost before the publicity dies away. This is a fatal compromise of the biblical standard. It is one of the most pernicious results of modern pragmatism.

Am I saying there should be no restoration for a leader who fails morally and genuinely repents? Certainly there should be restoration to fellowship, but not to the role of an elder or pastor. Churches cannot abandon biblical standards to accommodate their leaders' sin. The biblical requirements for leaders are *purposely* set high because leadership must be by example. Those who scandalize the church are not above reproach. They are disqualified from leadership as long as their reproach remains. In cases involving sexual scandal or unfaithfulness, that may mean a permanent disqualification (Prov. 6:32–33). The apostle Paul recognized that possibility. He wrote, "I discipline my body and keep it under control, lest after preaching to others I myself should be disqualified" (1 Cor. 9:27).

If a church's leaders fail in the matter of personal holiness, the church itself is discredited—no matter how orthodox its confession of faith. Those who ignore the biblical prerequisites for church leaders are building a structure with useless materials and not in accordance with the true foundation (cf. 1 Cor. 3:10–11). No matter how strongly a man may call for truth and righteousness, if his life doesn't back it up, many will reject his teaching as hypocritical or simply conclude that genuine godliness is optional.

---

[3]"This Must Be a Soldier's Battle," *The Sword and the Trowel* (December 1889), 634.

Biblical Goals

There is certainly nothing wrong with a church's setting goals. In fact, a church must have some functional goals or it will have no direction.

But our goals for the church must be *biblical*. Wrong goals set a wrong direction, and that is as bad as having *no* direction—maybe even worse. What are biblical goals? They include worship, fellowship, spiritual growth, and evangelism. Those would be primary goals. More specific goals—such as strengthening families, offering biblical counseling, providing childhood education, and similar purposes—must be seen in light of how they help accomplish the primary goals. And they must be kept subordinate to the primary goals. For example, a church might have a notable music ministry or operate a Christian elementary school. If it does so just to boost attendance figures or to make money, those are not worthy goals. But if it sees the ministry as a means to strengthen the church family spiritually or extend the reach of the gospel, that is a legitimate goal. If we can evaluate every church ministry in light of how it promotes the primary goals, that perspective will help keep the church on track.

Discipleship

The church is not an arena where a professional preacher/minister is cheered on by laypeople who are nothing more than spectators. The church should be discipling and training Christians for ministry. Church members, not just staff, are supposed to be ministering. That is the point of Ephesians 4:11–12. Apostles, prophets, evangelists, and pastor-teachers are given to equip the *saints* to do the work of ministry.

All of this results from discipleship. Discipleship is the ministry of developing deeply spiritual friendships focusing on teaching biblical truth, applying Scripture to life, and thus learning to solve problems biblically. It must be reinforced by a godly example, not just delivered as a set of academic precepts. Therefore, discipleship involves time and personal involvement with people. Jesus' earthly ministry to His own disciples is the biblical model. The church must provide an environment that encourages that kind of discipleship at every level, from the pastor to the newest convert.

Outreach

The church built by Christ will have a strong emphasis on evangelism, beginning with its own community and extending to the uttermost parts of the earth. The early church turned the world upside down (Acts 17:6).

The Jewish leaders told them, "You have filled Jerusalem with your teaching" (Acts 5:28). In a short time their message penetrated the entire community.

Too many Christians think they have fulfilled their responsibility to be witnesses if they drive to church in a car that has a fish sticker on the bumper! Effective churches emphasize the importance of regular, personal outreach on every level.

Our church has been labeled in some circles as non-evangelistic. Yet we have a baptismal service for new converts every Sunday night. As they are baptized, people give their testimonies before the entire congregation. Do you know what brings most of these people to a saving knowledge of Christ? Their personal contact with faithful Christians. People in our church witness to their neighbors, coworkers, other parents in Little League, friends at school, people in the markets, their doctors, their attorneys, and everyone they meet. And over the years the Lord has blessed that one-to-one evangelistic activity to bring more people to faith in Christ than any service, program, or event we sponsor.

If a church lacks this emphasis on outreach, it is doomed to stagnation, decline, and ultimately failure. The means Christ uses to build His church is the faithful witness of Christians on His behalf.

Concern for One Another

In the church that Christ is building, people are involved in one another's lives. The church is not a theater where people go to watch what happens. People are not supposed to come in, sit down, walk out, and have no other involvement with the fellowship. We are not supposed to encourage anonymity and uninvolvement. Instead, we're commanded to "consider how to stir up one another to love and good works, not neglecting to meet together, as is the habit of some, but encouraging one another" (Heb. 10:24–25).

"One another" is a repeated expression in the New Testament instructions to the church. Here is a sampling of some of these commandments.

- "Love one another with brotherly affection. Outdo one another in showing honor" (Rom. 12:10).
- "Be of the same [lowly] mind toward one another" (Rom. 12:16, NASB).
- "Let us not pass judgment on one another any longer, but rather decide never to put a stumbling block or hindrance in the way of a brother" (Rom. 14:13).

- "Be of the same mind with one another according to Christ Jesus" (Rom. 15:5, NASB).
- "Accept one another, just as Christ also accepted us to the glory of God" (Rom. 15:7, NASB).
- "Instruct one another" (Rom. 15:14).
- "Through love serve one another" (Gal. 5:13).
- "Bear with one another in love" (Eph. 4:2).
- "Be kind to one another, tenderhearted, forgiving one another, as God in Christ forgave you" (Eph. 4:32).
- "[Submit] to one another out of reverence for Christ" (Eph. 5:21).
- "Regard one another as more important than yourselves" (Phil. 2:3, NASB).
- "Do not lie to one another" (Col. 3:9).
- "Bear with one another . . . forgiving each other" (Col. 3:13).
- "Encourage one another and build one another up" (1 Thess. 5:11).
- "Confess your sins to one another and pray for one another" (Jas. 5:16).
- "Love one another earnestly from a pure heart" (1 Pet. 1:22).
- "Show hospitality to one another without grumbling" (1 Pet. 4:9).
- "As each has received a gift, use it to serve one another" (1 Pet. 4:10).
- "Clothe yourselves . . . with humility toward one another" (1 Pet. 5:5).

That list alone is infinitely more valuable than all the volumes on marketing techniques and user-friendliness that have ever been written. Those are the qualities of the church that Christ is building. Like the builder Himself, the church that puts those "one anothers" into practice will be a caring, sensitive, and loving church. Add to that the proper exercise of spiritual gifts (Rom. 12:3–8; 1 Cor. 12:4–11; 1 Pet. 4:10–11), and you have a community that will be conformed to the very image of Christ. But it will not be conformed to the world.

A Commitment to the Family

Modern society has unleashed an unprecedented onslaught against the family. Most of the major controversial issues in the news today—such as homosexuality, abortion, women's rights, divorce, youth gangs, and so on—are direct attacks against the family. People's families no longer are where their strongest loyalties lie. Families no longer function as units. And the fragmentation of the family has undermined morality and stability throughout all of society.

The church cannot tolerate or accommodate this devastation. It must confront and correct, then train its families. Strong families are the church's backbone. And strong families build strong individuals. We will pay a high price if we don't make the family a priority. That means we must help our people develop solid marriages and sturdy families by teaching husbands to love and lead their wives (Eph. 5:25), wives to submit to their husbands (5:22), children to obey their parents (6:1), and parents not to exasperate their children but to nurture them in the Lord (6:4).

Biblical Teaching and Preaching

No church can remain healthy long if the pulpit is not strong. And no pulpit is truly strong if the Bible is not the basis of the preaching. That, of course, has been the whole message of this book. But it is certainly worth emphasizing again. As D. Martyn Lloyd-Jones wrote:

> The moment you begin to turn from preaching to these other expedients you will find yourself undergoing a constant series of changes. One of the advantages of being old is that you have experience, so when something new comes up, and you see people getting very excited about it, you happen to be in the position of being able to remember a similar excitement perhaps forty years ago. And so one has seen fashions and vogues and stunts coming one after another in the Church. Each one creates great excitement and enthusiasm and is loudly advertised as *the* thing that is going to fill the churches, the thing that is going to solve the problem. They have said that about every single one of them. But in a few years they have forgotten all about it, and another stunt comes along, or another new idea; somebody has hit upon the one thing needful or he has a psychological understanding of modem man. Here is the thing, and everybody rushes after it; but soon it wanes and disappears and something else takes its place.
>
> This is, surely, a very sad and regrettable state for the Christian Church to be in, that like the world she should exhibit these constant changes of fashion. In that state she lacks the stability and the solidity and the continuing message that has ever been the glory of the Christian Church.[4]

Biblical preaching cannot be geared toward meeting felt needs, solving psychological problems, amusing the audience, making people feel good about themselves, or any of the other hollow fads that have commandeered pulpits in this entertainment-oriented age. Biblical preaching must uphold the truth of God and demand that it be heeded. There is plenty of room

---

[4]D. Martyn Lloyd-Jones, *Preaching and Preachers* (Grand Rapids, MI: Zondervan, 1971), 35.

for innovation and creativity within those guidelines, but the message cannot be altered or abridged in any way without prostituting the church's responsibility. Truth proclaimed powerfully from the Scriptures is the sine qua non of the church. Any other kind of preaching is not worthy of the church that Christ is building.

A Willingness to Change

Healthy churches must be willing to change.

Wait a minute! someone says. *Aren't you appealing for traditionalism in churches?* No. There's nothing sacred about human tradition. I'm not in favor of staid formalism or hackneyed custom. I agree with those who warn that stagnation can be fatal to the church. I just don't believe the church needs to abandon the centrality of the Word of God, the primacy of preaching, and the fundamentals of biblical truth in order to be fresh and creative.

Someone has said that the seven last words of the church are, "We've never done it that way before!" An inflexible attitude is the bane of a healthy church. We must be willing to grow and adapt and try new things— but never at the expense of biblical truth, and never to the detriment of the gospel message.

Worship

I've saved worship for last, certainly not because it is least crucial but because it sums up all the others. Several years ago I wrote a book on worship titled *The Ultimate Priority*.[5] I do believe that worship is the church's—and the individual Christian's—highest priority. True worship comprises and fulfills all these other characteristics of the church that Christ builds. The church that sets its focus on God will find that all other things fall naturally into place.

Here is precisely the problem with the market-oriented, user-friendly, pragmatic approach to ministry: it is man-centered, not God-centered. Its concern is what people desire, not what God demands. It sees the church as existing for people's sake rather than for God's sake. It works from a faulty blueprint rather than fulfilling the plan of the Master Builder.

User-friendly, entertainment-oriented, market-driven, pragmatic churches will probably continue to flourish for a while. Unfortunately, however, the whole movement is based on current fashion and therefore

---

[5](Chicago: Moody, 1983).

cannot last long. When the fickle winds finally change, one of three things may happen. These churches will fall out of vogue and wane; or they will opt to change with the spirit of the age and very likely abandon any semblance of biblical Christianity; or they will see the need to rebuild on a more sure foundation. My prayer, of course, is that most will take the third course of action and that they will not wait until worldliness and compromise have so permeated their fellowships that it becomes impossible to change.

Charles Spurgeon wrote, "It is hard to get leaven out of dough, and easy to put it in. . . . Oh that those who are spiritually alive in the churches may look to this thing, and may the Lord himself baffle the adversary!"[6]

---

[6]"Notes," *The Sword and the Trowel* (October 1888). Reprinted in *The "Down Grade" Controversy* (Pasadena, TX: Pilgrim, n.d.), 67.

10

INTERLUDE

On the "Down-Grade" the train travels very fast: another station has been passed. What next? And what next?

CHARLES HADDON SPURGEON[1]

What is the future of evangelicalism? In a perceptive series of articles on the church growth movement, Os Guinness points out that traditional evangelicalism not only resisted worldly influences but also stressed "cognitive defiance" of the world spirit. Evangelicals historically have understood that their calling is to be in the world but not of the world. Now, however, "at the high noon of modernity, the world has become so powerful, pervasive, and appealing that the traditional stance of cognitive defiance has become rare and almost unthinkable."[2] Somewhere along the line evangelicals decided to make friends with the world.

Guinness points out that although we are called to be in the world but not of the world (John 17:14–18), many Christians have reversed the formula, becoming *of* the world while not really being *in* the world. They did this by allowing cable television, VCRs, radio, and other forms of communication to infuse worldly values into their thinking, while isolating themselves from any personal involvement with the people in the world who most desperately need the gospel.

"Evangelicals are now outdoing liberals as the supreme religious modernizers—and compromisers—of today," Guinness writes.[3] He suggests that the market-driven philosophy so popular among modern evangelicals is nothing more than "a recycling of the error of classical liberalism."[4]

---

[1] "Notes," *The Sword and the Trowel* (May 1889). Reprinted in *The "Down Grade" Controversy* (Pasadena, TX: Pilgrim, n.d.), 76.
[2] "Recycling the Compromise of Liberalism," *Tabletalk* (May 1992), 51.
[3] Ibid.
[4] Ibid.

We noted earlier that the reason most evangelicals were caught unaware by modernism a hundred years ago is that liberals rose from within evangelical ranks, used evangelical vocabulary, and gained acceptance through relentless appeals for peace and tolerance. The new modernism is following precisely the same course, and that tactic seems likely to take evangelicals by surprise once again.

Most of the market-driven megachurches insist they would never compromise doctrine. They are attractive to evangelicals precisely because they claim to be as orthodox in their doctrine as they are unorthodox in their methodology. Multitudes are sufficiently reassured by such promises and simply abandon their critical faculties, thus increasing their vulnerability. Unfortunately, real discernment is in short supply among modern evangelicals.

The truth is, it wouldn't matter much *what* doctrinal position some of these churches took, because doctrine is simply a non-issue with them. A friend of mine wanted to learn how the user-friendly churches integrate doctrine into their ministries. He selected one of the largest and best-known churches in the movement and ordered several cassettes from their tape ministry. He asked for tapes that focused on biblical doctrine and was sent several tapes and a catalog. A survey of the catalog revealed that the sermons preached in the church—by a ratio of more than thirty to one—usually dealt with contemporary topics, psychological issues (depression, eating disorders, self-image), personal relationships, motivational themes, and other matters a la mode. Messages dealing with doctrine—even sermons based on any biblical text—were rare. A tape titled "The Cost of Commitment" dealt not with commitment to Christ but with the personal sacrifice required to build strong personal relationships with others. After listening to hours of tapes from this pastor, my friend concluded that it was impossible to tell what the man's positions were on any basic doctrinal issues. Most of the messages would have been immediately transferrable to any context—a sales convention, a school assembly, or a businessmen's luncheon. They simply avoided doctrinal or biblical issues altogether, using Scripture for illustrative purposes only, often reserving the scant biblical allusions for the very end.

Like the modernists a century ago, churches in the user-friendly movement have decided doctrine is divisive and peace is more important than sound teaching. Wanting to appeal to a modern age, they try to frame their message as a friendly, agreeable, and relevant dialogue. Unfortunately, it is often the most "relevant" topics that the church can ill afford to be agreeable on. The pet doctrines of our modern age—radicalism, abortion, women's rights, homosexuality, and other politically charged moral issues—pose the most obvious problems for user-friendly churches. Their undefined theology and seeker-sensitive philosophy does not permit them to take a firm biblical stance on such matters, because the moment they defy the spirit of the age, they forfeit their marketing appeal. They are therefore forced to keep mum or capitulate. Either way, they compromise the truth.

If a church is not even willing to take a firm stand against abortion, how will that church deal with subtle erosion of crucial doctrine? If a church lacks enough discernment to condemn such an overt error as homosexuality or feminism, how will that church handle a *subtle* attack on doctrinal integrity?

The landscape of evangelicalism is rapidly changing. The February 19, 1990 issue of *Christianity Today* included an article by Robert Brow entitled "Evangelical Megashift," reporting on a recent wave of radical thinking among evangelical theologians. "New-model" evangelicalism, as the article labeled the movement, turns out to be nothing more than "old-model" liberalism. By redefining key terms, this new-model theology seeks to fashion a kinder, gentler Christianity.

For example, new-model evangelicalism redefines *hell.* "No one could possibly be in hell who would rather be in heaven," the new view claims.[5] So hell is no longer thought of as a place of eternal torment. Instead, it is an exclusive refuge from God's presence, open only to those determined to get there.

There's more:

> In new-model theology . . . *wrath*—specifically God's wrath—similarly means something different from the old-model understanding. Wrath connotes not angry punishment, but the bad consequences God assigns, as any loving parent might, to destructive or wrongful behavior. The word *wrath* as used in the Old Testament, it is argued, is not primarily a law-court term. It never means sending people to an eternal hell. In fact, it can simply be translated "bad consequences"—the bad consequences of pestilence, drought, and famine, or the ravages of wild animals and invading armies, experienced in the here and now.[6]

That's still not all. "*Sin* also changes meaning. . . . In old-model theology, even one sin would be sufficient to condemn us to hell. New-model evan-

---

[5]"Evangelical Megashift," *Christianity Today* (February 19, 1990), 13.
[6]Ibid.

gelicals, on the other hand, cannot think about sin without reference to the fatherly care of God. For loving parents, sin or bad behavior requires discipline and correction, with a view to helping the child change. But the purpose is never to exclude the child from home."[7] That is, God would never cite sin as a reason for sending anyone to hell.

In new-model theology God's primary attribute is benevolence, which overrides and supersedes His holiness, justice, wrath, and sovereignty. The new-model God is a *judge* only in the sense of being a "defender of His people." His sole concern is "the freedom and peace of the people."[8] Moreover, the new-model church is called not to confront the world, but "to make known the love of God, to say, 'your sins are forgiven,' as Jesus did, and to offer the resources of the Spirit to all who want to learn how to love and enjoy God and their neighbors."[9]

If ever there was a user-friendly theology, this is it. But it is not biblical, and there is nothing really new about it. It is simply retreaded liberalism. These are the same arguments and the same teachings that liberals have promoted for years—only now they are designated "evangelical." Don't let the label fool you. Spurgeon wrote, "It is mere cant to cry, 'We are evangelical; we are all evangelical,' and yet decline to say what evangelical means."[10] "You may believe anything, everything, or nothing and yet be enrolled in the 'Evangelical' army—*so they say.* Will there arise no honest, out-spoken evangelicals among Dissenters to expose and repudiate this latitudinarianism? Are all the watchmen asleep? Are all the churches indifferent?"[11]

According to new-model theology, "the cross was not a judicial payment, but the visible expression in a space-time body of his eternal nature as Son."[12] That is simply a new way of stating the central tenet of liberal theology: Christ's saving work was not substitutionary atonement but His moral example. It is an attack on the central truth of evangelical theology. It proves beyond question that some who like to think of themselves as evangelicals have already passed the warning signs and are now freewheeling heedlessly down the slope.

User-friendly churches have no means of defense against trends like new-model theology. Their market-driven philosophy does not permit them to take firm enough doctrinal positions to oppose these teachings. Their

---

[7]Ibid.
[8]Ibid.
[9]Ibid., 14.
[10]"Notes," *The Sword and the Trowel* (October 1888). Reprinted in *The "Down Grade" Controversy*, 66.
[11]"Notes," *The Sword and the Trowel* (January 1889), 40.
[12]"Evangelical Megashift," 14.

outlook on leadership drives them to hire marketers who can sell rather than pastors who can teach. Their approach to ministry is so *un*doctrinal that they cannot educate their people against subtle errors. Their hatred of controversy puts them in a position where they cannot oppose false teaching that masquerades as evangelicalism. In fact, new-model theology seems *ideally suited* to the user-friendly philosophy. Why would the user-friendly church oppose such doctrines?

But oppose them we must, if we are to remain true to God's Word and maintain a gospel witness. Pragmatism does not hold answers to the dangers confronting biblical Christianity. Pragmatism is carnal wisdom— spiritually bankrupt and contrary to the Word of God. (See Appendix 4 for an eighteenth-century contrast between carnal and spiritual wisdom that applies particularly well to twentieth-century pragmatism.)

Marketing techniques offer nothing but the promise of popularity and worldly approval. They certainly offer no safeguard against the dangers of the down-grade.

The only hope is a return to Scripture and sound doctrine. As evangelicals we desperately need to recover our determination to be biblical, our refusal to comply with the world, our willingness to defend what we believe, and our courage to defy false teaching. Unless we collectively awaken to the current dangers that face our movement, the adversary will attack us from within, and we will not be able to withstand. History will repeat itself, and the same disaster that ravaged the church a hundred years ago will strike our generation.

> Yet, surely, there must be some who will fling aside the dastard love of peace, and speak out for our Lord, and for his truth. A craven spirit is upon many, and their tongues are paralyzed. Oh, for an outburst of true faith and holy zeal! (Charles Haddon Spurgeon)[13]

---

[13]"Notes" (May 1889). Reprinted in *The "Down Grade" Controversy*, 76.

11

CARRIED ABOUT BY EVERY WIND

Be ye not carried about by every wind of doctrine. Give not heed to every schismatic who would lead you aside. Hold fast by the oracles of the Most High. Ye know what ye have been taught, and whereunto ye have been called; and ye know the foundation whereupon ye have been built up. "Be ye steadfast, unmoveable, always abounding in the work of the Lord." Whatever may happen to dominations, whatever divisions we may live to see, let it be known still that for God and his truth we are prepared to hold our ground, at any expense or at any risk.

CHARLES HADDON SPURGEON[1]

We fast-forward now more than fifteen years since the preceding chapters were first written, and what lessons can we glean from the state of the church today? The message that stands out above all others is this: several decades of nonstop talk and strategizing about relevance, contextualization, and clever methods for engaging the culture have had no perceptible positive spiritual effect on the world in which we live. The influence of the church within our culture continues to diminish; our society has grown steadily darker; and the message the church is now giving to the world is more confused and confusing than perhaps any time since the Dark Ages.

What *has* happened is this: the church's true message is still being drowned out by slick, market-savvy masters of hype. Leadership in the church has been commandeered by carnival barkers rather than men who are serious-minded proclaimers of God's Word. There are today very few

---

[1] "The Church of God and the Truth of God," *The Metropolitan Tabernacle Pulpit*, Vol. 54 (London: Passmore & Alabaster, 1908), 242.

clarion voices declaring the gospel plainly and accurately to the world. Many who have risen to positions of prominence and influence in the evangelical community simply are not spiritually qualified to lead, and naturally they are not leading well.

Today more than ever, evangelical church leaders are held captive to the notion that their main duty toward the world is to study the trends of popular culture and try desperately to get on every passing bandwagon as quickly as possible. Some pastors literally devote most of their energies to learning whatever happens to be the latest worldly craze, and then they desperately seek a way to blend themes and references from those fads into their sermons and Sunday-school programs. The goal, still, is to woo people into the kingdom by making Christianity seem cool and contemporary. As a result, people in evangelical pews have become utterly obsessed with superficial trends and silly fashions. In fact, evangelical Christians may be more addicted to quickly passing fads than any other single demographic or subculture, including preteen girls.

To be blunt: the church has become a laughingstock with no moral authority to stand before the world and confront sin, declare Christ's lordship, and speak with any credibility about sin, righteousness, or judgment.

As a matter of fact, the marketing of evangelical fads has become a major commercial enterprise. Numerous publishing companies and Web sites peddle topical-sermon series in a box, complete with prefabricated PowerPoint slides, most of which are based on movies, television programs, popular music, or other icons of pop culture. Everything from Greenpeace to Ultimate Fighting has been harnessed by worldly church leaders in a misguided attempt to connect with "culture." No secular fad or catchphrase is too trite, too vulgar, or too frivolous to be expounded in the church.

In fact, evangelicals seem to have a knack for borrowing the most pointless and profane symbols of secular culture and pretending they are profound. Someone wrote an entire quarter's worth of adult Sunday-school curricula (complete with lesson plans, a leader's guide, an annotated textbook, and video clips) featuring "The Gospel According to Barney Fife." The series was so wildly popular that several Christian publishers developed extensive lines of similar material, featuring programs (mislabeled as "Bible studies") based on every insipid sitcom from *I Love Lucy* to *The Simpsons*. Recently the sitcom fad seems to be fading from popularity. Sex and social activism are becoming the current sermon topics of choice. (In other words, sixties fashions have finally caught the evangelical eye.)

Evangelicals hungrily devour fads like those—and more. Consider what has happened in the decade and a half between the first and this new edition of this book. In that relatively short period of time, the evangelical movement burned through more fads than I can count. There was a time when evangelicals everywhere were praying the prayer of Jabez, and the phenomenon was so large that someone issued an entire catalog chock-full of Jabez merchandise—jewelry and knickknacks with 1 Chronicles 4:10 imprinted on them like a talisman. Similar trends have come and gone: WWJD jewelry, truckloads of Rapture fiction, scary novels about demonic warfare, the Promise Keepers movement, "Forty Days of Purpose," and *The Passion of the Christ*.

Curiosities like those, as well as various other gewgaws of lesser import, have swept through the evangelical movement like relentless waves of mass hysteria. Each cycle of enthusiasm manages to capture the attention of the evangelical world for a few weeks—eight months at most. At the start of each new surge, you would think (from the level of breathless anticipation) that the craftsmen of contextualization have finally identified something that will revolutionize just about *everything*. At the peak of each fad's popularity, it will be practically the only thing anyone in the evangelical community wants to talk about. Then suddenly one day it will be gone because something newer is on the horizon.

At that point, the dead fad becomes fodder for ridicule. Like yesterday's Precious Moments figurines and Thomas Kinkade paintings, they become objects of scorn for today's more sophisticated holy hipsters. But be forewarned: criticism of *any* fad is deemed intolerable and uncharitable while the fad is still hot. On the other hand, to defend an old fad is to declare one's own irrelevance. So timing is everything, and it is a lot of work to keep up with what's hot and what's not.

If you are a pastor and your church isn't up-to-date and on board with the newest trend—if you are just one stage behind (like those who were caught still "doing" Jabez when everyone else had moved on to *The Purpose-Driven Life*)—you will very quickly be written off as hopelessly uncool, and the inveterate fad-chasers in your congregation will move to a church that's more hip.

Meanwhile, the fads are becoming much more sensational, and their life spans are shortening. They have gone from "Forty Days of Purpose" to "Seven Days of Sex." During the weeks I have been working on revisions to this new edition, I have read at least five stories from secular news sources about various churches that have literally issued sex-challenges to married couples. They typically advertise via deliberately suggestive billboards and flyers spread throughout the community. One church was prohibited from holding their Sunday services on city school board property because the church spread fliers around the community advertising sermons on sex, porn, and homosexuality. The fliers were deemed "obscene" by secular school officials.[2] The church complained that they were victims of persecution.

Of course, that is not at all what Scripture is talking about when it warns that the gospel is a stumbling-block and that the world will hate Christians.

FAD-CHASING AND APOSTASY

It is hard to think of a ministry philosophy more fundamentally in conflict with Scripture than chasing fads in order to keep in step with the world. It is a blatant form of friendship with the world, which James 4:4 likens to spiritual adultery. James also says those who follow such a course are God's enemies: "You adulteresses, do you not know that friendship with the world is hostility toward God? Therefore whoever wishes to be a friend of the world makes himself an enemy of God" (NASB).

Fad-chasing is the very thing Paul instructed Timothy to avoid in 2 Timothy 4. Building one's message around fictional themes borrowed from the entertainment industry not only caters to and cultivates audiences who have itching ears, it overlays and obscures the truth with Hollywood's mythology. Isn't that precisely what 2 Timothy 4:4 condemns? "[They] turn away from listening to the truth and wander off into myths." That verse is a description of *apostasy*—exactly where evangelical faddism invariably goes.

Some of the most popular and dangerous evangelical fads of the past fifteen years have involved waves of charismatic fervor that have sown confusion and discord in every culture where they have been embraced. I'm talking about the Toronto Blessing (where "holy laughter" and other forms of pseudo-drunkenness were declared to be signs that the Holy Spirit was moving), the Kansas City Prophets (a movement led by a group of self-appointed seers whose prognostications were usually false and whose private morals were even worse), the Pensacola Outpouring (whose major features were gold dust and gold tooth fillings that supposedly appeared miraculously, but the revival disbanded amid charges of fraud and embezzled funds). Then (most recently) those movements were all eclipsed by a supposed revival in Lakeland, Florida whose leader embodied all those

---

[2]Gary J. Kunich, "Unified Boots out Church over Flier: Sermons on Sex Deemed 'Obscene'; Parents Complain," *Kenosha News* (February 1, 2009).

errors and turned out to be twice as much a son of hell as all the religious scoundrels he imitated (cf. Matt. 23:15).[3]

You might think the cumulative effect of so many "prophetic" movements, *all* of them being totally discredited in fairly rapid succession, would heighten a craving for more careful discernment among evangelicals. But every new charismatic tsunami seems to grow larger and confound more people than the previous ones. Each wave is considerably more bizarre and certainly more grossly unbiblical than all its predecessors, yet each one pulls in Christians who previously seemed fairly mainstream. Craving something more than the shallow fare they are force-fed in the average evangelical church, they are eager patsies for a charlatan who promises supernatural signs and wonders instead of the superficial skits and tomfoolery to which they have grown accustomed.

Thus the evangelical mainstream relentlessly chases its own fringe. What sounds outlandish today will be canonized as an essential methodology tomorrow. It is a vivid reminder of the grave dangers that face sheep who have no shepherds.

It also ought to be a signal that the church of our day is the living embodiment of precisely what Paul said ear-tickling teachers would unleash into the church. The truth has been overthrown by mythologists and storytellers. The one remedy for the mess we are in would be a return to the *truth*. And that can happen only if church leaders will fulfill the central duty Paul set forth in his instructions to Timothy: "Preach the word . . . in season and out of season; reprove, rebuke, and exhort, with complete patience and teaching" (2 Tim. 4:2).

That has been the theme and the main message of this entire book. It is neither complex nor mysterious. It is amazing that after decades of fooling around with worldly diversions, so many evangelicals still do not seem to realize that worldly pragmatism is the very thing that has made the church so ineffectual. This is why we are not reaching the world for Christ. The

---

[3]The following quotation comments on this sad situation:

> [Lakeland Revival founder Todd] Bentley's faith and exuberance impressed seasoned, prominent revivalists while his wild tactics often tempered the enthusiasm of other leaders. When praying for healing, the tattooed evangelist was known to hit the sick in the stomach with his knee in a move more common among wrestlers than preachers. Bentley even recounted kicking a woman in the face in an act of "obedience to the Lord."
>
> Yet, with the exception of a few ministers, many charismatic leaders chose to overlook Bentley's peculiar methods for the sake of what they saw as "fruit." They claimed the revival stirred many Christians worldwide to pursue God with a renewed hunger.
>
> "Personally, I believe that the Lakeland Outpouring was another wave of revival like Toronto and Brownsville," said Los Angeles-area pastor [Ché] Ahn, referring to the Toronto Blessing and the Pensacola Revival, both of which occurred during the 1990s. "Each wave has its own life span." Paul Steven Ghiringhelli, "Lakeland Revival Officially Ends," *Charisma* (October 13, 2008).

church's own pragmatism has made the church subservient to the world's fashions and beliefs. The church (except for a faithful remnant) has become exactly like the world.

WE NEED TO RETURN TO THE WORD OF GOD

If you take just one lesson away from this book, let it be this: *the church needs to get back to the Word of God.* Scripture alone can give life and bring sanctification to a sinful soul. Scripture alone can fully equip us to discern between truth and error. Only by returning to the Bible and submitting to its truth can the church recover what she needs to resist the lure of the world's fads and ever-changing philosophies, to confront the world with life-changing truth, and to keep our message pure and accurate.

Scripture gives us both the means and the road map for true church growth. Gags and gimmicks may draw massive crowds for a while, but inflated attendance numbers do not necessarily constitute true church growth. As a matter of fact, in the book of Acts, even though we see the church steadily growing numerically, the actual progress of the church is measured by the advance of God's Word as it is proclaimed faithfully. "The word of God increased and multiplied" (Acts 12:24; cf. 19:20). "The word of God continued to increase, and the number of the disciples multiplied greatly" (6:7).

No wonder. "The word of God is living and active, sharper than any two-edged sword, piercing to the division of soul and of spirit, of joints and of marrow, and discerning the thoughts and intentions of the heart" (Heb. 4:12). Notice what that verse says about the vitality of God's Word: it "is living and active." It is not dead, and it will never be passé—no matter how unstylish it might seem to those who want to follow the world.

God's Word itself is not only living; it is a source of spiritual life to those who receive it as truth. The life-giving power of God's Word is the instrument through which the Holy Spirit imparts eternal life to those who were formerly dead in sin (cf. Eph. 2:1). That's what Jesus meant in John 6:63 when He said, "The words that I have spoken to you are spirit and life." The New Testament repeatedly tells us that the Word of God is the instrument of regeneration—the power by which God raises a spiritually dead soul to eternal life. "You have been born again, not of perishable seed but of imperishable, through the living and abiding word of God" (1 Pet. 1:23). This was an Old Testament truth as well, celebrated by David in Psalm 119:50: "Your word has revived me" (NASB).

James 1:18 stresses the absolute sovereignty of God. But it affirms that truth right alongside a statement that underscores how God uses *means*. "Of his own will he brought us forth by the word of truth." The doctrines of divine sovereignty and predestination do not mean that the elect will be saved whether they hear the gospel or not. Scripture says God has ordained the means as well as the end. He brings His chosen ones to repentance and faith *through the proclamation of His Word*. Quite simply, people cannot be saved unless they hear the Word of God: "How then will they call on him in whom they have not believed? And how are they to believe in him of whom they have never heard? And how are they to hear without someone preaching? And how are they to preach unless they are sent?" (Rom. 10:14–15). Therefore to substitute anything other than the preaching of the Word as a method of "outreach" is to stifle church growth, not stimulate it.

There is no other program, no other message, and no other book that is capable of transforming sinners' hearts. We've all heard preachers who are capable of making Scripture sound dry and tedious. Shame on them. But the backlash against that sort of ungifted, unqualified teaching can be even worse. You'll often hear pastors and Bible-study leaders talk about "making the Bible come alive"—by which they usually mean they are looking for ways to spice up the Bible by adding to it, altering it through illegitimate means of contextualization, or using the Bible as illustrative material while they exegete the latest popular movie.

That is faulty thinking, and it has led thousands of good and gifted teachers down the wrong path. We don't have to "make the Bible come alive"; it *is* both alive and active. It is *always* relevant. It is eternally applicable to the true needs of the human soul. And it is capable of speaking to fallen, hardened, and insensitive hearts with a power no human composition could possibly display.

The thoughts and opinions of men are weak and transitory and ultimately powerless. Human philosophies and worldly fads have preposterously short life spans. But the Word of God remains unchanging for all eternity. Jesus said, "Heaven and earth will pass away, but my words will not pass away" (Luke 21:33). Forever, "the word of God is living and active."

That's as true of the obscure portions of the Old Testament as it is of all the favorite verses of the New Testament. *All* of Scripture is living and active. *All* of it is "profitable for teaching, for reproof, for correction, and for training in righteousness" (2 Tim. 3:16). "Every word of God proves true" (Prov. 30:5). "Every word that comes from the mouth of God" (Matt. 4:4) is life-giving, life-sustaining spiritual bread for hungry souls.

I love to listen to the testimonies of believers when they describe how they came to salvation. In every authentic conversion, there is a point at which some truth of Scripture pierces the heart, rebukes the conscience, and awakens the soul from spiritual death. Several biographies of Spurgeon include the famous account of a woman who bought some butter at a farmer's market. The package was wrapped in a piece of newsprint that included a single page of one of Spurgeon's published sermons. Through that partial exposition of a single Bible verse, she came to faith in Christ.

Spurgeon himself was converted as a teenager when a lay preacher pointed his finger at Spurgeon and quoted a portion of Numbers 21:8: "Every one that is bitten, when he *looketh* upon it, shall live" (KJV, emphasis added). The preacher that morning was an ill-prepared, unlearned, modestly gifted layman who was called upon at the last minute to fill in for the pastor, who could not be there because of a blizzard. The replacement preacher took John 3:14–15 as his text: "[As] Moses lifted up the serpent in the wilderness, so must the Son of Man be lifted up, that whoever believes in him may have eternal life." When the preacher looked at Spurgeon and addressed him directly—"Young man, look to Jesus Christ"—Spurgeon said,

> I saw at once the way of salvation. I know not what else he said, I did not take much notice of it, I was so possessed with that one thought. Like as when the brazen serpent was lifted up, the people only looked and were healed, so it was with me. I had been waiting to do fifty things, but when I heard that word, "Look!" what a charming word it seemed to me! Oh! I looked until I could almost have looked my eyes away. There and then the cloud was gone, the darkness had rolled away, and that moment I saw the sun; and I could have risen that instant, and sung with the most enthusiastic of them, of the precious blood of Christ, and the simple faith which looks alone to Him. Oh, that somebody had told me this before, "Trust Christ, and you shall be saved."[4]

The word of God is *powerful*. The Greek word translated "active" in Hebrews 4:12 is *energes*. It means God's Word is dynamic, potent, full of life and vigor. The true power to draw people to Christ, awaken them to faith, and accomplish the work of regeneration is in the Word of God itself, not in

---

[4]*The Autobiography of Charles H. Spurgeon*, 4 vols. (London: Passmore and Alabaster, 1897), 1:106–108.

the efforts of clever admen to market the message to a worldly culture. In his first letter to the church at Thessalonica, Paul described the Word of God as a living force that "is at work in you believers" (1 Thess. 2:13).

The Word of God *always* accomplishes whatever purpose God intends—even when people hear it, harden their hearts, and turn away from it. God told Isaiah, "So shall my word be that goes out from my mouth; it shall not return to me empty, but it shall accomplish that which I purpose, and shall succeed in the thing for which I sent it" (Isa. 55:11). Here's the supreme reason for making sure the proclamation of God's Word is the heart and focus of our ministry, and it makes sense even from the perspective of a pragmatist: Scripture *always* accomplishes what God intends. It may not always get the result we hope for, but God's purposes are always fulfilled whenever His Word is declared.

The truth of God's Word is perceived differently by different people. To one it is "a fragrance from death to death, to the other a fragrance from life to life" (2 Cor. 2:16). God's purposes differ accordingly. Sometimes He blesses the hearers (Luke 11:28); sometimes He curses them (Mal. 2:2). Sometimes the Word instructs and edifies in a wholly positive way; other times it brings a harsh reproof or correction (2 Tim. 3:16). When the full counsel of God is proclaimed, it will do all those things—sometimes all at once. Whatever the result, God's Word never returns to Him void.

The task of the preacher is not a complex one. The substance of what he is to teach is Scripture. He could spend a lifetime preaching and not begin to exhaust it all. It is a sumptuous feast, prepared by God and ready to be served without adding foreign spices to the recipe. The preacher's duty, quite simply, is to put the meal on the table without messing it up.

Preachers need to concern themselves with how clear they are and how correctly they interpret the text, rather than how cool and creative they can be in the contextualization process. As John Piper frequently says, you cannot exalt Christ and show off your own cleverness at the same time. If we are faithful to preach the Word with clarity and power, God will be glorified and the Word will have its way in our and our hearers' hearts, whether the response looks like what the world would label success or not. God's Word is certainly more powerful than our cleverness and programs, and always more effective too, given that the central goal of our ministry (like Christ's) is to seek and save the lost, and not to be conformed to the world.

Notice that Hebrews 4:12 illustrates the power of God's Word by likening the Word to a sword. That is not a particularly popular comparison in these tolerant postmodern times, but it does nevertheless touch on an aspect of biblical ministry that churches today are all too prone to forget: we are not to imitate the world and thereby make friends with it; our task is to confront our culture—especially sin and unbelief. And that sometimes entails using the Word of God as a weapon.

WE NEED TO LAY HOLD OF THE SWORD OF THE SPIRIT

The wording of Hebrews 4:12 is deliberately both vivid and violent: "The word of God is . . . sharper than any two-edged sword, piercing to the division of soul and of spirit, of joints and of marrow."

A two-edged sword is a particularly dangerous weapon. The verse says Scripture is even sharper and more effective than that. Like a two-edged sword, it has no dull side. It will cut no matter how you swing it. It also has a sharp point on the business end, capable of "piercing" deeply. So whether it is swung like a saber or thrust like a rapier, it will cut to the bone and marrow—and there is nothing so hard that this blade cannot pierce it. Even in the hands of the most unskilled swordsman, it is capable of inflicting mortal wounds to human pride and self-righteousness.

None of the artificial instruments contemporary church leaders have labored so hard to concoct are like that. No mere psychotherapy can truly penetrate the human heart and discover the cause of human woe (much less offer a cure for it), and no clever amusement will ever lay bare the pride that is at the root of all unbelief. For such things, only the Word of God is effectual.

Contemporary Christians seem to lack confidence in the ability of the Word of God to penetrate sin-hardened hearts. One of the reasons given for so much of the nonsense that has made our churches so superficial is the idea that if we first entertain people and make them comfortable, they will be more open to the gospel. If we can convince them that our message poses no threat to their way of life and that they have nothing to fear from Christ, perhaps we can then break through that hard exterior and reach them. But (the conventional wisdom insists) they must be made ready by something *gentler* than Scripture itself. The plain proclamation of the unadulterated Word is too intimidating, we are told. A milder approach will soften people so that the Word can do its work. But (they say) that will not be until after we have persuaded them that church is fun, Christians are just like everyone else, and they have nothing whatsoever to fear from God.

Nonsense. Every aspect of that kind of thinking is wrong. *Nothing* penetrates a sin-hardened heart better than the Word of God itself. There is a legitimate, intimidating aspect of God's truth that we dare not tone down. There's a reason God's Word is compared to a sword rather than a pillow or a featherbed. Parts of the biblical message are unpleasant—even hostile to a carnal mind. The *law* has some very bad news for us before the *gospel* announces the good news. For those who neglect or reject the bad news (that we are utterly condemned and hopeless before God because of our sin), there simply is no good news—because Christ came for sinners, not the righteous (Mark 2:17).

To think that we have invented a strategy that can soften a sinner's heart more effectively than Scripture is the very height of arrogance. The Word of God alone can actually do what none of our "missional" schemes could ever accomplish: pierce to the very depths, "as far as the division of soul and spirit, of both joints and marrow, and [it is] able to judge the thoughts and intentions of the heart." God's Word probes to the deepest, darkest hollows of a human heart, no matter how hardened or how closed the heart might be. *Only* Scripture can do that.

We naturally recoil from the ideas of warfare, bloodshed, swordplay, and cutting through bone so deeply that it exposes the marrow. The sword is a shocking symbol for God's Word. But this is an important point. The same imagery is employed repeatedly in Scripture. We find it in Ephesians 6:17 as well: "The sword of the Spirit . . . is the word of God."

As a matter of fact, it is significant that every other instrument of warfare named in Ephesians 6 is defensive armor. The only offensive weapon available to us is the Word of God. It is by God's Word that we are to tear down the strongholds of false ideologies and belief systems (including *un*belief itself) that keep people captive to their sin. In 2 Corinthians 10:4–5 Paul writes, "The weapons of our warfare are not of the flesh but have divine power to destroy strongholds. We destroy arguments and every lofty opinion raised against the knowledge of God, and take every thought captive to obey Christ."

That is perhaps the key description of the nature and aim of spiritual warfare in Scripture. And notice: the battle is spiritual, not carnal. Its aim is not the *destruction* of people but rather their *liberation*. What we aim to destroy are the "strongholds" in which sinners have been imprisoned: wrong beliefs, ignorance, and worldly ideologies.

So despite all the violent-sounding imagery, the sword of the Spirit— the Word of God—is not a weapon by which we are to bludgeon, injure, or destroy people. It is, however, a weapon of immense power for tearing down falsehoods. Sometimes sinners will think *they* are being injured when their comfortable fortresses are being dismantled. Moreover, in the end the Word of God will indeed penetrate to the very heart and conscience of the one being delivered. When that happens, it usually inflicts great fear as well as great pain.

But it is not the kind of pain designed to kill; it is a healing pain. It is analogous to the pain inflicted by a skilled surgeon. A good cardiologist, for example, is quite capable of penetrating to the very heart (in a literal sense)—not to kill but to make whole.

That is how we need to put God's Word to work again in our churches.

LET'S USE IT FOR THE GOOD OF THE CHURCH

If we're going to restore God's Word to its rightful place in the church, we cannot try to tone it down to eliminate or alleviate the pain it sometimes causes (especially the pain we feel in *our own consciences*). We need to proclaim the truth of Scripture straightforwardly and unapologetically, while submitting ourselves to its cutting work, knowing that it is ultimately for our good.

It is not without significance that the Old Testament symbol of regeneration was circumcision—the cutting away of the flesh of the foreskin. This was a vivid symbol of cleansing and renewal. It pictured the kind of spiritual precision surgery involved in the renewal of the heart when the Holy Spirit regenerates us. It can be intensely painful, but the long-term aim is not to hurt us but to conform us to God's standard.

Ezekiel 11:19 describes regeneration in these terms: "I will give them one heart, and a new spirit I will put within them. I will remove the heart of stone from their flesh and give them a heart of flesh." That is precisely what circumcision symbolized—the cutting away of the defiled heart for the implantation of a new, pure one. God had told the Israelites, "Circumcise . . . your heart" (Deut. 10:16). The prophet Jeremiah echoed the command: "Circumcise yourselves to the LORD; remove the foreskin of your hearts" (Jer. 4:4).

The point of Ezekiel 11:19 is that God *himself* does this for us—and more. He doesn't merely remove the foreskin of the old heart; he gives us a whole new heart. Romans 2:28–29 says the regenerated heart, having undergone this radical spiritual circumcision, is what defines the authentic believer: "No one is a Jew [a true spiritual son of Abraham] who is merely one outwardly, nor is circumcision outward and physical. But a Jew is one inwardly, and circumcision is a matter of the heart, by the Spirit."

Hebrews 4:12 calls a similar imagery to mind. The two-edged sword cuts, and cuts accurately—not with the purpose of destroying us, but in order to remove (through spiritual surgery) whatever defiles. The sword of the Spirit—the Word of God—is the instrument God uses to that end.

That is why churches must not tone down the preaching of God's Word or relegate Scripture to the status of a footnote in our public worship. If we do not welcome the painful piercing of the two-edged sword, we close ourselves off from the means of sanctification. If we try to soften the truth of God's Word or to shield unbelievers from its hard truths because we are afraid of how someone will respond, we virtually guarantee that our churches will be weak, our ministry to the world will be hindered, and we will have much to answer for on that day when God calls us to give account for our work.

12

SPIRITUAL ADULTERY

We live in very singular times just now. The professing Church has been flattering itself that, notwithstanding all our divisions with regard to doctrine, we are all right in the main. A false and spurious liberality has been growing up which has covered us all, so that we have dreamed that all who bore the name of ministers were indeed God's servants—that all who occupied pulpits, of whatever denomination they might be, were entitled to our respect, as being stewards of the mystery of Christ. But, lately, the weeds upon the surface of the stagnant pool have been a little stirred and we have been enabled to look down into the depths. This is a day of strife—a day of division—a time of war and fighting between professing Christians! God be thanked for it! Far better that it should be so than that the false calm shall any longer exert its fatal spell over us!

CHARLES HADDON SPURGEON[1]

Sometime in the late 1980s I was writing an article about 1 Corinthians 9:22, where Paul says, "I have become all things to all people, that by all means I might save some."[2] The article was going to highlight the true lesson of that verse: we should not show contempt for the cultural and religious taboos of whatever civilization to which we are preaching. The gospel itself is enough of a stumbling block. As much as possible, therefore, we ought to avoid unnecessarily offending a culture's traditions and mores in matters that have nothing to do with gospel truth or biblical commandments.

Of course, 1 Corinthians 9:22 was already a favorite proof-text for

---

[1]"The Church of God and the Truth of God," *The Metropolitan Tabernacle Pulpit*, Vol. 54 (London: Passmore & Alabaster, 1908), 241.
[2]The article subsequently became the basis for Chapter 4 in this book.

evangelical trendsetters who were immersing the church in all kinds of worldly amusements. They insisted this was the only effective means of reaching an entertainment-addicted culture, and Paul himself had more or less endorsed the strategy in that key verse. Ironically, in contrast to Paul's actual intent, however, many of them seemed bent on *defying* as many cultural and religious taboos as possible.

So I wanted to illustrate the folly of over-contextualization and point out the danger of conformity to the world, especially for those who were pressing pragmatism to further and further extremes. I hoped to make that point without singling out any of the vanguards of seeker-sensitivity by name. I was therefore trying to invent a hypothetical illustration—something that made my point clearly but without resorting to gross caricature.

The problem was that every grotesque style of sideshow Christianity I could concoct in my own imagination had already been done in the real world. *Clowns in church?* Already commonplace. *Hollywood movies in the evening service, followed by an exposition of the films' artistic qualities and moral lessons?* Lots of churches were doing that. *Christian heavy metal with androgynous makeup and Spandex costumes?* Stryper was old news already.

My editor suggested this line: "What next? Shall we translate the gospel into four-letter words in order to reach people whose native language is profanity?"

I immediately rejected that. Not only did the idea offend me, it also seemed very far-fetched. It was just the sort of extreme caricature I was trying to avoid. No one would ever think of going *that* far. Right?

Never in my wildest imagination could I have conceived that in less than a decade, a new breed of pragmatists would be vying with one another to see who could push the limits of polite language in the pulpit to the very breaking point—justifying the practice by an appeal to 1 Corinthians 9:22.

PRAGMATISM REMIXED

In the early 1990s, evangelical pragmatism met and married postmodernism. The eventual result was the Emerging Church. This was a vast, bewildering, theologically confused swarm of opinions. It never really jelled into an authentic *movement* with identifiable leaders and a clear direction. And yet its influence among evangelicals continues to be profound.[3]

---

[3]In *The Truth War* (Nashville: Thomas Nelson, 2007), I described and analyzed the Emerging Church movement in much more detail than space will permit here. Readers seeking to understand the basic ideas underlying the postmodern shift, how it has shaped Emerging trends, and what it does to the very concept of truth will find my analysis of all those things in that earlier work.

The Emerging trend has radically changed the face and direction of seeker-sensitivity and market-driven ministry. The underlying principle is as pragmatic as ever, but the look and feel of Emerging Christianity is drastically different. It's the same old utilitarian philosophy with a postmodern makeover and a bad-boy attitude.

Describing postmodernized evangelicalism and finding terminology that fits the trend has been a pesky problem from the start. In the early 1990s, the embryonic community where it all began was an informal worldwide network of similarly minded people with no real structure. Early participants were enlightened young people and recent college graduates who were keenly aware of the postmodern shift in secular thinking. They were seeking ways to contextualize Christianity for postmodern cultures. Many of these young people openly embraced postmodern values, but some were more cautious. All were convinced that postmodern times demanded major changes in the church. Some wanted a new social agenda; some wanted new worship styles; some wanted new doctrines; and some wanted all of the above. As those trends gained momentum, people within the network began to speak of "the Emerging Church." They seemed convinced that a radical new kind of Christianity was just on the horizon.

Around 2001, a group of key leaders in the network's American wing formed an organization named Emergent, whose Web site, EmergentVillage.com, became a hub for the Emerging community and a meeting point for the exchange of ideas. For the next few years, the movement was commonly referred to as either the Emerg*ing* Church or the Emerg*ent* Church. The terms were interchangeable.

In fact, a 2004 article in *Christianity Today* treated the two expressions as synonymous.[4] That article brought the burgeoning movement to the attention of many evangelicals who were previously unaware of it. The article also provoked grave concerns about the movement. Some of the most prominent voices in the Emerging community were profiled in that article. All of them had a shockingly low view of Scripture and an infatuation with uncertainty. The effects of postmodern skepticism were all too obvious. From that point on, the Emerging Church movement seemed to unravel.

Shortly after the *CT* feature, key figures in the Emerging community declared that their network was more of a "conversation" than a *church* or a *movement*. They began correcting people who continued to speak about "the Emerging Church movement." It was now to be known as "the Emerging Conversation."

---

[4] Andy Crouch, "The Emergent Critique," *Christianity Today* (November 2004), 36–41.

Within a year, the Conversation seemed hopelessly hung up on terminology. For example, in keeping with the postmodern contempt for authority and clarity, Emergent Village had never really adopted any identifiable structure. But in June 2005, the organization's Web site announced that Tony Jones (an early, influential participant in the original network) had been appointed national director. An angry backlash ensued.[5] Within days, the organization's Web site featured this follow-up memo: "Some of you read the last post regarding the recent appointment of Tony Jones as 'National *Director.*' Before the official press release was sent out the decision was made to instead use the title 'National *Coordinator.*' This felt more in keeping with both the spirit of Emergent and the overall purpose of the role."

Less than four years later, however, Tony Jones stepped away from the role, and Emergent Village sponsored a campaign encouraging all of their members to "stand up and claim the role of National Coordinator."[6] A stream of mock press releases followed on Emergent blogs and YouTube videos, announcing dozens of new "National Coordinators." In effect, the role was dissolved in favor of egalitarian anarchy.

The constant redefinition of terms and renaming of everything mirrors secular postmodernism's obsession with language and relativism. To the postmodern mind, words have tremendous social implications but no fixed meaning. Language is a tool of repression that needs to be dismantled. Therefore a conspicuous feature in any postmodern "conversation" is wordplay whereby word-meanings are questioned, words themselves are endlessly redefined, and new, indecipherable jargon is invented. The point is to demonstrate that all truth-claims are questionable, nothing is really clear or certain, and no one can legitimately speak with authority about anything. Language itself is something to be *deconstructed*. Supposedly, this empowers the disenfranchised by dismantling the oppressive power of words. "The raison d'être for deconstruction is always *justice*," according to Tony Jones.[7]

That sort of deconstruction has had two significant effects on language in these postmodern times. First, new language taboos have been invented: the rules of political correctness. Anyone who uses any of the newly banned

---

[5]A typical commenter at the Emergent Village Web site wrote, "I think we are going in a horribly dangerous direction. We aren't becoming a 'conversation,' we're becoming an institution. A 'National Director?' for a conversation? Give me a break"; http://emergent-us.typepad.com/emergentus/2005/06/report_from_eme.html.

[6]See http://www.emergentvillage.com/weblog/who-is-the-new-national-coordinator-of-emergent-village.

[7]Tony Jones, "Why is the Emerging Church drawn to deconstructive theology?"; http://churchand pomo.typepad.com/conversation/2007/03/why_is_the_emer.html.

words or expressions is marginalized in exactly the same the way people would have been for using profane language in polite society a few decades ago. Second, the old taboos are being systematically overturned. Words and subject matter that used to be considered profane or inappropriate are now supposed to be acceptable in any context.

Even in the pulpit.

Tony Jones, one-time National Coordinator of Emergent Village, wrote an anecdotal history of the Emerging Church movement. He describes one incident in which a Texas pastor invited one of the best-known figures in the Emerging network to speak to his congregation. He forewarned the guest speaker that although his people were reasonably savvy about the postmodern shift, "swearing from the pulpit in Texas just wouldn't fly. He asked [the Emerging fellow] to please keep his language clean. [In defiance, the guest speaker] used the f-word in the first sentence."[8]

Question: why would a pastor even think to caution a guest speaker not to cuss in the pulpit? Answer: because free-flowing profanity has long been a staple of the Emerging Conversation. Postmodernized evangelicals deliberately mingle cusswords, "filthiness and silly talk, [and] coarse jesting" (cf. Eph. 5:4, NASB), with biblical terms and quasi-spiritual jargon. They have thus designed a stylish new kind of religious dialect. It is the postmodern equivalent of the previous generation's decision to substitute the language of clinical psychology in place of biblical terms about sin and guilt.

Emergent blogs and Web forums are peppered with expletives ranging from mild profanity to the most obscene kinds of sexual references. An associate of mine tried listening to some of the early Emergent podcasts, and every one he heard contained multiple instances of casual profanity.

Even using the Lord's name as an expletive is evidently not frowned upon in some quarters of Emergent Village. Some of the online meeting-places where Emergent Christians gather are so liberally sprinkled with cusswords that they get banned by Web filters screening for inappropriate language. A number of Emergent blogs have discussed the issue at length, and invariably they staunchly defend the use of profanity as a badge of "authenticity."[9] It is considered hopelessly naive to imagine that Scripture

---

[8]Tony Jones, *The New Christians: Dispatches from the Emergent Frontier* (San Francisco: Jossey-Bass, 2008), 48. Tony Jones himself used the f-bomb in the article quoted earlier: "Why is the Emerging Church drawn to deconstructive theology?"

[9]For example, "Out of Ur," a weblog sponsored by *Christianity Today*, featured an article by "Skye Jethani" (writers at "Out of Ur" use pseudonyms) titled "Expletive Undeleted: Dropping the F-bomb in Church." The article describes how the pastor of an Emergent-style assembly (they named their gathering "Scum o' the Earth") wrestled with the question of whether to allow a member to read a poem she had

still forbids believers in these enlightened postmodern times to pepper their speech with irreverent words and obscene subject matter. The biblical standard of sound speech according to Ephesians 5:4 (cf. also 4:29; Col. 3:8) is simply dismissed as unworkable for Emergents bent on communicating with a postmodern culture in its native tongue.

Thus the very thing I considered unthinkable in the 1980s has come to pass. People who profess to be Christians have translated their message into profanity. In the name of contextualization, some preachers have even begun to speak about Christ Himself in terms that *anyone* would have considered obscene (and therefore certainly blasphemous) just a decade ago. Evangelical pragmatism is scraping bottom.

DECONSTRUCTING DOCTRINE

Profane language is by no means the only unhealthy side effect of postmodern pragmatism. It's not even the worst—by a long shot. The postmodern idea begins with the assumption that settled certainty was a purely "modern" goal—a goal that has proved unattainable. Once someone buys into that premise, the only possible outcome is a pervasive and cynical skepticism about *everything*. Even the clearest biblical propositions ultimately get deconstructed, including articles of faith that are essential to Christianity itself—truths to which every Christian is supposed to be unshakably committed.

In the realm of doctrine, therefore, the Emerging Church movement has proved to be a veritable mudslide, obliterating the familiar, well-paved route of the down-grade and sweeping everyone caught in its channel directly into a dark valley of error, indecision, skepticism, and outright unbelief. Some obviously slide more quickly than others, but all in that current are headed in the same direction. The only way to escape the hard drop at the end of the slide is to get out of that current, and the earlier the better because it doesn't take long to reach the point of no return.

It would be hard to think of any tenet of Christian doctrine that has not been challenged at some point by one or another of the dominant voices in the Emerging Conversation. The authority of Scripture and the

---

written for the Christmas Eve service. "It's really, really good, but it's got the F-bomb in it several times," an associate told him. After pondering the issue, this Emergent trailblazer decided that "asking [the young woman] to clean this poem up before presenting it in church would be like asking the widow to wipe off her coins before dropping them in the offering plate." Commenters on the blog were overwhelmingly supportive of that decision, and most were outraged at the few who suggested that using such language and calling it an act of "worship" would be an abomination. The final commenter scolded such people for "recriminat[ing] the pastor of Scum o' the Earth with your 'moral clarity'"; http://blog.christianity today.com/outofur/archives/2005/11/expletive_undel_1.html.

doctrine of substitutionary atonement have been the movement's favorite targets. But in a movement where every definitive affirmation is automatically subject to deconstruction and doubt, *nothing* can ever be considered settled, certain, clear, or authoritative. No statement of Scripture (much less any historic creed or confession of faith) is truly accepted at face value. *Everything* is perpetually on the table for debate. That is a recipe for all kinds of apostasy.

One of the best-known early participants in the Emerging Conversation wrote a book titled *A Heretic's Guide to Eternity*.[10] It is a fitting title because the book is essentially a renunciation of biblical Christianity, an attack on all doctrine, and a call for a vague, New-Agey notion of "spirituality." It turns out that this self-styled heretic's notion of eternity is the same as any old-fashioned universalist's. He denies the exclusivity of Christ, affirms panentheism (the belief that all creation is part of the being of God), and says he isn't sure he believes in God as a Person anymore.[11] This man created and still operates the original Emerging Web site, and his voice remains influential in the Conversation.[12]

That author is no minor background player in the passage between old-style, program-driven pragmatism and the newer postmodern pragmatism. He helped steer multitudes through that treacherous strip of the down-grade. He was at one time a pastor on the staff of a well-known seeker-sensitive megachurch in Southern California. He tells the story of his transition from the evangelical mainstream to the Emergent fringe in *Stories of Emergence: Moving from Absolute to Authentic*—a book in which each chapter tells a similar tale.[13] It reads, frankly, like a travelogue describing one of the steepest sections of the down-grade.

But this former megachurch pastor admits that he had been wracked by nagging doubts throughout all his years in the ministry. The hypocrisy of that, understandably, wore him out. "I eventually grew tired of keeping up appearances. After 18 years in ministry, the evangelical package started to unwrap. Swallowing my questions for the sake of the status quo no longer was a viable option. . . . Eventually I knew something had to give. When the pain of staying at [the church] began to seem worse than the pain of leaving, I submitted my resignation. I packed up my desk, loaded up my car, and drove home to my 700-square-foot beach shack. Five years later, here I

---

[10]Spencer Burke with Barry Taylor, *A Heretic's Guide to Eternity* (San Francisco: Jossey-Bass, 2006).
[11]Ibid., 195.
[12]Theooze.com was founded in 1998.
[13]Mike Yaconelli, ed., *Stories of Emergence: Moving from Absolute to Authentic* (Grand Rapids, MI: Zondervan, 2003).

sit."[14] His goal with the Web site is to provide "a safe place" where people "trying to be on the edge" can question anything they like. The whole point is to "'unpackage' rather than 're-package' theology."[15]

That pastor's metamorphosis from a seeker-sensitive evangelical leader to a self-styled heretic shows in microcosm where postmodern pragmatism will inevitably lead. Subjecting every proposition of Scripture to endless deconstructive interrogation cannot possibly produce anything but a deep-seated skepticism. That approach is more like a leap off the cliffs of existentialism than a freewheeling descent on the down-grade. The end result is destructive—usually fatal—either way, but the wreckage at the foot of that postmodern cliff is much worse, and considerably harder to clean up.

WHAT PRAGMATISM HAS BROUGHT TO THE EVANGELICAL MOVEMENT

The old-style, entertainment-intoxicated pragmatism that prompted me to write this book several years ago is already in its death throes. The largest, oldest, best-known sanctuary of seeker-sensitivity acknowledged in 2007 that its programs had failed to produce authentic, growing, committed disciples. On a videotape announcing a change of direction, that church's executive pastor admitted, "I sit there Sunday after Sunday, and I wonder: Are we spending those folks' money in the right way? Really? Would they feel great about how we're investing their resources? Some days I'm not quite so sure we're making the right decisions. Some days I'm just not quite so sure. . . . These questions I've been wresting with for more than a decade."[16]

The church's senior pastor then explained the results of a survey designed to determine whether the church's programs were really helping people grow spiritually. "That survey just rocked my world," he said. "It was one of the hardest things I've ever had to digest as a leader. Because some of the stuff that we have put millions of dollars in, thinking it would really help our people grow and develop spiritually—when the data actually came back, it wasn't helping people that much. Other things that we didn't put much money into (and didn't put much staff against) is stuff that our people are crying out for."[17] Data showed that non-Christians rated the church's style of ministry "very high" (around nine on a scale of ten); but

---

[14]Ibid., 28–29.
[15]See http://www.theooze.com/about/index.cfm.
[16]Greg Hawkins in a video promo for the Leadership Summit, August 9–11, 2007.
[17]Bill Hybels, "The Wakeup Call of My Adult Life" (video from the Leadership Summit, August 9–11, 2007).

with people who described themselves as fully devoted followers of Christ, the pastor said, scores got "scarily low."

"That bothers me," he said. "That really bothers me. Like, we're not helping them that much." He went on to report that people in the "devoted" category were saying "they're not being fed, that they want more meat of the Word of God. They want more serious-minded Scripture taught to them. They want to be challenged more."[18]

"That's hard for me to hear," he acknowledged. He said his first thought was, *I'll feed those people. I'll hire some old seminary prof. I'll feed 'em till they barf.* Church staff concluded they needed to teach their people to be "self-feeders."

A few months later *Christianity Today* erroneously reported that the church "now plans to gear its weekend services toward mature believers seeking to grow in their faith."[19] The real truth is practically the opposite. The church is making a move toward the postmodern style of pragmatism.

In a video replying to the erroneous *CT* article, the pastor flatly denied that the church's recent statements about the failure of their strategy were expressions of "repentance." He reaffirmed his commitment to the seeker-sensitive philosophy. But he also noted that "seekers have changed in a lot of ways, and we are committed to being *relevant* to the seeker of 2008 like we were in 1978."[20]

A few months later the church sponsored a conference for student ministry leaders called Shift, featuring speakers drawn mainly from the radical wing of the Emerging Conversation.[21] Every session at the conference featured some speaker, video, or topic associated with postmodernism and Emerging spirituality.

After prepping people for months with announcements of shifts and philosophical changes, there is no doubt about which direction America's flagship seeker-sensitive church has now shifted. Hundreds of other churches will follow its lead. The trend watchers in the evangelical megachurch movement will hustle to climb aboard the bandwagon of postmodern pragmatism.

---

[18]Ibid.

[19]Matt Branaugh, "Willow Creek's 'Huge Shift,'" *Christianity Today* (June 2008), 13.

[20]"Bill Hybels Responds" (video); http://revealnow.com/story.asp?storyid=63.

[21]For example, the keynote speakers that day were Brian McLaren, Shane Claiborne, and Mike Yaconelli. Regarding the opening session, Taylor Birkey, a blogger who writes professionally for the Willow Creek Association, said: "McLaren, who was the featured speaker of that first session, gave a talk on, among other things, the church, global paradigms, the environment and the emerging postmodern generation. Brian is an extremely controversial guy within the Christian world due to some very liberal theology and biblical interpretation. Still, his talk at Shift left out most of those sensitive subjects, and focused on more concrete things. 'Whether or not Jesus is the only way to heaven' did not come up"; http://www.taylorbirkey.com/?p=144.

Ironically, these evangelical trend watchers are nearly two decades late to the postmodern party. Even worse for them, as we are about to see, they are arriving just as the Emerging Conversation seems to be breaking up.

THE END OF THE EMERGING CONVERSATION

As of this writing, the Emerging juggernaut has nearly ground to a halt. The wheels seem to be coming off. The cacophony of contradictory points of view within the movement, the mingling of self-styled "heretics" with people who say they just want to be innovative, not unorthodox, and the rising tide of critics have all taken their toll. Several influential authors and pastors (including several members of the original network) have now foresworn the word "Emerging" altogether.

The *Next-Wave* e-zine, an online digest of trends in church and culture (with strong sympathies for all things Emerging) led off its first issue of 2009 with a ten-year retrospective on the Emerging Conversation. The article began with this: "January . . . finds us at a crossroads for the emerging church in North America. There's increasing discomfort with the term 'emerging church' itself, with a number of leading lights in the movement expressing hesitations about the term."[22]

In a similar vein, the "Out of Ur" blog at *Christianity Today* recently published a post titled "R.I.P. Emerging Church: An overused and corrupted term now sleeps with the fishes."[23] The article cited an anonymous executive from a major evangelical publishing house who said the company was planning to drop its Emerging brand. "The emerging church is dead—at least in nomenclature, if not in spirit," the article concluded.

Andrew Jones, Britain's best-known cheerleader for all things Emergent, "conducted a poll on his blog asking whether or not to dump the emerging church term. The results were 60/40 in favor of killing the expression."[24] Dan Kimball, one of the pioneers in the Conversation and author of a book titled *The Emerging Church*,[25] explained why he was dropping the term: "In my opinion, the definition has changed. I am not wedded to any term and I don't think most people are."[26]

Some of the more moderate voices in the movement now want out,

---

[22]Stephen Shields, "Ten Years Out: A Retrospective on the Emerging Church in North America"; http://the-next-wave-ezine.info/bin/_print.cfm?id=44&ref=COVERSTORY.
[23]Url Scaramanga, "R.I.P. Emerging Church: An overused and corrupted term now sleeps with the fishes"; http://blog.christianitytoday.com/outofur/archives/2008/09/rip_emerging_ch.html.
[24]Ibid.
[25]Dan Kimball, *The Emerging Church: Vintage Christianity for New Generations* (Grand Rapids, MI: Zondervan/Youth Specialties, 2003).
[26]Dan Kimball, "The Emerging Church: 5 years later: The definition has changed"; http://www.dankimball.com/vintage_faith/2008/09/the-emerging-ch.html.

too. They are looking for a new name and a tighter network, because they are tired of being associated with (and criticized for tolerating) the radical views of some of the movement's best-known writers and spokespersons. Out of Ur reported recently that "news has been leaking about a new network being formed by Dan Kimball, Erwin McManus, and Scot McKnight among others. I understand further meetings will be happening this week to help solidify the group. The still unnamed network has agreed to start with the inclusive but orthodox theological foundation of the Lausanne Covenant, and they intend to emphasize mission and evangelism."[27]

In typically postmodern fashion, however, the focus seems to be on terminology more than substance. One of those seeking to form that new network, an author and seminary professor who has frequently defended the radical wing of Emergent, says, "I like the diversity of 'emerging' but the problem is that the term has been so abused *by its critics* that embracing the term leads to endless discussions of just how one is part of that emerging conversation. I've basically given up on using the term except in audiences where I think it is understood."[28] Notice: the problem as he sees it is not the pragmatic philosophy or doctrinal chaos in the Emerging Conversation itself, but the way the critics have ruined the movement's *name*.

That is an incredibly myopic assessment. The fact is, as long as pragmatism underlies the strategy, and "diversity" and "inclusivity" remain key goals, no mere cosmetic change will ever be for the better. The Emerging Conversation may fragment and diffuse, but its influence within evangelical Christianity will always be destructive. Until these theological tinkerers stop trying to design a religion that stays in step with the times, there is no way for them to escape the gravitational pull of the down-grade.

Put simply, the pragmatic and postmodern values that have shaped the Emerging Conversation from the start are contrary to any definitive statement of faith. The idea of an immovable "theological foundation" (even one as broad and inclusive as the Lausanne Covenant) is a contradiction of the core principles that made the Emerging Conversation distinctive in the first place. As one disillusioned Emerger pointed out to those talking about forming a whole new network,

> I, and many of like mind, are convinced that the principles of "Emerging Church" (in its original, unadulterated form; and all further references to EC will imply that form) are contrary to its reduction to a "statement of faith," no matter how inclusive-yet-orthodox that statement

[27]Scaramanga, "R.I.P. Emerging Church."
[28]Cited in Stephen Shields, "Ten Years Out."

is. It was my understanding that the "statement of faith" of the EC was contained in Genesis 1 to Rev. 22. I was under the impression that one of the central stimuli for the EC was the injury caused by the attempted reduction of God's narrative into bite-sized nuggets, no matter how "true" those nuggets.

The EC was never about having true beliefs with less certainty, leaving room for others.

The EC was never about replacing terms like "true" with less in-your-face terms like "coherent" or "sound."[29]

And so as former leaders in the Conversation try to salvage something meaningful from the detritus of their movement, it appears that they themselves don't get it after all. The contradiction between pragmatic postmodernism and the fundamental creeds of Christendom should be obvious to all. But those writing the most books and influencing the most people press further down the slippery slope.

THE LANDSCAPE AHEAD

What does the future look like? If history is any indication, the unlikely marriage of seeker-sensitive megachurches with the radical wing of Emergent will eventually lead to the total demise of those churches. They are following the same route on the down-grade taken by most of the mainline denominations in the first half of the twentieth century. Liberalism killed those denominations, and the neo-liberalism of the radical Emergents will have the same effect on the pragmatic megachurches.

My greater concern involves the potential influence of those who are leaving the Emerging Conversation without leaving their pragmatic and postmodern values behind. Many of them are moving into established churches and denominations. Authors and speakers who are glib and clever and cool enough will continue to have a substantial influence in whatever context to which they migrate. Presently evangelicalism's biggest "growth market" is the "Young, Restless, and Reformed." That was the title of a 2006 CT article (later a book) by Collin Hansen.[30] The article pointed out that biblical preaching and classic Reformation doctrine were having a stronger influence among today's young people than either the gimmickry of old-style pragmatism or the hipness of postmodern pragmatism. "While the Emergent 'conversation' gets a lot of press for its appeal to the young,

---

[29]Raffi Shahinian, "An Open Letter to Dan Kimball, Erwin McManus and Scot McKnight"; http://www.parablesofaprodigalworld.com/2008/09/open-letter-to-dan-kimball-erwin.html.
[30]Collin Hansen, "Young, Restless, and Reformed," *Christianity Today* (September 2006); *Young, Restless, Reformed: A Journalist's Journey with the New Calvinists* (Wheaton, IL: Crossway Books, 2008).

the new Reformed movement may be a larger and more pervasive phenomenon. It certainly has a much stronger institutional base." [31]

In the first quarter of 2009, *Time* magazine ran a cover story titled "10 Ideas Changing the World Right Now."[32] Number three on their list was "The New Calvinism."

All of this, obviously, is strong motivation for evangelical and postmodern pragmatists to jump on the Calvinist bandwagon. (Why wouldn't those who think of religion as a product to be marketed—as well as those addicted to popularity—want to get into the fastest-growing demographic?) Prepare yourself for a wave of erstwhile Emergents and evangelical pragmatists to run to the crowd and declare themselves the true representatives of neo-Calvinism. They will bring every pragmatic tool in their arsenal and will exert all their energies toward making "the New Calvinism" seem even more stylish—until the glow fades and something else becomes stylish, and they will run after that.

The "restless" aspect of the "Young, Restless, and Reformed" community is what makes them dangerously susceptible to such influences. The sober, biblically minded remnant in their midst need to remain on guard.

What should Christian leaders among that remnant do to stay off the slippery precipice that leads to the down-grade? That question is best answered by the text that was the starting point for this book and has been our theme throughout: "Preach the word; be ready in season and out of season; reprove, rebuke, and exhort, with complete patience and teaching. For the time is coming when people will not endure sound teaching, but having itching ears they will accumulate for themselves teachers to suit their own passions, and will turn away from listening to the truth and wander off into myths. As for you, always be sober-minded, endure suffering, do the work of an evangelist, fulfill your ministry" (2 Tim. 4:2–5).

To my readers who are laypeople rather than church leaders: pray for your pastors; labor alongside them with your own gifts; encourage them; assist them; and you yourselves "be steadfast, immovable, always abounding in the work of the Lord, knowing that in the Lord your labor is not in vain" (1 Cor. 15:58).

Spurgeon said it this way:

> Let us be zealous: "Let not thine hands be slack." . . . Now is the hour
> for redoubled prayers and labors. Since the adversaries are busy, let

[31]"Young, Restless, and Reformed."
[32]*Time*, March 23, 2009.

us be busy also. If they think they shall make a full end of us, let us resolve to make a full end of their falsehoods and delusions. I think every Christian man should answer the challenge of the adversaries of Christ by working double tides, by giving more of his substance to the cause of God, by living more for the glory of God, by being more exact in his obedience, more earnest in his efforts, and more importunate in his prayers. "Let not thine hands be slack" in any one part of holy service. Fear is a dreadful breeder of idleness; but courage teaches us indomitable perseverance. Let us go on in God's name.[33]

There are, thankfully, many knees that have not yet bowed to the Baal of pragmatism. May God bless them and make them fruitful. I for one have absolute confidence that no matter how many religious hucksters and marketeers may come and go, and no matter how much wood, hay, and stubble is going to burn up, the Lord is building *His* church, "and the gates of Hades [margin] shall not prevail against it" (Matt. 16:18).

---

[33]"A Sermon for the Time Present," *The Metropolitan Tabernacle Pulpit*, Vol. 33 (London: Passmore and Alabaster, 1887), 612.

APPENDIX 1

SPURGEON AND THE DOWN-GRADE CONTROVERSY

[At the end of the Puritan age] by some means or other, first the ministers, then the Churches, got on "the down grade," and in some cases, the descent was rapid, and in all, very disastrous. In proportion as the ministers seceded from the old Puritan godliness of life, and the old Calvinistic form of doctrine, they commonly became less earnest and less simple in their preaching, more speculative and less spiritual in the matter of their discourses, and dwelt more on the moral teachings of the New Testament, than on the great central truths of revelation. Natural theology frequently took the place which the great truths of the gospel ought to have held, and the sermons became more and more Christless. Corresponding results in the character and life, first of the preachers and then of the people, were only too plainly apparent.

THE SWORD AND THE TROWEL[1]

In March 1887, Charles Spurgeon published the first of two articles entitled "The Down Grade" in his monthly magazine, *The Sword and the Trowel*. The articles were published anonymously, but the author was Robert Shindler, Spurgeon's close friend and fellow Baptist pastor. Shindler wrote the articles with input from Spurgeon, who footnoted the first article with a personal endorsement: "Earnest attention is requested for this paper. We are going down hill at breakneck speed."[2]

Tracing the state of evangelicalism from the Puritan age to his own era, Shindler noted that every revival of true evangelical faith had been

---

[1] Robert Shindler, "The Down Grade," *The Sword and the Trowel* (March 1887), 122.
[2] Ibid., 122n.

followed within a generation or two by a drift away from sound doctrine, ultimately leading to wholesale apostasy. He likened this drifting from truth to a downhill slope and thus labeled it "the down-grade."

"DOWN-GRADE" I

In that first article, Shindler recounted the history of the major Protestant denominations in England since the beginning of Puritanism's decline in 1662. He noted that in the first generation after the Puritan era, virtually every nonconformist (non-Anglican Protestant) denomination in England drifted from orthodoxy toward an ancient form of theological liberalism called *Socinianism* (which denies original sin and questions Christ's deity). Shindler recounted how hundreds of post-Puritan churches had abandoned sound doctrine in favor of rationalistic skepticism, Unitarianism, and other liberal beliefs. The downward slide usually began slowly, almost imperceptibly. He suggested that denominations often "got on the down-grade" when they abandoned Calvinism (which emphasizes God's sovereignty in salvation) in favor of Arminianism (which makes human will the decisive factor). Other groups embraced *Arianism* (which denies the full deity of Christ). Still others simply became enamored with scholarship and worldly wisdom; consequently they lost their zeal for truth.

"The Presbyterians were the first to get on the down line," Shindler wrote. They took the route of worldly wisdom: "They paid more attention to classical attainments and other branches of learning. . . . It [was therefore] an easy step in the wrong direction to pay increased attention to academical attainments in their ministers, and less to spiritual qualifications; and to set a higher value on scholarship and oratory, than on evangelical zeal and ability to rightly divide the word of truth."[3]
Shindler further stated:

> As is usual with people on an incline, some who got on "the down grade" went further than they intended, showing that it is easier to get on than to get off, and that where there is no brake it is very difficult to stop. Those who turned from Calvinism may not have dreamed of denying the proper deity of the Son of God, renouncing faith in his atoning death and justifying righteousness, and denouncing the doctrine of human depravity, the need of Divine renewal, and the necessity for the Holy Spirit's gracious work, in order that men might become new creatures; but, dreaming or not dreaming, this result became a reality.[4]

[3]Ibid., 123.
[4]Ibid., 124.

Some who abandoned the faith did so openly, Shindler said. But many purposely concealed their skepticism and heresy, preferring to sow seeds of doubt while posing as orthodox believers. "These men deepened their own condemnation, and promoted the everlasting ruin of many of their followers by their hypocrisy and deceit; professing to be the ambassadors of Christ, and the heralds of his glorious gospel, their aim was to ignore his claims, deny him his rights, lower his character, rend the glorious vesture of his salvation, and trample his crown in the dust."[5]

Many of those who remained true to the faith were nevertheless reluctant to fight for what they believed in. Evangelical preaching was often cold and lifeless, and even those who held to sound doctrine were careless about where they drew the line in their associations with others: "Those who were really orthodox in their sentiments were too often lax and unfaithful as to the introduction of heretical ministers into their pulpits, either as assistants or occasional preachers. In this way the Arian and Socinian heresies were introduced into the Presbyterian congregations in the city of Exeter."[6]

Thus within only a few decades, the Puritan fervor that had so captured the soul of England gave way to dry, listless, apostate teaching. Churches became lax in granting membership privileges to the unregenerate. People who were, in Shindler's words, "strangers to the work of renewing grace" nevertheless claimed to be Christians and were admitted to membership— even leadership—in the churches. These people "chose them pastors after their own hearts, men who could, and would, and did, cry 'Peace, peace,' when the only way of peace was ignored or denied."[7]

Shindler concluded that first paper on "The Down Grade" with these words: "These facts furnish a lesson for the present times, when, as in some cases, it is all too plainly apparent men are willing to forego the old for the sake of the new. But commonly it is found in theology that that which is true is not new, and that which is new is not true."[8]

"DOWN-GRADE" II

In April, *The Sword and the Trowel* carried a second article entitled "The Down Grade." In it, Robert Shindler continued his overview of the history of the decline of Puritanism. He laid the blame for the downhill slide at the feet of the church leaders. Even those who were orthodox in their teaching were not earnestly contending (Jude 3), but were weak in defending the faith,

---

[5]Ibid., 125.
[6]Ibid.
[7]Ibid., 126.
[8]Ibid.

Shindler said. As one example, he cited Philip Doddridge (1702–1751), best known today as the hymn-writer who penned "O Happy Day" and "Grace, 'Tis a Charming Sound." Doddridge, according to Shindler, "was as sound as he was amiable; but perhaps he was not always judicious; or more probably still, he was too judicious, and not sufficiently bold and decided."[9]

Doddridge had been principal of the academy where most non-conformist ministers went for training in the mid-1700s. Shindler's judgment was that "[Doddridge's] amiable disposition permitted him to do what men made of sterner stuff would not have done. He sometimes mingled in a fraternal manner, even exchanging pulpits, with men whose orthodoxy was called in question. It had its effect on many of the younger men, and served to lessen in the estimate of the people generally the growing divergence of sentiment."[10] In other words, Shindler felt that Doddridge's tolerance of unorthodox teachers obscured from his ministerial students the awful reality that these men were guilty of serious error and left the students exposed to the deadly effects of their heresy. But, Shindler hastened to add, no one could "insinuate even the suspicion of heresy" against Doddridge himself.

Because of the attitude of tolerance implanted by Doddridge, the academy at last succumbed to Socinianism, then was dissolved in the generation after Doddridge's passing.[11]

Shindler paraphrased Hosea 4:9 ("Like priest, like people") and wrote, "Little good can be expected of such ministers, and little hoped for of the hearers who approve their sentiments."[12] He warned against such tolerance, suggesting it is better to err on the side of caution:

> In too many cases sceptical daring seems to have taken the place of evangelical zeal, and the husks of theological speculations are preferred to the wholesome bread of gospel truth. With some the endeavour seems to be not how steadily and faithfully they can walk in the truth, but how far they can get from it. To them divine truth is like a lion or a tiger, and they give it "a wide berth." Our counsel is—Do not go too near the precipice; you may slip or fall over. Keep where the ground is firm; do not venture on the rotten ice.[13]

He gave specific examples of how tolerance had led to disaster, noting that the "tadpole of Darwinism was hatched . . . [in a pew] of the old chapel

---

[9]"The Down Grade" (second article), *The Sword and the Trowel* (April 1887), 166.
[10]Ibid., 167.
[11]Ibid.
[12]Ibid., 168.
[13]Ibid.

in High Street, Shrewsbury," where Charles Darwin had first been introduced to skepticism by a pastor who was enthralled with Socinianism. And he noted that the chapel once pastored by Matthew Henry, author of the famous commentary on the whole Bible, had for years been teaching "full-blown Socinianism."[14]

The Baptists, Shindler noted, had seen their share of churches on the down-grade. He named several churches in the county of Kent that had embraced Socinianism: those at Dover, Deal, Wingham, and Yalding.

But, he noted, there were a few notable exceptions to the rule. Those churches willing to fight for the faith and uphold the doctrines of grace and God's sovereignty had managed to avoid the fate of those on the down-grade. They were singular illustrations of the up-grade, Shindler said, showing the down-grade in bold relief.

How did so many Bible-believing churches go astray? And why does this happen again and again in human history? Shindler raised these questions:

> In the case of every errant course there is always a first wrong step. If we can trace that wrong step, we may be able to avoid it and its results. Where, then, is the point of divergence from the "King's highway of truth"? What is the first step astray? Is it doubting this doctrine, or questioning that sentiment, or being sceptical as to the other article of orthodox belief? We think not. These doubts and this scepticism are the outcome of something going before.[15]

What was that "something"? What was the common denominator of all those who started on the down-grade?

> The first step astray is a want of adequate faith in the divine inspiration of the sacred Scriptures. All the while a man bows to the authority of God's Word, he will not entertain any sentiment contrary to its teaching. "To the law and to the testimony" is his appeal concerning every doctrine. He esteems that holy Book, concerning all things, to be right, and therefore he hates every false way. But let a man question or entertain low views of the inspiration and authority of the Bible, and he is without chart to guide him and without anchor to hold him.
>
> In looking carefully over the history of the times, and the movement of the times, of which we have written briefly, this fact is apparent: that where ministers and Christian churches have held fast to the truth that the Holy Scriptures have been given by God as an authoritative

---

[14]Ibid.
[15]Ibid., 170.

and infallible rule of faith and practice, they have never wandered very seriously out of the right way. But when, on the other hand, reason has been exalted above revelation, and made the exponent of revelation, all kinds of errors and mischiefs have been the result.[16]

Shindler noted a correlation between Calvinistic doctrine and a high view of Scripture, suggesting that the great majority of those who remained committed to the authority of Scripture were "more or less Calvinistic in doctrine."[17] In the "Notes" section of that same issue of *The Sword and the Trowel*, Spurgeon added this: "We care far more for the central evangelical truths than we do for Calvinism as a system; but we believe that Calvinism has in it a conservative force which helps to hold men to the vital truth."[18] The clear implication to both Spurgeon and Shindler was that a high view of Scripture goes hand in hand with a high view of divine sovereignty. Moreover, Shindler noted, those churches that held firmly to sound doctrine remained healthy and flourished, while those that embraced Socinianism inevitably began to dwindle and die. Shindler quoted the Rev. Job Orton, a man who evidently had Socinian leanings himself but nonetheless wrote a warning to pastors flirting with liberal theology:

> "I have long since found," says [Orton] "(and every year that I live increases my conviction of it), that when ministers entertain their people with lively and pretty things, confine themselves to general harangues, insist principally on moral duties, without enforcing them warmly and affectionately by evangelical motives; while they neglect the peculiars of the gospel, never or seldom display the grace of God, and the love of Christ in our redemption; the necessity of regeneration and sanctification by a constant dependence on the Holy Spirit of God for assistance and strength in the duties of the Christian life, their congregations are in a wretched state; some are dwindling to nothing, as is the case with several in this neighbourhood, where there are now not as many scores as there were hundreds in their meeting-places, fifty years ago. . . . There is a fatal deadness spread over the congregation. They run in 'the course of this world,' follow every fashionable folly, and family and personal godliness seems in general to be lost among them. There is scarcely any appearance of life and zeal."[19]

Shindler wryly added, "It would seem that Orton had seen the folly of

---

[16]Ibid.
[17]Ibid.
[18]Ibid., 195.
[19]Ibid., 171–172.

'the down grade' course, and was anxious to bear his testimony, to deter others."[20]

Then he closed that article with an appeal to the centrality and sufficiency of God's Word:

> But leaving men and their opinions, the Word of the Lord standeth fast forever; and that Word to every one who undertakes to be God's messenger, and to speak the Lord's message to the people, is "He that hath my word, let him speak my word faithfully. What is the chaff to the wheat? saith the Lord."
>
> The Lord help us all to be "steadfast, immovable, always abounding in the work of the Lord, forasmuch as we know our labour shall not be in vain in the Lord.'"[21]

With that the two-part series ended.

Shindler appended it with a third article for the June *Sword and Trowel*. The June article offered an analysis of a heresy trial in America involving some professors from Andover Theological Seminary, Andover, New York. Andover had been founded less than a hundred years earlier in response to Socinianism at Harvard. Andover's founders, Shindler wrote, "were sound Calvinists of the Cotton Mather type, and the College was instituted for the special purpose of training men in that faith."[22] Shindler accused "the five gentlemen who now fill professorial chairs" with having "seriously departed from the faith of the founders." They did this by deceit, Shindler said. Having subscribed to the school's doctrinal statement, they were now undermining it by their teaching, which had been labeled "Progressive Orthodoxy" by some. Shindler had his own assessment: "Indeed the *progression* is so considerable that the 'orthodoxy' is lost sight of."[23] He went on to chronicle the heresies taught by these men, which, though considered subtle in the late nineteenth century, were indeed serious defections from the faith.

Shindler saw the Andover disaster as an object lesson on the dangers of the down-grade, and he did not hesitate to make the point, using American Baptists as an illustration, that The Baptist Union in England was headed down the same road.

Three months later, Charles Haddon Spurgeon himself would write about "the down-grade." The controversy was only beginning to heat up.

---

[20]Ibid., 172.
[21]Ibid.
[22]Robert Shindler, "Andover Theology," *The Sword and the Trowel*, Vol. 23 (June 1887), 274.
[23]Ibid.

"DOWN-GRADE" III

In August *The Sword and the Trowel* carried an article by Spurgeon entitled "Another Word Concerning the Down-Grade." The tone of this article was more urgent than Shindler's had been. The earlier articles had evidently provoked two basic responses—displeasure from those who believed Shindler's analysis was too pessimistic, and hearty agreement from many who were also troubled about the trends in British evangelicalism.

Those who agreed with Shindler's warning blasts responded by offering more proof of apostasy and compromise in formerly sound churches. Spurgeon read these responses, and his outrage grew. One man reported that "two ministers had derided him because he thought we should pray for rain." A woman told Spurgeon that "a precious promise in Isaiah which had comforted her had been declared by her minister to be uninspired."[24] The editorial office of *The Sword and the Trowel* was inundated with such accounts.

From the opening paragraph, Spurgeon's tone was more militant, more intense than Shindler's had been in the earlier articles. In the weeks since those first two articles were published, Spurgeon had evidently come to feel that *The Sword and the Trowel* had underestimated the gravity of "The Down-Grade":

> Our solemn conviction is that things are much worse in many churches than they seem to be, and are rapidly tending downward. Read those newspapers which represent the Broad School of Dissent, and ask yourself, How much farther could they go? What doctrine remains to be abandoned? What other truth to be the object of contempt? A new religion has been initiated, which is no more Christianity than chalk is cheese; and this religion, being destitute of moral honesty, palms itself off as the old faith with slight improvements, and on this plea usurps pulpits which were erected for gospel preaching.[25]

In place of gospel preaching, this "new-and-improved" variety of Christianity was substituting amusements. Spurgeon warned that many were turning the church into a "play-house," allowing the values and techniques of the theater to invade the sanctuary of the Lord.

Spurgeon noted that many churches were no longer having prayer meetings. Spiritual fervor was dwindling, congregations were thinning, and enthusiasm for the gospel was quickly becoming extinct. "Alas! many are returning to the poisoned cups which drugged that declining [post-Puritan]

---

[24]"Another Word Concerning the Down-Grade," *The Sword and the Trowel* (August 1887), 399.
[25]Ibid., 397.

generation. . . . Too many ministers are toying with the deadly cobra of 'another gospel,' in the form of 'modern thought.'"[26]

Who was chiefly to blame for the decline? Spurgeon believed it was the preachers: "The case is mournful. Certain ministers are making infidels. Avowed atheists are not a tenth as dangerous as those preachers who scatter doubt and stab at faith. . . . Germany was made unbelieving by her preachers, and England is following in her tracks."[27]

Spurgeon made no effort to disguise his contempt for the modernists:

> These destroyers of our churches appear to be as content with their work as monkeys with their mischief. That which their fathers would have lamented they rejoice in: the alienation of the poor and simple-minded from their ministry they accept as a compliment, and the grief of the spiritually-minded they regard as an evidence of their power.[28]

To those who might be put off by such frankness, Spurgeon wrote,

> A little plain-speaking would do a world of good just now. These gentlemen desire to be let alone. They want no noise raised. Of course thieves hate watch-dogs, and love darkness. It is time that somebody should spring his rattle, and call attention to the way in which God is being robbed of his glory, and man of his hope.[29]

At the end of the article, Spurgeon fired this shot, which for the first time raised the issue that would become the focus of all the subsequent controversy:

> It now becomes a serious question how far those who abide by the faith once delivered to the saints should fraternize with those who have turned aside to another gospel. Christian love has its claims, and divisions are to be shunned as grievous evils; but how far are we justified in being in confederacy with those who are departing from the truth? It is a difficult question to answer so as to keep the balance of the duties. For the present it behooves believers to be cautious, lest they lend their support and countenance to the betrayers of the Lord. It is one thing to overleap all boundaries of denominational restriction for the truth's sake: this we hope all godly men will do more and more. It is quite another policy which would urge us to subordinate the maintenance of truth to denominational prosperity and unity. Numbers of

---

[26]Ibid., 398.
[27]Ibid., 399.
[28]Ibid., 399–400.
[29]Ibid., 400.

easy-minded people wink at error so long as it is committed by a clever man and a good-natured brother, who has so many fine points about him. Let each believer judge for himself; but, for our part, we have put on a few fresh bolts to our door, and we have given orders to keep the chain up; for, under colour of begging the friendship of the servant, there are those about who aim at robbing the Master.[30]

Spurgeon was now suggesting that true believers might have reason to sever their organizational ties with those who were promulgating the new theology. In his estimation the truth of the Word had been so seriously compromised that true Christians needed to consider the command of 2 Corinthians 6:17: "Go out from their midst, and be separate from them, says the Lord, and touch no unclean thing."

This was not a call for a new denomination. Spurgeon clearly distrusted earthly organizations:

We fear it is hopeless ever to form a society which can keep out men base enough to profess one thing and believe another; but it might be possible to make an informal alliance among all who hold the Christianity of their fathers. Little as they might be able to do, they could at least protest, and as far as possible free themselves of that complicity which will be involved in a conspiracy of silence. If for a while the evangelicals are doomed to go down, let them die fighting, and in the full assurance that their gospel will have a resurrection when the inventions of "modern thought" shall be burned up with fire unquenchable.[31]

The article rocked the evangelical world. Spurgeon, who for decades had been almost universally revered by evangelicals, was suddenly besieged with critics from within the camp. What he was proposing was diametrically opposed to the consensus of evangelical thought. All the trends were toward unification, harmony, amalgamation, and brotherhood. Suddenly here was a lone voice—but the most influential voice of all—urging true believers to become separatists. The church was neither prepared nor willing to receive such counsel, not even from the Prince of Preachers.

"DOWN-GRADE" IV

Despite pleas from some of the brethren that he soften his rhetoric or tone down his complaints, Spurgeon ratcheted up the intensity in a September

---

[30]Ibid.
[31]Ibid.

Sword and Trowel article. Reader response to the earlier articles vindicated his position, Spurgeon believed. Letters had been pouring in to corroborate his worst allegations. In fact, he was now wondering if his alarm had been too little, too late:

> According to the best of our ability we sounded an alarm in Zion concerning the growing evils of the times, and we have received abundant proof that it was none too soon. Letters from all quarters declare that the case of the church at this present is even worse than we thought it to be. It seems that, instead of being guilty of exaggeration, we should have been justified in the production of a far more terrible picture. This fact causes us real sorrow. Had we been convicted of mis-statement we would have recanted with sincerely penitent confessions, and we should have been glad to have had our fears removed. It is no joy to us to bring accusations; it is no pleasure to our heart to seem to be in antagonism with so many.[32]

Instead of answering Spurgeon's charges, the critics had declared them vague (although both Shindler and Spurgeon had been anything but vague). Spurgeon was now struggling with recurring kidney ailments and had been absent from the pulpit. Some insinuated that the Down-Grade articles were the rantings of someone who was desperately sick. Clearly, Spurgeon was personally grieved by that allegation:

> Our opponents have set to work to make sneering allusions to our sickness. All the solemn things we have written are the suggestions of our pain, and we are advised to take a long rest. With pretended compassion, but with real insolence, they would detract from the truth by pointing to the lameness of its witness. Upon this trifling we have this much to say:—In the first place, our article was written when we were in vigorous health, and it was in print before any sign of an approaching attack was discoverable. In the second place, if we were in a debate with Christians we should feel sure that, however short they might run of arguments, they would not resort to personalities.[33]

His opponents had attacked him personally, though he and Shindler both had taken extreme care to avoid making personalities the subject of his censures. What is more, Spurgeon's adversaries utterly ignored the substance of his strictures. "No one has set himself to disprove our allegations,"

---

[32]"Our Reply to Sundry Critics and Enquirers," *The Sword and the Trowel* (September 1887), 461.
[33]Ibid, 462.

Spurgeon wrote.[34] No one had denied any of his charges. Indeed, no one could. Though few wanted to admit it, English evangelicalism was indeed on the down-grade.

Employing the vivid imagery that was the hallmark of Spurgeon's preaching, he wrote, "The house is being robbed, its very walls are being digged down, but the good people who are in bed are too fond of the warmth, and too much afraid of getting broken heads, to go downstairs and meet the burglars; they are even half vexed that a certain noisy fellow will spring his rattle, or cry, 'Thieves!'"[35]

Spurgeon was beginning to think more seriously and speak more explicitly about breaking fellowship with those who he believed were opposing the gospel. For several decades Spurgeon had been the most visible and influential member of the Baptist Union. Yet it seemed he was now seriously pondering withdrawal from the Union as a matter of conscience.

> The divergence is every day becoming more manifest. A chasm is opening between the men who believe their Bibles and the men who are prepared for an advance upon Scripture. Inspiration and speculation cannot long abide in peace. Compromise there can be none. We cannot hold the inspiration of the Word, and yet reject it; we cannot believe in the atonement and deny it; we cannot hold the doctrine of the fall and yet talk of the evolution of spiritual life from human nature; we cannot recognise the punishment of the impenitent and yet indulge the "larger hope." One way or the other we must go. Decision is the virtue of the hour.
>
> Neither when we have chosen our way can we keep company with those who go the other way.[36]

Spurgeon apparently hoped the evangelical leaders of the Baptist Union would see his side and opt for reform. The Union had never required adherence to a doctrinal statement of any kind. From the beginning, it had more or less been the assumption that members of the Union were all evangelical. The only point of doctrine required for membership, therefore, dealt with the mode of baptism. Spurgeon believed that was an insufficient guard against the erosion of truth, so he appealed to the Baptist Union to affirm a new structure that would ensure doctrinal integrity among its members.

Faced with the possibility of losing Spurgeon versus the certainty of

---

[34]Ibid., 461.
[35]Ibid., 465.
[36]Ibid.

splitting the Union, denominational leaders began looking for a way of compromise.

But Spurgeon refused to compromise:

> Let those who will keep the narrow way keep it, and suffer for their choice; but to hope to follow the broad road at the same time is an absurdity. What communion hath Christ with Belial?
>
> Thus far we come, and pause. Let us, as many as are of one mind, wait upon the Lord to know what Israel ought to do. With steadfast faith let us take our places; not in anger, not in the spirit of suspicion or division, but in watchfulness and resolve. Let us not pretend to a fellowship which we do not feel, nor hide convictions which are burning in our hearts. The times are perilous, and the responsibility of every individual believer is a burden which he must bear, or prove a traitor. What each man's place and course should be the Lord will make clear unto him.[37]

And thus Spurgeon ended his article. He had thrown down the gauntlet. His mind and heart were set. He would not be moved.

"DOWN-GRADE" V

The October issue of *The Sword and the Trowel* carried the third of Spurgeon's articles about the down-grade. This article, entitled "The Case Proved," consisted mostly of excerpts from letters and reviews Spurgeon had received in response to the earlier articles. These fell into two categories. The first were from readers who saw controversy brewing and wanted to still the storm. Spurgeon characterized them as "esteemed friends" who wanted to "rush in between the combatants, and declare that there was no cause for war, but that our motto might continue to be 'Peace, peace!'"[38] Spurgeon accused such people of being "so supremely amiable that they see all things through spectacles of tinted glass."[39]

The second category included responses from people affirming Spurgeon's assessment of the dismal state of affairs. Many described specific examples of compromise and false teaching among those who classified themselves as evangelical.

Again Spurgeon asked the question, "Are brethren who remain orthodox prepared to endorse such sentiments by remaining in union with those

---

[37]Ibid.
[38]*The Sword and the Trowel* (October 1887), 509.
[39]Ibid., 510.

who hold and teach them?"[40] Believing that the Baptist Union would take up these issues at their annual autumn meetings at Sheffield, Spurgeon made his position clear one final time:

> What action is to be taken we leave to those who can see more plainly than we do what Israel ought to do. One thing is clear to us: we cannot be expected to meet in any Union which comprehends those whose teaching is upon fundamental points exactly the reverse of that which we hold dear. . . . To us it appears that there are many things upon which compromise is possible, but there are others in which it would be an act of treason to pretend to fellowship. With deep regret we abstain from assembling with those whom we dearly love and heartily respect, since it would involve us in a confederacy with those with whom we can have no communion in the Lord.[41]

But at Sheffield the issue never even came up.

WITHDRAWAL FROM THE UNION

On October 28, 1887, Spurgeon wrote to Samuel Harris Booth, General Secretary of the Baptist Union:

> DEAR FRIEND,—I beg to intimate to you, as the secretary of the Baptist Union, that I must withdraw from that society. I do this with the utmost regret; but I have no choice. The reasons are set forth in *The Sword and the Trowel* for November, and I trust you will excuse my repeating them here. I beg you not to send anyone to me to ask for reconsideration. I fear I have considered too long already; certainly every hour of the day impresses upon me the conviction that I am moving none too soon.
>
> I wish also to add that no personal pique or ill-will has in the least degree operated upon me. I have personally received more respect than I desired. It is on the highest ground alone that I take this step, and you know that I have long delayed it because I hoped for better things.—Yours always heartily,
>
> C. H. SPURGEON[42]

Spurgeon evidently had already written his November *Sword and Trowel* article when he wrote the letter to Booth. He began the article "A Fragment upon the Down-Grade Controversy" with these words: "By this

---

[40]Ibid., 513.
[41]Ibid., 515.
[42]Cited in G. Holden Pike, *The Life and Work of Charles Haddon Spurgeon*, 6 vols. (London: Cassell and Company, n.d.), 6:287.

time many of our readers will be weary of the Down-Grade controversy: they cannot be one-tenth so much tired of it, or tried by it, as we are."[43] The controversy had consumed Spurgeon's thoughts and emotions as he deliberated whether to withdraw from the Union. But Spurgeon felt he was left no choice. Severing ties with the enemies of the gospel was no option as far as he was concerned: "Fellowship with known and vital error is participation in sin."[44] The force of his rhetoric is an insight into Spurgeon's heart: "To be very plain, we are unable to call these things Christian Unions, they begin to look like Confederacies in Evil. Before the face of God we fear that they wear no other aspect. To our inmost heart this is a sad truth from which we cannot break away."[45]

Spurgeon saw no reason true Christians should accommodate those who doubted the authority and sufficiency of Scripture. "If these men believe such things, let them teach them, and construct churches, unions, and brotherhoods for themselves! Why must they come among us?"[46]

He felt he had no choice other than the course of action he had taken:

> During the past month many have put to us the anxious question, *"What shall we do?"* To these we have had no answer to give except that each one must act for himself after seeking direction of the Lord. In our own case we intimated our course of action in last month's paper. We retire at once and distinctly from the Baptist Union.[47]

That announcement must have come as a jolt to many readers. Few had believed Spurgeon would carry through with his threats. Peace and unity were almost universally esteemed as the highest of Christian virtues. It was unthinkable that Charles H. Spurgeon, the most visible and popular British evangelical of his day, would become a schismatic. Yet that was the popular perception of the course Spurgeon had pursued.

SPURGEON AND THE BAPTIST UNION

But Spurgeon had not withdrawn capriciously or hastily. On November 23 he wrote from the south of France to explain his actions to a fellow pastor, Mr. Mackey: "It was encumbent upon me to leave the Union, as my private remonstrances to officials, and my repeated pointed appeals to the whole

---

[43]*The Sword and the Trowel* (November 1887), 557.
[44]Ibid., 559.
[45]Ibid., 558.
[46]Ibid., 559–560.
[47]Ibid., 560.

body, had been of no avail. My standpoint had become one from which, as an earnest man, I could see no other course but to withdraw."[48]

The private letter to Mackey was shared with the hundred-member Council of the Baptist Union. Eighty of these men met December 13 to discuss Spurgeon's accusations. Most of them were outraged at Spurgeon's charges and his subsequent withdrawal from their group. They accused him of making charges based on inaccurate information, and the officers of the Union flatly denied that Spurgeon had ever come to them with "private remonstrances" or concerns of any kind about the doctrinal state of the Union.

One officer in particular, General Secretary Booth, knew better. Booth and Spurgeon had had many private conversations and exchanged many letters about the deplorable state of the Union. In fact, Booth himself had urged Spurgeon to speak out against the modernism that was running rampant in the Union. Booth evidently had even given Spurgeon details about the widespread compromise and names of men whose orthodoxy he had reason to doubt.[49] But Booth had sworn Spurgeon to secrecy about their correspondence. "My letters to you were not official but in confidence," Booth wrote when he thought Spurgeon was about to blow the whistle on him. "As a matter of honor you cannot use them."[50]

The Council minutes show that Booth misled the Council as to the nature of his conversations with Spurgeon. He told them, "Again I say that whatever conversations I have had with Mr. Spurgeon were not of a kind to formulate charges against brethren in order that I might submit them to this council. It never entered my mind that Mr. Spurgeon intended the things which passed in conversation to be brought here and formulated as charges."[51] While strictly speaking that was true, it was far from the whole truth. Booth, after all, had first come to Spurgeon with concerns. Their dialogue on the issues was far more than passing conversation. Booth more than anyone else had known about—and as far as Spurgeon believed, shared—the great preacher's profound concern over the drift of the Union.

But even when the Baptist Union Council, including Booth himself, accused Spurgeon of misrepresenting the truth, Spurgeon honored Booth's wishes to keep their correspondence confidential. "Spurgeon could have summarily proved the extent of his prior consultation with Union officials

---

[48]*Letters of Charles Haddon Spurgeon* (Edinburgh: Banner of Truth, 1992), 183.
[49]Lewis Drummond, *Spurgeon: Prince of Preachers* (Grand Rapids, MI: Baker, 1992), 671.
[50]Ibid., 697.
[51]Ibid.

by producing correspondence from Booth."[52] Instead, he bore the abuse and false accusations—even when Booth himself became one of the accusers.

"For Dr. Booth to say I never complained, is amazing," Spurgeon wrote his wife. "God knows all about it, and He will see me righted."[53]

But as one biographer pointed out, "Spurgeon was never righted. The impression in many quarters still remains that he made charges which could not be substantiated, and when properly called upon to produce his evidence he resigned and ran away. Nothing is further from the truth. Spurgeon might have produced Dr. Booth's letters. I think he should have done so."[54]

The Baptist Union Council accused Spurgeon of having breached Jesus' instructions in Matthew 18 by failing to go privately first to those with whom he had grievances. In another letter to his wife, Spurgeon responded to that charge: "What a farce about my seeing these brethren, privately, according to Matt. xviii. 15! Why, I saw the Secretary and the president again and again; and then I printed my plaint, and only left the Union when nothing could be done."[55]

To Dr. James Culross, president of the Union, Spurgeon wrote,

> I have followed out our Lord's mind as to private remonstrances by seeing Presidents and Secretary on former occasions, and I have written my remonstrances again and again without avail. I had no course but to withdraw. Surely, no sane person thinks that I should have made a tour to deal with the individual errorists. I have no jurisdiction over them, and should have been regarded as offensively intrusive if I had gone to them; and justly so. My question is with the Union, and with that alone. I have dealt with it all along.[56]

By raising the Matthew 18 question and by accusing Spurgeon of failure to bring his concerns properly before the Union's leaders, the Council was clearly evading the real issues. They proposed sending a delegation of four men to confront Spurgeon and wrote him to try to arrange a visit while Spurgeon was in France. Spurgeon declined, saying he would meet with the men when he returned to England.

Spurgeon saw the Council's response as a transparent attempt to make *him* the issue and to draw the controversy away from the doctrinal drift

[52]Iain Murray, *The Forgotten Spurgeon* (Edinburgh: Banner of Truth, 1966), 145.
[53]Susannah Spurgeon and J. W. Harrald, eds., *C. H. Spurgeon's Autobiography*, 4 vols. (London: Passmore and Alabaster, 1897), 4:257.
[54]J. C. Carlisle, *C. H. Spurgeon—An Interpretive Biography* (London: Religious Tract Society, 1933), 247.
[55]*C. H. Spurgeon's Autobiography*, 4:256.
[56]Ibid., 4:263.

within the Union. Furthermore, he had carefully avoided making any of his attacks personal, and now the Council was using even that against him, claiming that since he had not mentioned specific names and details, his charges were too vague for them to address. In an uncharacteristically defensive letter, Spurgeon sent a letter to the editor of the main organ of the Union:

> *To the Editor of "The Baptist."*
>
> DEAR SIR—I would not occupy your columns with a personal matter were it not of considerable importance that I should do so. In the letter to Mr. Mackey I wrote: "It was incumbent upon me to leave the Union, as my private remonstrances to officials, and my repeated pointed appeals to the whole body, had been of no avail." This is not untrue, nor inaccurate. After a painful occurrence at Leicester [in 1883 a Unitarian minister was permitted to preach at the Baptist Union meetings there] I made serious complaint to the secretary, the president (Mr. Chown), and others of the Council. At the Orphanage, to which he kindly came, Mr. Chown made to me a pathetic appeal to regard it as a solitary incident, and hoping that I had been mistaken. I did not go further with this matter, for which, possibly, I am blameworthy.
>
> Since then I have repeatedly spoken to the secretary [Booth] upon the subject, as he will willingly admit. I think each year either himself or Mr. Baynes has waited upon me to preach for the Union, or to preach at the mission services connected with the Union gatherings. On each occasion one or other has heard my complaints till they must, I fear, have been wearied. Here I beg to add that I do not confound the mission with the Union; but it so happens that these good secretaries call upon me while making arrangements for the same series of meetings, and therefore I have regarded that which I said to one as said to both. The fact has remained that I have declined to take a public part in the meetings, because I could not feel sure that I should not be compromised thereby. This is surely an action which spoke more loudly than words. With Mr. Williams and Dr. Maclaren I had considerable correspondence, which on their part, at any rate, was most admirable.
>
> My friend Mr. Williams says my letters were marked "Private," and that is just what I said to Mr. Mackey. Mr. Booth did not regard my communications as made to him *officially*, neither did I ever say that he did. The complaints were, however, made by me to him, while I tried to compromise the matter with my judgment by joining in the *work*, and not in the *talk*, of the Union, and I wish it could have been a possible middle way. I will not venture to say definitely how many

of the Council knew my views and feelings by hearing me utter them at various times, but more than enough to justify my statement to Mr. Mackey.

Please note that the first clause of the sentence only is taken, and it is made to be more prominent than I intended by the remainder being left out—"my repeated pointed appeals to the whole body." My letters on "The Down-grade" do not deal exclusively with the Baptist denomination, which I have all along admitted to be far less tainted than another; but they did so far concern it that the republished articles were submitted to the entire ministry and posted to all. "The organ of the Baptist denomination" likened the affair to a "big gooseberry," and stated that certain ministers on the road to Sheffield regarded it as a "great joke." At the meetings no public notice was taken except to assail me before a public meeting, where there was no opportunity of reply. Of other expressions of an unkind character then used by individuals I will not write; but the whole together made it clear to me that no one thought my appeals worthy of notice. Had any one of the brethren judged them to be serious he could have mentioned them to the Council, and could have asked that private statements should become public ones; but no one thought this wise. Of this I am not complaining; but it must not be said that I have not spoken the truth in the lines quoted above.

The fact seems to be that the question asked was not, "Is that statement made by Mr. Spurgeon true?" but the real inquiry made was, *"Has he so written that the officials felt bound to lay the matter before the Council?"* This is quite another subject, as anyone can see with half an eye. Thus I can exonerate questioners, repliers, and others by the theory that *they* meant one thing and *I* meant another; and I at once do so.

But this is a sad beginning for a brotherly conference. The charge was not that I was knowingly untruthful, but that I said what was not true—I suppose through the failure of my mental powers. The inference should be that it is a waste of time to send a deputation to confer with so imbecile a person. I will not, however, draw the inference. I have not descended, I trust, to personalities. I do not even impute motives; but I hope I may write thus much without seeming to be disrespectful to the honoured brethren who request a conference with me.—Yours truly,

C. H. Spurgeon.
Menton, December 19.[57]

The letter was never published.

---

[57]Cited in Pike, *The Life and Work of Charles Haddon Spurgeon*, 6:292–293.

THE BAPTIST UNION CENSURE

Spurgeon's reluctance to meet with the Union delegation in France stemmed from his fear that they were simply trying to make him appear disagreeable and obstinate. He wrote Susannah, "Think of four doctors of divinity coming all this way to see me! I was in great perplexity, and knew not what to reply. I don't quite see what it all means. I lay awake till one o'clock. . . . I do not fear four doctors, but I think it a very wise move on their part. If it means they will surrender, it is well; but if it is meant to fix on me the odium of being implacable, it is another matter."[58]

On January 13, 1888, Spurgeon was back in London and met with the Union delegation at the Tabernacle. The group included General Secretary Booth, outgoing President James Culross, and President-elect John Clifford. Alexander Maclaren, the fourth member of the appointed panel—and the most likely to be sympathetic to Spurgeon—was ill and did not attend.[59] The men asked Spurgeon to reconsider his withdrawal. Spurgeon proposed that the Union adopt an evangelical statement of faith. The delegation refused. Neither side felt anything was accomplished by the meeting.

Five days later the full Baptist Union Council met again. This time they voted to accept Spurgeon's withdrawal. Then they voted to censure him.

Only five of the nearly one hundred members supported Spurgeon in the vote. A surprisingly lopsided majority approved the censure against their best-known member. The Council passed this resolution:

> The Council recognises the gravity of the charges which Mr. Spurgeon has brought against the Union previous to, and since, his withdrawal. It considers that the public and general manner in which they have been made reflects on the whole body, and exposes to suspicion brethren who love the truth as dearly as he does. And as Mr. Spurgeon declines to give the names of those to whom he intended them to apply, and the evidence supporting them, those charges, in the judgment of the council, ought not to have been made.[60]

One writer at the time, Richard Glover, accurately assessed the issues in the *Evangelical Nonconformist*:

> The policy which they adopted was to attempt to put the responsibility for disturbing the peace of the Union back on Spurgeon. They took

---

[58]*C. H. Spurgeon's Autobiography*, 4:257.
[59]"Brief Notes," *The Baptist* (February 1888), 84.
[60]Ibid., 85.

the position that his charges were too vague to merit serious investigations, that he had failed to substantiate them by naming any ministers who were guilty. However useful this policy might have been politically, it can only be described as dishonest trifling with the subject.[61]

The fact is, as we have seen, Spurgeon *could* have named names. He could have produced Booth's letters and thereby not only exonerated himself but also forced Booth into the role of a second witness against the heretics. Moreover, Spurgeon could have simply cited the published works of some of his fellow Baptists. "Spurgeon had plenty of evidence; there were the utterances of well-known men which had been published in the pages of the *Christian World*, and the *Independent*, the *Freeman*, the *British Weekly*, and the *Baptist*. Reference to the files of these journals for 1887 and 1888 can still be made, and will provide ample proof of the truth of Spurgeon's general charge."[62]

Why didn't Spurgeon simply name those who had abandoned evangelicalism? For one thing, he did not want to wage a dispute over individuals. He feared that the debate would degenerate into a personal war: "If we were not extremely anxious to avoid personalities, we could point to other utterances of some of these esteemed writers which, if they did not contradict what they have now written, would be such a supplement to it that their entire mind would be better known."[63] "The warfare has been made too personal; and certain incidents in it, upon which I will not dwell, have made it too painful for me to feel any pleasure in the idea of going on with it."[64]

But more important, Spurgeon felt the clamoring for names was simply an attempt to deflect from the real issue, which was the policy of the Baptist Union. As he pointed out, the Union had no doctrinal statement and therefore no authority to discipline anyone for false teaching: "No one can be heterodox under this constitution, unless he should forswear his baptism."[65] So even if he had named names, nothing could be done about the heretics unless the Union was willing to adopt an evangelical statement of faith and require all members to abide by it. That is precisely what the Union had heretofore refused to do.

Spurgeon sincerely hoped that the Down-Grade Controversy would

---

[61]Cited in Drummond, *Spurgeon: Prince of Preachers*, 700–701.
[62]Carlisle, *C. H. Spurgeon—An Interpretive Biography*, 248.
[63]"The Case Proved," *The Sword and the Trowel* (October 1887), 27.
[64]"The Baptist Union Censure," *The Sword and the Trowel* (February 1888), 83.
[65]Ibid., 81.

stir the Union's rank-and-file membership to demand that the Council institute such a policy.

THE FINAL COMPROMISE

"No creed but Christ" was a popular sentiment among evangelicals in Spurgeon's day. There were many who felt creeds and doctrinal statements were somehow sub-Christian. And there is a legitimate sense in which we ought to guard against elevating any creed above Scripture. When that happens, the creed itself can become an idol, something that actually hinders true worship.

But Spurgeon pointed out that if the creed itself is *true*—that is, if it is in harmony with Scripture and subject to Scripture—no such danger exists:

> To say that "a creed comes between a man and his God," is to suppose that it is not true; for truth, however definitely stated, does not divide the believer from his Lord. So far as I am concerned, that which I believe I am not ashamed to state in the plainest possible language; and the truth I hold I embrace because I believe it to be the mind of God revealed in his infallible Word. How can it divide me from God who revealed it? It is one means of my communion with my Lord, that I receive his words as well as himself, and submit my understanding to what I see to be taught by him. Say what he may, I accept it because he says it, and therein pay him the humble worship of my inmost soul.
>
> I am unable to sympathize with a man who says he has no creed; because I believe him to be in the wrong by his own showing. He ought to have a creed. What is equally certain, he has a creed—he must have one, even though he repudiates the notion. His very unbelief is, in a sense, a creed.
>
> The objection to a creed is a very pleasant way of concealing objection to discipline, and a desire for latitudinarianism. What is wished for is a Union which will, like Noah's Ark, afford shelter both for the clean and for the unclean, for creeping things and winged fowls.[66]

In the theological climate of late nineteenth-century England, it was impossible not to see that Spurgeon had a point. Even after their censure of Spurgeon, the Union Council knew it would have to deal with the issue of a creed at the April 23 Assembly meeting.

Spurgeon had guarded hopes for the Union Assembly meeting. In the April *Sword and Trowel* "Notes," he wrote,

---

[66]Ibid., 82.

Prayer should be continually offered by the people of God at this time. The Baptist Union meets in full assembly on April 23, and the great question then before it will be—"Is this Union to have an Evangelical basis or not?" We trust the question will be discussed with good temper, and that the decision will be of the right kind. Surely, as every other body of Christians avows its faith, the Baptist Union should do the same. Whatever its belief is, let it own it.[67]

Spurgeon appealed for clarity above all. He sent a letter to the editor of the *Baptist* that said in part, "Whatever the Council does let it above all things avoid the use of language which could legitimately have two meanings contrary to each other. Let us be plain and outspoken. *There are grave differences*—let them be avowed honestly."[68]

In Iain Murray's words, "This was almost precisely the policy which the council did not follow."[69] Meeting before the April Union Assembly, the Council prepared a brief, somewhat vague, but essentially evangelical doctrinal statement. When the statement was read at the Assembly meeting, however, it was introduced with a statement disclaiming that the Union had any authority to enforce doctrinal standards on its members. Worse, a footnote had been appended that said some "brethren in the Union . . . have not held the common interpretation" on passages regarding the resurrection and final judgment.[70]

Nevertheless, many evangelicals at the Assembly meetings—Spurgeon's brother James included—believed the statement as read was an acceptable compromise. Certainly it was clear that the Union would go no further.

A proponent of the "New Theology," Charles Williams (not the famous novelist), moved that the Assembly adopt the compromised statement. Williams took the opportunity to deliver a passionate plea in favor of liberal ideas. James Spurgeon "seconded Mr. Williams's resolution, but not his speech."[71] *The Baptist* reported that "The sincerity, the courage, and manliness of Mr. Spurgeon's speech deeply impressed the audience, and did much towards gaining substantial unanimity in the subsequent vote."[72] The resolution passed 2,000 to 7.

Henry Oakley was there that day. Years later, he recalled the bedlam in the auditorium:

---

[67]Ibid., 197–198.
[68]"Notes," *The Sword and the Trowel* (March 1888), 148.
[69]Murray, *The Forgotten Spurgeon*, 147.
[70]Cited in Drummond, *Spurgeon: Prince of Preachers*, 704.
[71]"A Welcome Conclusion," *The Baptist* (May 1888), 230.
[72]Ibid., 231.

I was present at the City Temple when the motion was moved, seconded, and carried. Possibly the City Temple was as full as it could
be. I was there very early, but found only a "standing seat" in the
aisle of the back gallery. I listened to the speeches. The only one
of which I have any distinct remembrance was that of Mr Charles
Williams. He quoted Tennyson in favour of a liberal theology and
justification of doubt. The moment of voting came. Only those in
the area were qualified to vote as members of the assembly. When
the motion of censure was put, a forest of hands went up. "Against,"
called the chairman, Dr Clifford. I did not see any hands, but history
records that there were *seven*. Without any announcement of numbers the vast assembly broke into tumultuous cheering, and cheering
and cheering yet. From some of the older men their pent-up hostility
found vent; from many of the younger men wild resistance of "any
obscurantist trammels," as they said, broke loose. It was a strange
scene. I viewed it almost with tears. I stood near a "Spurgeon's
[College] man," whom I knew very well. Mr Spurgeon had welcomed
him from a very lowly position. He went wild almost with delight at
this censure of his great and generous master. I say it was a strange
scene, that that vast assembly should be so outrageously delighted
at the condemnation of the greatest, noblest, and grandest leader of
their faith.[73]

It is almost certain, however, that most evangelicals present that day did
not see as clearly as Oakley. They could not have understood the vote
as another censure of Spurgeon. Certainly James Spurgeon intended no
affront to his brother when he seconded the motion. But like most of the
evangelicals there that day, James was so eager for reconciliation that he
mistakenly believed a doctrinal statement—any statement at all—was
something of a victory for their side.

Charles Spurgeon knew otherwise. He wrote to a friend, "My brother
thinks he has gained a victory, but I believe we are hopelessly sold. I feel
heart-broken. Certainly he has done the very opposite of what I should
have done. Yet he is not to be blamed, for he followed his best judgment.
Pray for me, that my faith fail not."[74]

THE AFTERMATH

G. Holden Pike wrote, "As the sequel proved, the peace gained [by the
Assembly vote] was not that abiding peace which many had anticipated.

---

[73]Cited in Murray, *The Forgotten Spurgeon*, 149–150.
[74]Ibid., 148.

The rupture with the Union . . . was never to be repaired."[75] Just as Charles Spurgeon had warned all along, nothing was to be gained by compromising with the enemies of the gospel. The Baptist Union's decline was, if anything, accelerated. Those who embraced the "New Theology" were emboldened after the Union Assembly. They now held the reins of the Union.

Spurgeon wrote,

> The resolution, with its footnote, with the interpretation of its mover, and the re-election of the old council, fairly represent the utmost that would be done when everybody was in his best humour. Is it satisfactory? Does anybody understand it in the same sense as anybody else? Does not the whole virtue of the thing lie in its pleasing both sides a little? And is not this the vice and the condemnation of it?[76]

Spurgeon understood what most evangelicals who voted at the Assembly meeting did not—that the last-minute modifications utterly negated the whole point of having a doctrinal statement:

> The points mentioned were certainly elementary enough, and we did not wonder that one of the brethren exclaimed, "May God help those who do *not* believe these things! Where must they be?" Indeed, little objection was taken to the statements which were tabulated, but the objection was to a belief in these being made indispensable to membership. It was as though it had been said, "Yes, we believe in the Godhead of the Lord Jesus; but we would not keep a man out of our fellowship because he thought our Lord to be a mere man. We believe in the atonement; but if another man rejects it, he must not, therefore, be excluded from our number."[77]

Spurgeon hated schism. He did not want to be divisive. But his conscience would not permit him to align with the enemies of the gospel. In the end he concluded that separating from the Union was actually the best way to promote true unity: "Nothing has ever more largely promoted the union of the true than the break with the false."[78]

Spurgeon saw separation as a biblical *necessity* for himself. "Whether others do so or not, I have felt the power of the text, 'Come out from among them, and be ye separate,' and have quitted both Union and Association

---

[75]Pike, *The Life and Work of Charles Haddon Spurgeon*, 302.
[76]"Notes," *The Sword and the Trowel* (June 1888). Reprinted in *The "Down Grade" Controversy* (Pasadena, TX: Pilgrim, n.d.), 56.
[77]"Attempts at the Impossible," *The Sword and the Trowel* (December 1888), 618.
[78]"Notes," *The Sword and the Trowel* (May 1888). Reprinted in *The Down Grade Controversy*, 55.

once for all. . . . This is forced upon me, not only by my convictions, but also by the experience of the utter uselessness of attempting to deal with the evil except by personally coming out from it."[79]

Spurgeon did not actively seek to pull others out of the Union, but he could not understand why men who wanted to remain faithful to the Scriptures would continue to belong to an organization that was so obviously barreling down the down-grade:

> Numbers of good brethren in different ways remain in fellowship with those who are undermining the gospel; and they talk of their conduct as though it were a loving course which the Lord will approve of in the day of his appearing. We cannot understand them. The bounden duty of a true believer towards men who profess to be Christians, and yet deny the Word of the Lord, and reject the fundamentals of the gospel, is to come out from among them. If it be said that efforts should be made to produce reform, we agree with the remark; but when you know that they will be useless, what is the use? Where the basis of association allows error, and almost invites it, and there is an evident determination not to alter that basis, nothing remains to be done inside, which can be of any radical service. The operation of an evangelical party within can only repress, and, perhaps, conceal, the evil for a time; but meanwhile, sin is committed by the compromise itself, and no permanently good result can follow. To stay in a community which fellowships all beliefs in the hope of setting matters right, is as though Abraham had stayed at Ur, or at Haran, in the hope of converting the household out of which he was called.
>
> Complicity with error will take from the best of men the power to enter any successful protest against it. . . . Our present sorrowful protest is not a matter of this man or that, this error or that; but of principle.[80]

The Down-Grade Controversy was a perpetual grief to Spurgeon until his death on January 31, 1892. Close friends, and even some of the students from his Pastors' College, turned against him. But Spurgeon declared to the end that he did not regret the stand he had taken.

It was surely difficult for Spurgeon himself, and even his early biographers, to assess the value of the Down-Grade Controversy. In those last years of Spurgeon's life, the strife was so much in the foreground that it obscured for most observers the real importance of the stand Spurgeon had taken. Spurgeon was the first evangelical with international influence

---

[79] "Notes," *The Sword and the Trowel* (June 1888), 56.
[80] "Notes," *The Sword and the Trowel* (October 1888). Reprinted in *The "Down Grade" Controversy*, 66.

to declare war on modernism. The Baptist Union was never the same. But the Evangelical Alliance, an interdenominational fellowship, stood with Spurgeon and gained strength. Spurgeon's actions helped alert evangelicals worldwide to the dangers of modernism and the down-grade.

Robert Shindler, author of those original "Down Grade" articles in *The Sword and the Trowel*, wrote a biography of Spurgeon that was published the year of the great preacher's death. Recalling a scene in those final, tumultuous years when Spurgeon was invited to address the Evangelical Alliance, Shindler wrote,

> The reception given by the audience to Mr. Spurgeon when he rose to speak was almost overpowering in its fervor and heartiness. We occupied a seat on the platform near enough to witness the powerful emotions that agitated his soul, and the tears that streamed down his cheeks as he listened to previous speakers; and though only a very few of his Baptist brethren were present, there was not wanting such a display of hearty sympathy as must have been cheering to his heart, and comforting to his soul. Since then time has revealed much; and following months and years will, no doubt, make more and more evident how needful was the protest which fidelity to God and to the gospel would not allow him to withhold.
>
> The Lord graciously purge His Church of all false doctrine, all false teachers, and all who are traitors in the camp of Israel! And may the Spirit from on high be poured out upon all flesh, that all the ends of the earth may see, and own, and rejoice in, the salvation of our God![81]

---

[81]*From the Usher's Desk to the Tabernacle Pulpit: The Life and Labors of Charles Haddon Spurgeon* (New York: A. C. Armstrong and Son, 1892), 274.

APPENDIX 2

SPURGEON SPEAKS TO OUR TIME

Spurgeon was never afraid to sound like a polemicist. His boldness in standing for what he believed is one of the major characteristics highlighted in virtually every biography of the Prince of Preachers. Iain Murray's excellent short biography of Spurgeon, *The Forgotten Spurgeon*,[1] chronicles and measures the key periods of Spurgeon's life with an outline of the major controversies in which he became embroiled. Given the number of controversies and the way they spanned the course of practically his whole ministry, one might think Spurgeon was a full-time controversialist or that he loved controversy. Both would be inaccurate assessments.

One thing can be said of Spurgeon: he picked his battles well. He was not one to engage in controversy over inconsequential points of disagreement. Though his enemies sometimes accused him of fighting over trifles, history has vindicated Spurgeon in every battle he waged. Many of those controversies were tied together by a common theme: the danger of doctrinal compromise in the name of charity, unity, and brotherhood. Though Spurgeon's theological adversaries constantly badgered him with the charge that he lacked those characteristics, the charge was untrue. Spurgeon simply knew that some things were more important than artificial charity. He refused to be intimidated. He never did back down. And the church—even today—is richer because of his courage.

As the following collection of excerpts will show, we need to draw the line today exactly where Spurgeon drew the line with regard to doctrinal compromise. His words come to us across the decades and ring true and timely, because the very same kind of spiritual decline and doctrinal

---

[1]Edinburgh: Banner of Truth, 1972.

compromise Spurgeon stood against in his day is threatening the church today. The remainder of this appendix consists of verbatim excerpts from Spurgeon's published works.

NO, ADJUST THE AGE TO THE BIBLE

Brethren, we shall not adjust our Bible to the age; but before we have done with it, by God's grace, we shall adjust the age to the Bible.

We shall not fall into the error of that absent-minded doctor who had to cook for himself an egg; and, therefore, depositing his watch in the saucepan, he stood steadfastly looking at the egg. The change to be wrought is not for the Divine chronometer, but for the poor egg of human thought. We make no mistake here; we shall not watch our congregation to take our cue from it, but we shall keep our eye on the infallible Word, and preach according to its instructions.

Our Master sits on high, and not in the chairs of the scribes and doctors, who regulate the theories of the century. We cannot take our key-note from the wealthier people, nor from the leading officers, nor even from the former minister.

How often have we heard an excuse for heresy made out of the desire to impress "thoughtful young men"! Young men, whether thoughtful or otherwise, are best impressed by the gospel, and it is folly to dream that any preaching which leaves out the truth is suitable to men, either old or young. We shall not quit the Word to please the young men, nor even the young women.

This truckling to young men is a mere pretence; young men are no more fond of false doctrine than are the middle-aged; and if they are, there is so much the more necessity to teach them better. Young men are more impressed by the old gospel than by ephemeral speculations.

If any of you wish to preach a gospel that will be pleasing to the times, preach it in the power of the devil, and I have no doubt that he will willingly do his best for you. It is not to such servants of men that I desire to speak just now.

I trust that, if ever any of you should err from the faith, and take up with the new theology, you will be too honest to pray for power from God with which to preach that mischievous delusion; if you should do so, you will be guilty of constructive blasphemy.

No, brethren, it is not our object to please men, but our design is far nobler.[2]

---

[2]*An All-Round Ministry: Addresses to Ministers and Students* (London: Passmore & Alabaster, 1906), 230.

PEOPLE WITH ITCHING EARS

In reference to ministers, many church-members are indifferent as to the personal piety of the preacher; what they want is talent or cleverness. What the man preaches does not matter now; he must draw a crowd, or please the elite, and that is enough. Cleverness is the main thing. One would think they were looking for a conjurer rather than a pastor. Whether he preaches truth or error, the man is held in admiration so long as he can talk glibly, and keep up a reputation as a speaker.

If we had truer piety in members and deacons, pretenders would soon take their wares to other markets. Alas! I fear there has been great laxity in the admission of members, and the quality of our churches has become defiled and debased by "the mixed multitude," among whom all manner of evil finds a congenial dwelling-place. Unhappy leader, who has an Achan in his own camp! Better that Demas should forsake us, than that he should abide with us, and import the world into the church.[3]

DIFFERENT FROM THE WORLD

The church is a separate and distinct thing from the world. I suppose there is such a thing as "the Christian world"; but I do not know what it is, or where it can be found. It must be a singular mixture. I know what is meant by *a worldly Christian*; and I suppose *the Christian world* must be an aggregate of worldly Christians. But the church of Christ is not of the world. "Ye are not of the world," says Christ, "even as I am not of the world."

Great attempts have been made of late to make the church receive the world, and wherever it has succeeded it has come to this result, the world has swallowed up the church. It must be so. The greater is sure to swamp the less.

They say, "Do not let us draw any hard-and-fast lines. A great many good people attend our services who may not be quite decided, but still their opinion should be consulted, and their vote should be taken upon the choice of a minister, and there should be entertainments and amusements, in which they can assist."

The theory seems to be, that it is well to have a broad gangway from the church to the world: if this be carried out, the result will be that the nominal church will use that gangway to go over to the world, but it will not be used in the other direction.

It is thought by some that it would perhaps be better to have no distinct

---

[3]Ibid., 215.

church at all. If the world will not come up to the church, let the church go down to the world; that seems to be the theory. Let the Israelites dwell with the Canaanites, and become one happy family. Such a blending does not appear to have been anticipated by our Lord in the chapter which was read just now: I mean the fifteenth of John. Read verses eighteen and nineteen: "If the world hate you, ye know that it hated me before it hated you. If ye were of the world, the world would love his own: but because ye are not of the world, but I have chosen you out of the world, therefore the world hateth you."

Did he ever say—"Try to make an alliance with the world, and in all things be conformed to its ways"? Nothing could have been further from our Lord's mind. Oh, that we could see more of holy separation; more dissent from ungodliness, more nonconformity to the world! This is "the dissidence of Dissent" that I care for, far more than I do for party names and the political strife which is engendered by them.

Let us, however, take heed that our separateness from the world is of the same kind as our Lord's. We are not to adopt a peculiar dress, or a singular mode of speech, or shut ourselves out from society. He did not so; but he was a man of the people, mixing with them for their good. He was seen at a wedding-feast, aiding the festivities: he even ate bread in a Pharisee's house, among captious enemies. He neither wore phylacteries, nor enlarged the borders of his garments, nor sought a secluded cell, nor exhibited any eccentricity of manner.

He was separate from sinners only because he was holy and harmless, and they were not.

He dwelt among us, for he was of us. No man was more a man than he; and yet, he was not of the world, neither could you count him among them. He was neither Pharisee, nor Sadducee, nor Scribe; and at the same time, none could justly confound him with publicans and sinners. Those who reviled him for consorting with these last did, by that very reviling, admit that he was a very different person from those with whom he went.

We want all members of the church of Christ to be, manifestly and obviously, distinct persons, as much as if they were of a separate race, even when they are seen mingling with the people around them. We are not to cut ourselves off from our neighbors by affectation and contempt. God forbid. Our very avoiding of affectation, our naturalness, simplicity, sincerity, and amiability of character, should constitute a distinction. Through Christians being what they seem to be, they should become remarkable in an age of pretenders. Their care for the welfare of others, their anxiety to do good, their forgiveness of injuries, their gentleness of manner—all these should distinguish them far more than they could be distinguished by a livery, or by any outward signs.

I long to see Christian people become more distinct from the world than ever, because I am persuaded that, until they are so, the church will never become such a power for blessing men as her Lord intended her to be. It is for the world's good that there should be no alliance between the church and the world by way of compromise, even to a shade. See what came to pass when the church and the world became one in Noah's day: when "the sons of God saw the daughters of men that they were fair," and were joined with them. Then came the deluge. Another deluge, more desolating even than the former, will come, if ever the church forgets her high calling, and enters into confederacy with the world.

The church is to be a garden, walled, taken out of the common, and made a separate and select plot of ground. She is to be a spring shut up, and a fountain sealed, no longer open to the fowl of the air, and the beasts of the field. Saints are to be separate from the rest of men, even as Abraham was when he said to the sons of Seth, "I am a stranger and a sojourner with you."

Come now, my dear friends, are you of this sort? Are you foreigners in a country not your own? You are no Christians, remember, if you are not so. "Come out from among them, and be ye separate, saith the Lord, and touch not the unclean thing." That is the Lord's own word to you. Did not he himself suffer without the gate that you might go forth unto him without the camp?

Are you at one with the rest of mankind? Could anybody live with you, and never see that any alteration had taken place in you? Would they think that you were just the same as any other man? Then, by your fruits ye shall be known. If there is no difference of life between you and the world, the text does not address you as the "sister" and the "spouse" of Christ. Those who are such are enclosed from the world, and shut up for Christ.

"I wish I were more so," cries one. So do I, my friend, and may you and I practically prove the sincerity of that desire by a growing separateness from the world![4]

THE CHANGEABLENESS OF MODERN THOUGHT

If man makes a gospel—and he is very fond of doing it, like children making toys—what does he do? He is very pleased with it for a few moments,

---

[4]From "The Lord's Own View of His Church and People," *The Metropolitan Tabernacle Pulpit*, Vol. 33 (London: Passmore and Alabaster, 1887), 205–216.

and then he pulls it to pieces, and makes it up in another way; and this continually.

The religions of modern thought are as changeable as the mists on the mountains. See how often science has altered its very basis! Science is notorious for being most scientific in destruction of all the science that has gone before it. I have sometimes indulged myself, in leisure moments, in reading ancient natural history, and nothing can be more comic. Yet this is by no means an abstruse science.

In twenty years time, some of us may probably find great amusement in the serious scientific teaching of the present hour, even as we do now in the systems of the last century. It may happen that, in a little time, the doctrine of evolution will be the standing jest of schoolboys.

The like is true of the modern divinity which bows its knee in blind idolatry of so-called science. Now we say, and do so with all our heart, that the gospel which we preached forty years ago we will still preach in forty years time if we are alive. And, what is more, that the gospel which was taught of our Lord and his apostles is the only gospel now on the face of the earth.

Ecclesiastics have altered the gospel, and if it had not been of God it would have been stifled by falsehood long ago; but because the Lord has made it, it abideth for ever. Everything human is before long moon-struck, so that it shifts with every phase of the lunar orb; but the Word of the Lord is not after men, for it is the same yesterday, to-day, and for ever.[5]

GOD'S TRUTH EXPOSES HERESY, BRINGS WARFARE

What is the reason why yon man hates me, because I preach what I believe to be right? If I do speak the truth am I responsible for his hating me? Not in the least degree.

I am sometimes told by my people that I attack certain parties very hard. Well, I cannot help it; if they are not right, it is not my fault—if they come in my way, that I am compelled to run over them. Suppose two of you should be driving in the road to-morrow, and one of you should be on the right side of the road, and some accident should occur, you would say, "Sir, the other man ought to have pulled up, he must pay the damages, for he had no business there at all on his wrong side." And it will be the same with us if we preach God's truth; we must go straight on; if the greatest ill feeling in the world rise up we have nothing to do with it.

[5]From "Our Manifesto," *The Metropolitan Tabernacle Pulpit*, Vol. 37 (London: Passmore and Alabaster, 1891), 37–50.

God's truth will sometimes bring about warfare; Jesus Christ, you know, said himself that he came to put warfare between man and man; to set the mother-in-law against the daughter-in-law, and the daughter-in-law against the mother-in-law; and that a man's foes should be those of his own household. But if there be ill-feeling, if there be clamoring of sects, to whom is it due? Who is responsible for it? Why, the man who makes the new sects, not the man who abides fast and firm by the old one.

If I am safely moored by a good strong anchor of fundamental truth, and some other shall strike my vessel and sink himself, I will not pay the damages. I stand firm: if others choose to go away from the truth, to cut their cables and slip their moorings, then let them. God grant that we may not do the same. Hold the truth, my friends, and hold it as the easiest method of sweeping away heresies and false doctrines.

But now-a-days, you know, you are told, "Oh, it does not matter what you believe; doctrines are nothing"; and they have tried lately to make a very happy family of us, like the happy family near Waterloo Bridge, where all kinds of creatures are shut up together; but they are only kept in order by a lath which the man, when we turn our heads, applies between the bars of the cage.

Just so with denominations, they want to amalgamate us all. We differ in various doctrines, and therefore some of us must be wrong, if we hold doctrines which are directly hostile to each other. But we are told, "It does not signify; doubtless, you are all right."

Now, I cannot see that. If I say one thing, and another man says another, how, by all that is holy, can both speak the truth? Shall black and white be the same color? Shall falsehood and truth be the same? When they shall be, and fire shall sleep in the same cradle with the waves of the ocean, then shall we agree to amalgamate ourselves with those who deny our doctrines, or speak evil of what we believe to be the gospel.

My brethren, no man has any right to absolve your judgment from allegiance to God; there is liberty of conscience between man and man, but there is none between God and man.

No man has a right to believe what he likes; he is to believe what God tells him; and if he does not believe that, though he is not responsible to man, or to any set of men, or to any government, yet mark you, he is responsible to God. I beseech you, therefore, if you would avoid heresies, and bring the church to a glorious union, read the Scriptures.

Read not so much man's comments, or man's books, but read the Scriptures, and keep your faith on this,—"God has said it."[6]

INFIDELITY IN THE PULPIT

To-day the revelation of God is treated with indifference, or talked of as if it deserved no reverence or credit. Unbelief has sapped the foundations of the social fabric. Worst of all,—I must not hold back the charge, many of the avowed ministers of Christ are no ministers of faith at all, but promoters of unbelief. The modern pulpit has taught men to be infidels.

What truth is there which has not been doubted by divines, questioned by doctors of divinity, and at length been denounced by the priests of "modern thought"? Nothing remains upon which a certain school of preachers have not spit their scepticism. The experience of the unbelief of Germany is being repeated here.

Among those who are ordained to be the preachers of the gospel of Christ there are many who preach not faith but doubt, and hence they are servants of the devil rather than of the Lord. Think not that I am aiming at the Church of England. With all my objection to a state-church, I am not so unjust as to conceal my belief, that I see in the Episcopal Church at this time less of unbelief than among certain Dissenters: in fact, Nonconformity in certain quarters is eaten through and through with a covert Unitarianism, less tolerable than Unitarianism itself. So frequently are the fundamental doctrines of the gospel assailed, that it becomes needful, before you cross the threshold of many a chapel, to ask the question, "Shall I hear the gospel here to-day, or shall I come out hardly knowing whether the Bible is inspired or not? Shall I not be made to doubt the atonement, the work of the Holy Ghost, the immortality of the soul, the punishment of the wicked, or the deity of Christ?"

I know I shall stir a hornet's nest by these honest rebukes but I cannot help it. I am burdened and distressed with the state of religion; a pest is in the air; no truth is safe from its withering infection.

No signs can be more alarming than the growing infidelity and worldliness which I see among those who call themselves Christians. Does this nation really intend to cast off the fear of God and the doctrines of Holy Scripture to follow the vain imaginings of the sophists and the fashionable follies of the great? Are we to see again unbelief and luxurious sin walking hand in hand? If so, there be some of us who mean to take up our sorrow-

---

[6]From "The Plea of Faith," *The New Park Street Pulpit*, Vol. 2 (London: Passmore and Alabaster, 1856), 273–280.

ful parable, and speak as plainly as we can for truth and holiness, whether we offend or please. Be it ours still to thunder out the law of God, and proclaim with trumpet clearness the gospel of Jesus, not batting one jot of firm belief in the revelation of God, nor winking at sin, nor toning down truth, even though we fear that the only result will be to make this people's hearts gross, and their ears heavy, and their eyes blind.

If it must be so, my soul shall weep in secret; but still, Oh Lord, here am I, send me. Be of good courage, oh my heart, for the faithful have not ceased from among men; other voices will cry aloud and spare not, if haply our land may be purged of its present defilement.[7]

WHATEVER CONTRADICTS TRUTH IS FALSE: HOW COMPLEX IS THAT?

Some things are true and some things are false.

I regard that as an axiom; but there are many persons who evidently do not believe it. The current principle of the present age seems to be, "Some things are either true or false, according to the point of view from which you look at them. Black is white, and white is black according to circumstances; and it does not particularly matter which you call it. Truth of course is true, but it would be rude to say that the opposite is a lie; we must not be bigoted, but remember the motto, 'So many men, so many minds.'"

Our forefathers were particular about maintaining landmarks; they had strong notions about fixed points of revealed doctrine, and were very tenacious of what they believed to be scriptural; their fields were protected by hedges and ditches, but their sons have grubbed up the hedges, filled up the ditches, laid all level, and played at leap-frog with the boundary stones.

The school of *modern* thought laughs at the ridiculous positiveness of Reformers and Puritans; it is advancing in glorious liberality, and before long will publish a grand alliance between heaven and hell, or, rather, an amalgamation of the two establishments upon terms of mutual concession, allowing falsehood and truth to lie side by side, like the lion with the lamb.

Still, for all that, my firm old-fashioned belief is that some doctrines are true, and that statements which are diametrically opposite to them are not true,—that when "No" is the fact, "Yes" is out of court, and that when "Yes" can be justified, "No" must be abandoned. I believe that the gentleman who has for so long a time perplexed our courts is either Sir Roger Tichborne or somebody else; I am not yet able to conceive of his being the

[7]From "Israel and Britain. A Note of Warning," *The Metropolitan Tabernacle Pulpit*, Vol. 31 (London: Passmore and Alabaster, 1885), 313–324.

true heir and an impostor at the same time. Yet in religious matters the fashionable standpoint is somewhere in that latitude.

We have a faith to preach, my brethren, and we are sent forth with a message from God. We are not left to fabricate the message as we go along. We are not sent forth by our Master with this kind of general commission—"As you shall think in your heart and invent in your head as you march on, so preach. Keep abreast of the times. Whatever the people want to hear, tell them that, and they shall be saved." Verily, we read not so. There is something definite in the Bible. It is not quite a lump of wax to be shaped at our will, or a roll of cloth to be cut according to the prevailing fashion.

Your great thinkers evidently look upon the Scriptures as a box of letters for them to play with, and make what they like of, or a wizard's bottle, out of which they may pour anything they choose from atheism up to spiritualism. I am too old-fashioned to fall down and worship this theory. There is something told me in the Bible—told me for *certain*—not put before me with a "but" and a "perhaps," and an "if," and a "maybe," and fifty thousand suspicions behind it, so that really the long and the short of it is, that it may not be so at all; but revealed to me as infallible fact, which must be believed, the opposite of which is deadly error, and comes from the father of lies.

Believing, therefore, that there is such a thing as truth, and such a thing as falsehood, that there are truths in the Bible, and that the gospel consists in something definite which is to be believed by men, it becomes us to be decided as to what we teach, and to teach it in a decided manner. We have to deal with men who will be either lost or saved, and they certainly will not be saved by erroneous doctrine. We have to deal with God, whose servants we are, and he will not be honored by our delivering falsehoods; neither will he give us a reward, and say, "Well done, good and faithful servant, thou hast mangled the gospel as judiciously as any man that ever lived before thee."

We stand in a very solemn position, and ours should be the spirit of old Micaiah, who said, "As the Lord my God liveth, before whom I stand, whatsoever the Lord saith unto me, *that will I speak*." Neither less nor more than God's word are we called to state, but that we are bound to declare in a spirit which lets the sons of men know that, whatever they may think of it, we believe God, and are not to be shaken in our confidence in him.[8]

---

[8]From "The Need of Decision for the Truth," *Sword & Trowel* (March 1874).

THE "CHARITY" OF UNCERTAINTY

If it could be proved to be, as certain cultivated teachers would have us believe, that there is nothing very sure, that although black is black it is not very black, and though white is white it is not very white, and from certain standpoints no doubt black is white and white is black—if it could be proved, I say, that there are no eternal verities, no divine certainties, no infallible truths—then might we willingly surrender what we know or think we know, and wander about on the ocean of speculation, the waifs and strays of mere opinion.

But while we have the truth, taught to our very souls by the Holy Ghost, we cannot drift from it, *nor will we*—though men count us fools for our stedfastness.

Brethren, aspire not to the "charity" which grows out of uncertainty. There are saving truths, and there are damnable heresies. Jesus Christ is not yea and nay. His gospel is not a cunning mixture of the gall of hell and the honey of heaven, flavoured to the taste of bad and good.

There *are* fixed principles and revealed facts. Those who know anything experimentally about divine things have cast their anchor down, and as they heard the chain running out, they joyfully said, "This I know, and have believed. In this truth I stand fast and immovable. Blow winds and crack your cheeks, you will never move me from this anchorage. Whatsoever I have attained by the teaching of the Spirit, I will hold fast as long as I live."[9]

I KNOW

In certain circles of society it is rare nowadays to meet with anybody who believes anything. It is the philosophical, the right, the fashionable thing nowadays to doubt everything which is generally received; indeed those who have any creed whatever are by the liberal school set down as old-fashioned dogmatists, persons of shallow minds, deficient in intellect, and far behind their age. The great men, the men of thought, the men of high culture and refined taste, consider it wisdom to cast suspicion upon revelation, and sneer at all definiteness of belief.

"Ifs" and "buts," "perhapses" and "peradventures," are the supreme delight of this period. What wonder if men find everything uncertain, when they refuse to bow their intellects to the declarations of the God of truth?

---

[9]From "The Anchor," *The Metropolitan Tabernacle Pulpit*, Vol. 22 (London: Passmore and Alabaster, 1876), 277–288.

Note then, with admiration, the refreshing and even startling positiveness of the apostle—"I know," says he. And that is not enough—"I am persuaded." He speaks like one who cannot tolerate a doubt. There is no question about whether he has believed or not. "I know whom I have believed." There is no question as to whether he was right in so believing. "I am persuaded that he is able to keep that which I have committed to him." There is no suspicion as to the future; he is as positive for years to come as he is for this present moment. "He is able to keep that which I have committed to him against that day."[10]

THE TRUTH WAR

To be a Christian is to be a warrior. The good soldier of Jesus Christ must not expect to find ease in this world: it is a battle-field. Neither must he reckon upon the friendship of the world; for that would be enmity against God. His occupation is war. As he puts on piece by piece of the panoply provided for him, he may wisely say to himself, "This warns me of danger; this prepares me for warfare; this prophesies opposition."

Difficulties meet us even in standing our ground; for the apostle, two or three times, bids us—"Stand." In the rush of the fight, men are apt to be carried off their legs. If they can keep their footing, they will be victorious; but if they are borne down by the rush of their adversaries, everything is lost. You are to put on the heavenly armor in order that you may stand; and you will need it to maintain the position in which your Captain has placed you.

If even to stand requires all this care, judge ye what the warfare must be! The apostle also speaks of withstanding as well as standing. We are not merely to defend, but also to assail. It is not enough that you are not conquered; you have to conquer: and hence we find, that we are to take, not only a helmet to protect the head, but also a sword, with which to annoy the foe. Ours, therefore, is a stern conflict, standing and withstanding; and we shall want all the armor from the divine magazine, all the strength from the mighty God of Jacob.

It is clear from our text that our defense and our conquest must be obtained by sheer fighting. Many try compromise; but if you are a true Christian, you can never do this business well. The language of deceit fits not a holy tongue. The adversary is the father of lies, and those that are with him understand the art of equivocation; but saints abhor it. If we discuss

---

[10]From "Assured Security in Christ," *The Metropolitan Tabernacle Pulpit*, Vol. 16 (London: Passmore and Alabaster, 1870), 1–12.

terms of peace, and attempt to gain something by policy, we have entered upon a course from which we shall return in disgrace. We have no order from our Captain to patch up a truce, and get as good terms as we can. We are not sent out to offer concessions.

It is said that if we yield a little, perhaps the world will yield a little also, and good may come of it. If we are not too strict and narrow, perhaps sin will kindly consent to be more decent. Our association with it will prevent its being so barefaced and atrocious. If we are not narrow-minded, our broad doctrine will go down with the world, and those on the other side will not be so greedy of error as they now are. No such thing. Assuredly this is not the order which our Captain has issued. When peace is to be made, he will make it himself, or he will tell us how to behave to that end; but at present our orders are very different.

Neither may we hope to gain by being neutral, or granting an occasional truce. We are not to cease from conflict, and try to be as agreeable as we can with our Lord's foes, frequenting their assemblies, and tasting their dainties. No such orders are written here. You are to grasp your weapon, and go forth to fight.

Neither may you so much as dream of winning the battle by accident. No man was ever holy by a happy chance. Infinite damage may be done by carelessness; but no man ever won life's battle by it. To let things go on as they please, is to let them bear us down to hell. We have no orders to be quiet, and take matters easily. No; we are to pray always, and watch constantly.

The one note that rings out from the text is this:—TAKE THE SWORD! TAKE THE SWORD! No longer is it, talk and debate! No longer is it, parley and compromise! The word of thunder is—Take the sword. The Captain's voice is clear as a trumpet—Take the sword! No Christian man here will have been obedient to our text unless with clear, sharp, and decisive firmness, courage, and resolve, he takes the sword. We must go to heaven sword in hand, all the way. "TAKE THE SWORD."[11]

ERROR REVEALING ITSELF: NOW WE PERCEIVE ITS SHAPE

I mourn the terrible defections from the truth which are now too numerous to be thought of in detail; nevertheless, I am not disquieted, much less dispirited. That cloud will blow over, as many another has done.

I think the outlook is better than it was. I do not think the devil is any

---

[11]From "The Sword of the Spirit," *The Metropolitan Tabernacle Pulpit*, Vol. 37, 229–240.

better: I never expected he would be; but he is older. Brethren, whether that is for the better or for the worse, I do not know; but, assuredly, the arch-enemy is not quite such a novelty among us as he was. We are not quite so much afraid of that particular form of devilry which is raging now, because we begin to perceive its shape.

The unknown appeared to be terrible; but familiarity has removed alarm. At the first, this "modern thought" looked very like a lion; the roaring thereof was terrible, though to some ears there was always a suspicion of braying about it. On closer inspection, the huge king of beasts looked more like a fox, and now we should honor it if we likened it to a wild cat.

We were to have been devoured of lions, but the monsters are not to be seen. Scientific religion is empty talk without either science or religion in it. The mountain has brought forth its mouse, or, at any rate, the grand event is near. Very soon, "advanced thought" will only be mentioned by servant girls and young Independent ministers. It has gradually declined till it may now be carried off with the slops [food waste fed to animals]. There is nothing in the whole bag of tricks.

At this hour, I see the tide turning;—not that I care much for that, for the rock on which I build is unaffected by ebb, or flood of human philosophy. Still, it is interesting to remark that the current is not setting in quite the same direction as heretofore. Young men who have tried modern doubt have seen their congregations dwindle away beneath its withering power; and they are, therefore, not quite so enamored of it as they were.

It is time they should make a change; for Christian people have observed that these advanced men have not been remarkable for abundant grace, and they have even been led to think that their loose views on doctrine were all of a piece with looseness as to religion in general. Want of soundness in the faith is usually occasioned by want of conversion. Had certain men felt the power of the gospel in their own souls, they would not so readily have forsaken it to run after fables.

Lovers of the eternal truth, you have nothing to fear! God is with those who are with Him. He reveals Himself to those who believe His revelation. Our march is not to and fro, but onward unto victory. "The Egyptians whom ye have seen today, ye shall see them again no more for ever." Other enemies will arise, even as Amalekites, Hivites, Jebusites, Perizzites, and all the rest of them, rose up against Israel; but, in the Name of the Lord, we shall pass on to possess the promised heritage.

Meanwhile, it is for us quietly to labor on. Our daydreams are over: we shall neither convert the world to righteousness, nor the church to orthodoxy. We refuse to bear responsibilities which do not belong to us, for our real responsibilities are more than enough. Certain wise brethren are hot to reform their denomination. They ride out gallantly. Success be to the champions! They are generally wiser when they ride home again.

I confess great admiration for my Quixotic brethren, but I wish they had more to show for their valor. I fear that both church and world are beyond us; we must be content with smaller spheres. Even our own denomination must go its own way. We are only responsible so far as our power goes, and it will be wise to use that power for some object well within reach. For the rest, let us not worry and weary about things beyond our line. What if we cannot destroy all the thorns and thistles which curse the earth; we can, perhaps, cleanse our own little plot. If we cannot transform the desert into a pasture, we may at least make two blades of grass grow where only one grew before; and that will be something.

Brethren, let us look well to our own steadfastness in the faith, our own holy walking with God. Some say that such advice is selfish; but I believe that, in truth, it is not selfishness, but a sane and practical love of others which leads us to be mindful of our own spiritual state. Desiring to do its level best, and to use its own self in the highest degree to God's glory, the true heart seeks to be in all things right with God. He who has learned to swim has fostered a proper selfishness, for he has thereby acquired the power of helping the drowning. With the view of blessing others, let us covet earnestly the best blessings for ourselves.[12]

THE BEST RESPONSE TO THE NEW THEOLOGY

There is something so enticing and yet so flimsy in the modern theological school, that I feel constrained to warn you constantly against it.

Its mystery is absurdity, and its depth is pompous ignorance. There is no theology in it; it is a futile device to conceal the want of theological knowledge.

A man with an education that may be complete in every department except that in which he should excel, stands up and would teach Christians that all they have learned at the feet of Paul has been a mistake, that a new theology has been discovered, that the old phrases which we have used are out of date, the old creeds broken up.

Well, what shall we do to this wiseacre and his fellow sages? Serve them, wherever you meet them or their disciples, as Job did Zophar: laugh

---

[12]*An All-Round Ministry: Addresses to Ministers and Students*, 188.

at them, dash their language to pieces, and remind them that the best things they tell us are only what the fishes of the sea, or the fowls of the air, knew before them, and that their grandest discoveries are but platitudes which every child has known before, or else they are heresies that ought to be scouted from the earth.[13]

BAD FADS

Till we are rooted and grounded in the truth, new things have great charms for us, especially if they have about them a great show of holiness and zeal for God.

Listen, then, dear children but newly born into the Savior's family: "Let that therefore abide in you, which ye have heard from the beginning."

Alas, even those who are older in grace than you are have shown a sad readiness to be duped by plausible persons who have invented fresh notions and methods. I have lived long enough to have seen a considerable variety of follies and manias in the religious world. They have sprung up, grown great, declined, and vanished. One day it has been one thing, another another.

I have lived to see those things justly ridiculed which a few years before were cried up as the wonders of the age. I thank God I have not been moved by any of these periodical fits of frenzy, but have been content to keep to the one old truth which I have gathered from the Scriptures and made my own by experience, and by the teaching of the Holy Spirit.

I have not had to tack about, for I have been enabled to steam ahead; and I hope I shall do so to the end. I have no respect for these upstart inventions; but I regard them as so many phases of human delusion. One never knows what will come next; but of this we are pretty sure, that every now and then a new doctrine is brought forth which turns out to be an old heresy with a fresh coat of varnish on it; or else some new method of saving souls is found out, and the work blazes away like a house on fire till it dies out in smoke.

Let us not be carried off our feet by every wind of doctrine. We may live to see the present craze ended and another or two after it; only be it ours to be steadfast, immovable. "Little children, let that therefore abide in you, which ye have heard from the beginning": leave to others the soon-exhausted novelties and do you keep to the eternal unchangeable truth which is taught you in God's word and in your own soul's experience.[14]

---

[13]*The New Park Street Pulpit*, Vol. 4 (London: Passmore and Alabaster, 1858), 317–324.
[14]From "A Sermon to the Lord's Little Children," *The Metropolitan Tabernacle Pulpit*, Vol. 29 (London:

JARGON

I would we had another Job, to chastise the high-sounding language of modern theologians.

There are starting up in our midst men, who if they are not heretics in doctrine, are aliens in speech. They are men described by the old preachers, who say, "Mark!" and there is nothing to mark, and who shout, "Observe!" and there is nothing to observe, except the want of everything that is worth observing.

We know ministers who cannot speak in the common language of mankind, but must needs adopt the jargon of Carlyle, who sets language on its head, and puts the last word first. These men must needs make the English language a slave to the German—the glorious grand old Saxon must buckle to their heresies and conceal the depths of their falsehoods.

I pray God the time may come when some man may unmask them, when all these wind-bags may be rent, and all these bladders may be pricked, when if teachers have anything to tell us they will deliver themselves so that all can understand. If they cannot use plain language let their tongues go to school till they have learned it.[15]

METAPHYSICAL BECLOUDMENT

Is it not very possible for a man to talk without knowing what he is saying?

Certain "modern thought" teachers appear before us as a luminous haze. It is "not light, but darkness visible." Like M. De Biran, our learned lumberer, might say, "I wander like a somnambulist in the world of affairs." He has an idea, but he does not quite know where to find it; and so all through his talk he hunts for it, "upstairs, downstairs, and in my lady's chamber."

We once heard a sermon which for half an hour did not convey to us a single thought. We whispered to our neighbour, and found that he was equally befogged, and so we concluded that the density was not in our brain, but in the discourse; yet the preacher was no fool, and we therefore concluded that he had been taking an overdose of metaphysics.

It did not matter much, for the sermon was not upon a subject of any material importance to man or beast; but when a person is preaching the gospel of our Lord Jesus Christ it does matter a great deal.

It is treason to men's souls to conceal the plain truth of salvation

Passmore and Alabaster, 1883), 157–168.

[15]From "Everywhere and Yet Forgotten," *The Metropolitan Tabernacle Pulpit*, Vol. 6 (London: Passmore and Alabaster, 1860), 317–324.

beneath a cloud of words: where God's honour and man's eternal destiny are concerned, everything should be as clear as the sun at noonday. Metaphysical becloudment, when a soul is at stake, is diabolical cruelty.[16]

PREACH DISTINCTLY

We must preach the gospel so distinctly that our people know what we are preaching. "If the trumpet give an uncertain sound, who shall prepare himself for the battle?" Don't puzzle your people with doubtful speeches.

"Well," said one, "I had a new idea the other day. I did not enlarge upon it; I just threw it out."

That is a very good thing to do with most of your new ideas. Throw them out, by all means; but mind where you are when you do it; for if you throw them out from the pulpit they may strike somebody, and inflict a wound upon faith. Throw out your fancies, but first go alone in a boat a mile out to sea. When you have once thrown out your unconsidered trifles, leave them to the fishes.

We have nowadays around us a class of men who preach Christ, and even preach the gospel; but then they preach a great deal else which is not true, and thus they destroy the good of all that they deliver, and lure men to error. They would be styled "evangelical" and yet be of the school which is really anti-evangelical.[17]

THE VIRTUE OF PLAIN LANGUAGE

Never was there a sermon more commonplace than that of Peter, and let me tell you that it is one of the blessed effects of the Holy Spirit to make ministers preach simply.

You do not want the Holy Spirit to make them ride the high horse and mount up on the wings of the spread-eagle to the stars; what is wanted is to keep them down, dealing with solemn subjects in an intelligible manner.

What was the theme of this sermon? Was it something so intellectual that nobody could comprehend it, or so grand that few could grasp it? No, Peter just rises up and delivers himself somewhat like this—"Jesus Christ of Nazareth lived among you; he was the Messias promised of old; you crucified him, but in his name there is salvation, and whosoever among you will repent and be baptized shall find mercy." That is all! I am sure Mr. Charles

---

[16]"Be Plain," *Sword & Trowel* (May 1885).
[17]"The Greatest Fight in the World" (London: Passmore & Alabaster, 1891), 38–39.

Simeon in his "Skeleton Sermons" would not have inserted it as a model, and I do not suppose that any college professor alive would ever say to his students—"If you want to preach, preach like Peter."

Why, I do not perceive firstly, secondly, thirdly, and fourthly, to which some of us feel compelled to bind ourselves. It is in fact a commonplace talking about sublime things—sublime things which in this age are thought to be foolishness and a stumbling-block. Well then, may the Spirit of God be poured out to teach our ministers to preach plainly, to set our young men talking about Jesus Christ, for this is absolutely necessary.

When the Spirit of God goes away from a Church it is a fine thing for oratory, because then it is much more assiduously cultivated. When the Spirit of God is gone, then all the ministers become exceedingly learned, for not having the Spirit they need to supply the emptiness his absence has made, and then the old-fashioned Bible is not quite good enough; they must touch it up a bit and improve upon it, and the old doctrines which used to rejoice their grandmothers at the fire-side are too stale for them; they must have an improved and a new theology, and young gentlemen now-a-days show their profound erudition by denying everything that is the ground, and prop, and pillar of our hope, and starting some new will-o'- the-wisp which they set their people staring at.

Ah! well, we want the Spirit of God to sweep all that away. Oh that my dear sister who conducts the female class, and all who are in the Sunday-school, may be helped just to talk to you about Christ. When you get the Spirit of God to come upon you like fire and like a rushing mighty wind it will not be to make you doctors of divinity, and scholars, and great elocu-tionists; it will only be just for this, to make you preach Christ, and preach him more simply than ever you did before.[18]

DON'T BE TOO POLITE

Men are perishing, and if it be unpolite to tell them so, it can only be so where the devil is the master of the ceremonies.

Out upon your soul-destroying politeness; the Lord give us a little honest love to souls, and this superficial gentility will soon vanish. I could with considerable refreshment to myself pour sarcasm after sarcasm upon religious cowardice. I would cheerfully sharpen my knife and dash it into the heart of this mean vice. There is nothing to be said in its favor.

---

[18]From "Pentecost," *The Metropolitan Tabernacle Pulpit*, Vol. 9 (London: Passmore and Alabaster, 1863), 289–300.

It is not even humble; it is only pride of too beggarly a sort to own itself.[19]

ON LAYING FOUNDATIONS

Beware of a religion without holdfasts. But if I get a grip upon a doctrine they call me a bigot. Let them do so. Bigotry is a hateful thing, and yet that which is now abused as bigotry is a great virtue, and greatly needed in these frivolous times. I have been inclined lately to start a new denomination, and call it "the Church of the Bigoted."

Everybody is getting to be so oily, so plastic, so untrue, that we need a race of hardshells to teach us how to believe. Those old-fashioned people who in former ages believed something and thought the opposite of it to be false, were truer folk, than the present timeservers.

I should like to ask the divines of the broad school whether any doctrine is worth a man's dying for it. They would have to reply, "Well, of course, if a man had to go to the stake or change his opinions, the proper way would be to state them with much diffidence, and to be extremely respectful to the opposite school."

But suppose he is required to deny the truth?

"Well, there is much to be said on each side, and probably the negative may have a measure of truth in it as well as the positive. At any rate, it cannot be a prudent thing to incur the odium of being burned, and so it might be preferable to leave the matter an open question for the time being."

Yes, and as these gentlemen always find it unpleasant to be unpopular, they soften down the hard threatenings of Scripture as to the world to come, and put a color upon every doctrine to which worldly-wise men object.

The teachers of doubt are very doubtful teachers. A man must have something to hold to, or he will neither bless himself nor others.

Bring all the ships into the pool; but do not moor or anchor one of them; let each one be free! Wait you for a stormy night, and they will dash against each other, and great mischief will come of this freedom. Perfect love and charity will not come through our being all unmoored, but by each having his proper moorings and keeping to them in the name of God. You must have something to hold to.[20]

---

[19]"The War-Horse," *Sword & Trowel* (May 1866).
[20]From "On Laying Foundations," *The Metropolitan Tabernacle Pulpit*, Vol. 29 (London: Passmore and Alabaster, 1883), 49–60.

DON'T PREACH MERE MORALITY

The minister ought to preach Christ in opposition to mere morality. How many ministers in London could preach as well out of Shakespeare as the Bible, for all they want is a moral maxim. The good man never thinks of mentioning regeneration. He sometimes talks of moral renovation. He does not think of talking about perseverance by grace. No, continuance in well-doing is his perpetual cry.

He does not think of preaching "believe and be saved." No; his continual exhortation is, "Good Christian people, say your prayers, and behave well, and by these means you shall enter the kingdom of heaven." The sum and substance of his gospel is that we can do very well without Christ, that although certainly there is a little amiss in us, yet if we just mend our ways in some little degree, that old text, "except a man be born again," need not trouble us.

If you want to be made drunkards, if you want to be made dishonest, if you want to be taught every vice in the world, go and hear a moral preacher. These gentlemen, in their attempts to reform and make people moral, are the men that *lead them from morality*.

Hear the testimony of holy Bishop Lavington, "We have long been attempting to reform the nation by moral preaching. With what effect? None. On the contrary, we have dexterously preached the people into downright infidelity. We must change our voice; we must preach Christ and him crucified; nothing but the gospel is the power of God unto salvation."[21]

THROW OUT THE ATONEMENT?

We are told that we ought to give up a part of our old-fashioned theology to save the rest. We are in a carriage travelling over the steppes of Russia. The horses are being driven furiously, but the wolves are close upon us! Can you not see their eyes of fire?

The danger is pressing. What must we do? It is proposed that we throw out a child or two. By the time they have eaten the baby, we shall have made a little headway; but should they again overtake us, what then? Why, brave man, *throw out your wife!*

"All that a man hath will he give for his life"; give up nearly every truth in hope of saving one. Throw out inspiration, and let the critics devour it.

---

[21]From "Christ Lifted Up," *The New Park Street Pulpit*, Vol. 3, 260; http://www.spurgeon.org/sermons/0139.htm.

Throw out election, and all the old Calvinism; here will be a dainty feast for the wolves, and the gentlemen who give us the sage advice will be glad to see the doctrines of grace torn limb from limb. Throw out natural depravity, eternal punishment, and the efficacy of prayer.

We have lightened the carriage wonderfully. Now for another drop. *Sacrifice the great sacrifice!* Have done with the atonement!

Brethren, this advice is villainous, and murderous; we will escape these wolves with everything, or we will be lost with everything. It shall be "the truth, the whole truth, and nothing but the truth," or none at all. We will never attempt to save half the truth by casting any part of it away.[22]

NEW THEOLOGY ATTACKS THE JUSTICE OF THE ATONEMENT

Some time ago an excellent lady sought an interview with me, with the object as she said, of enlisting my sympathy upon the question of "Anti-Capital Punishment." I heard the excellent reasons she urged against hanging men who had committed murder, and though they did not convince me, I did not seek to answer them.

She proposed that when a man committed murder, he should be confined for life.

My remark was, that a great many men who had been confined half their lives were not a bit the better for it, and as for her belief that they would necessarily be brought to repentance, I was afraid it was but a dream.

"Ah," she said, good soul as she was, "that is because we have been all wrong about punishments. We punish people because we think they deserve to be punished. Now, we ought to show them," said she, "that we love them; that we only punish them to make them better."

"Indeed, madam," I said, "I have heard that theory a great many times, and I have seen much fine writing upon the matter, but I am no believer in it. The *design* of punishment should be amendment, but the *ground* of punishment lies in the positive guilt of the offender. I believe that when a man does wrong, he ought to be punished for it, and that there is a guilt in sin which justly merits punishment."

Oh no; she could not see that. Sin was a very wrong thing, but punishment was not a proper idea. She thought that people were treated too cruelly in prison, and that they ought to be taught that we love them. If they were treated kindly in prison, and tenderly dealt with, they would grow so much better, she was sure.

---

[22]*The Greatest Fight in the World*, 33.

With a view of interpreting her own theory, I said, "I suppose, then, you would give criminals all sorts of indulgences in prison. Some great vagabond who has committed burglary dozens of times—I suppose you would let him sit in an easy chair in the evening before a nice fire, and mix him a glass of spirits and water, and give him his pipe, and make him happy, to show him how much we love him."

Well, no, she would not give him the spirits, but, still, all the rest would do him good.

I thought that was a delightful picture certainly. It seemed to me to be the most prolific method of cultivating rogues which ingenuity could invent. I imagine that you could grow any number of thieves in that way; for it would be a special means of propagating all manner of roguery and wickedness.

These very delightful theories to such a simple mind as mine, were the source of much amusement; the idea of fondling villains, and treating their crimes as if they were the tumbles and falls of children, made me laugh heartily. I fancied I saw the government resigning its functions to these excellent persons, and the grand results of their marvellously kind experiments. The sword of the magistrate transformed into a gruel-spoon, and the jail become a sweet retreat for injured reputations.

Little, however, did I think I should live to see this kind of stuff taught in pulpits; I had no idea that there would come out a divinity, which would bring down God's moral government from the solemn aspect in which Scripture reveals it, to a namby-pamby sentimentalism, which adores a Deity destitute of every masculine virtue.

But we never know to-day what may occur to-morrow. We have lived to see a certain sort of men—thank God they are not Baptists—though I am sorry to say there are a great many Baptists who are beginning to follow in their trail—who seek to teach now-a-days, that God is a universal Father, and that our ideas of his dealing with the impenitent as a Judge, and not as a Father, are remnants of antiquated error.

Sin, according to these men, is a disorder rather than an offence, an error rather than a crime. Love is the only attribute they can discern, and the full-orbed Deity they have not known. Some of these men push their way very far into the bogs and mire of falsehood, until they inform us that eternal punishment is ridiculed as a dream.

In fact, books now appear, which teach us that there is no such thing as the Vicarious Sacrifice of our Lord Jesus Christ. They use the word *atonement*, it is true, but in regard to its meaning, they have removed the ancient landmark. They acknowledge that the Father has shown his great love to poor sinful man by sending his Son, but not that God was inflexibly just in the exhibition of his mercy, not that he punished Christ on the behalf of his people, nor that indeed God ever will punish anybody in his wrath, or that there is such a thing as justice apart from discipline.

Even *sin* and *hell* are but old words employed henceforth in a new and altered sense. Those are old-fashioned notions, and we poor souls who go on talking about election and imputed righteousness, are behind our time.[23]

SOME NEW THING

Just as they say fish go bad at the head first, so modern divines generally go bad first upon the head and main doctrine of the substitutionary work of Christ. Nearly all our modern errors, I might say all of them, begin with mistakes about Christ.

Men do not like to be always preaching the same thing. There are Athenians in the pulpit as well as in the pew who spend their time in nothing but hearing some new thing. They are not content to tell over and over again the simple message, "He that believeth in the Lord Jesus Christ hath everlasting life." So they borrow novelties from literature, and garnish the Word of God with the words which man's wisdom teacheth.

The doctrine of atonement they mystify. Reconciliation by the precious blood of Jesus ceases to be the cornerstone of their ministry. To shape the gospel to the diseased wishes and tastes of men enters far more deeply into their purpose, than to remould the mind and renew the heart of men that they receive the gospel as it is.

There is no telling where they will go who once go back from following the Lord with a true and undivided heart, from deep to deep descending; the blackness of darkness will receive them unless grace prevent. Only this you may take for a certainty:

> "They cannot be right in the rest,
> Unless they speak rightly of Him."

If they are not sound about the purpose of the cross, they are rotten everywhere.

"Other foundation can no man lay than that is laid, which is Jesus Christ." On this rock there is security. We may be mistaken on any other

---

[23]From "Christ Our Substitute," *The Metropolitan Tabernacle Pulpit*, Vol. 6, 189–196.

point with more impunity than this. They who are builded on the rock, though they build wood, and hay, and stubble, thereupon to their sore confusion, for what they build shall be burned, themselves shall be saved yet so as by fire.

Now that grand doctrine which we take to be the keystone of the evangelical system, the very corner-stone of the gospel, that grand doctrine of the atonement of Christ we would tell to you again, and then, without attempting to prove it, for that we have done hundreds of times, we shall try to draw some lessons of instruction from that truth which is surely believed among us.

Man having sinned, God's righteousness demanded that the penalty should be fulfilled. He had said, "The soul that sinneth shall die"; and unless God can be false, the sinner must die. Moreover, God's holiness demanded it, for the penalty was based on justice. It was just that the sinner should die. God had not appended a more heavy penalty than he should have done. Punishment is the just result of offending. God, then, must either cease to be holy, or the sinner must be punished. Truth and holiness imperiously demanded that God should lift his hand and smite the man who had broken his law and offended his majesty.

Christ Jesus, the second Adam, the federal head of the chosen ones, interposed. He offered himself to bear the penalty which they ought to bear; to fulfill and honor the law which they had broken and dishonored. He offered to be their day's-man, a surety, a substitute, standing in their room, place, and stead. Christ became the vicar of his people; vicariously suffering in their stead; vicariously doing in their stead that which they were not strong enough to do by reason of the weakness of the flesh through the fall.

This which Christ proposed to do was accepted of God. In due time Christ actually died, and fulfilled what he promised to do. He took every sin of all his people, and suffered every stroke of the rod on account of those sins. He had compounded into one awful draught the punishment of the sins of the elect. He took the cup; he put it to his lips; he sweat as it were great drops of blood while he tasted the first sip thereof, but he never desisted, but drank on, on, on, till he had exhausted the very dregs, and turning the vessel upside down he said, "It is finished!" and at one tremendous draught of love the Lord God of salvation had drained destruction dry. Not a dreg, not the slightest residue was left; he had suffered all that ought to have been suffered; had finished transgression, and made an end of sin.

Moreover, he obeyed his Father's law to the utmost extent of it; he fulfilled that will of which he had said of old—"Lo, I come to do thy will, O God: thy law is my delight"; and having offered both an atonement for sin and a complete fulfillment of the law, he ascended up on high, took his seat on the right hand of the Majesty in heaven, from henceforth expecting till his enemies be made his footstool, and interceding for those whom he bought with blood that they may be with him where he is.

The doctrine of the atonement is very simple. It just consists in the substitution of Christ in the place of the sinner; Christ being treated as if he were the sinner, and then the transgressor being treated as if he were the righteous one.[24]

SPIRITUAL VAGRANTS

Let us get clearer views of what we believe. . . . Many are spiritual gypsies. They camp behind any hedge, but they abide nowhere; their theology consists of a few sticks and bits of canvas. It is easily upset, but then it is as easily set up. Well may they sing,—"We've no abiding city here"!

They prefer the chase after truth to truth itself; it is clear that such a chase has not much of reality in it, for the man is pleased that his prey should perpetually escape him. In olden times, the prophet was a seer; but, nowadays, a prophet is one who is too cultured to see anything. A man who protests that he has too much light to be sure that he sees anything is the favourite of certain intellectual hearers. David said, "I believed, therefore have I spoken"; but he was peculiar: our "thoughtful men" now speak because they doubt, and not because they believe.[25]

THE EFFEMINATE DEITY OF THE MODERN SCHOOL

This generation has made a god of its own. The effeminate deity of the modern school is no more the true God than Dagon or Baal. I know him not, neither do I reverence him. But Jehovah is the true God: he is the God of love, but he is also robed in justice; he is the God of forgiveness, but he is also the God of atonement; he is the God of heaven, but he is also the God who sends the wicked down to hell.

We, of course, are thought to be harsh, and narrow-minded, and bigoted: nevertheless, this God is our God for ever and ever. There has been no change in Jehovah. He has revealed himself more clearly in Christ Jesus;

---

[24]From "The Old, Old Story," *The Metropolitan Tabernacle Pulpit*, Vol. 8 (London: Passmore and Alabaster, 1862), 230–240.
[25]*An All-Round Ministry: Addresses to Ministers and Students*, 243.

but he is the same God as in the Old Testament, and as such we worship him.[26]

THE CRUELTY OF THE LARGE-HEARTED

The second persecution of the church, in which all the apostles were put into the common prison, was mainly brought about by the sect of the Sadducees. These, as you know, were the Broad School, the liberals, the advanced thinkers, the modern-thought people of the day.

If you want a bitter sneer, a biting sarcasm, or a cruel action, I commend you to these large-minded gentlemen. They are liberal to everybody, except to those who hold the truth; and for those they have a reserve of concentrated bitterness which far excels wormwood and gall.

They are so liberal to their brother errorists, that they have no tolerance to spare for evangelicals.

We are expressly told that "the high priest, and all they that were with him (which is the sect of the Sadducees,) were filled with indignation." That which had been done deserved their admiration, but received their indignation. Such gentlemen as these can be warm at a very short notice, when the doctrine of the cross is spreading, and God the Holy Spirit is bearing witness with signs following. Let them display their indignation, it is according to their nature.

To them the only answer which God gave was spoken by his angel: "Go, stand and speak in the temple to the people all the words of this life." Argument will be lost upon them; go on with your preaching. They have lost the faculty of believing: go and speak to the people. They are so given over to their doubts, that it is like rolling the stone of Sisyphus to persuade them to faith. They are so eaten up with objections, that to attempt to answer all the questions they raise would be as vain as the labor of filling a bottomless tub.

Go on with your preaching, you apostles; but address yourselves mainly to the people. Extend as widely as possible the range of the truth, and thus answer the opposition of its adversaries. It is better to evangelize than to controvert. The preaching of the word of life is the best antidote to the doctrine of death.

Clearly enough, if they had known it, and had been capable of seeing it, these blind Sadducees were answered at every point when the apostles were brought out of prison and bore witness to their Lord. Here was the creed

---

[26]From "The Bond of the Covenant," *The Metropolitan Tabernacle Pulpit*, Vol. 31, 265–276.

of the Sadducees: they said that "there was no resurrection, neither angel, nor spirit"; but these apostles stood up and witnessed to the resurrection of Jesus Christ from the dead. What did they make of that?

An angel had come from heaven and had brought these apostles out of prison. Then there were angels.

As these apostles were set free while the sentries remained standing before the doors, and those doors were afterwards found fastened, if there were no spirit, assuredly materialism had acted in a singular fashion.

Every item of their negative creed had been made to fall like Dagon before the ark. The Lord always arranges Red Seas for Pharaohs. All that the apostles had to do was to go on with their preaching, and this they did; for "daily in the temple, and in every house, they ceased not to teach and preach Jesus Christ."[27]

WORDS OF LOVE AND SOBERNESS DURING THE DOWN-GRADE

A certain newspaper paragraph very kindly attempts to comfort "Mr. Spurgeon at his worst stage of depression concerning the doubts of the day," by the assurance that religion can never pass away.

We can assure our friend that we never thought it could. No fear as to the ultimate victory of the truth of God ever disturbs our mind. We are sure that the doctrines of the gospel will outlive all the dotings of "modern thought."

The trouble is that, for the moment, error is having its own way in certain parts of the visible church, where better things once ruled; and, worse still, that good men will not see the evil, or, seeing it, wink at it, and imagine that it will do no very great deal of harm. It is ours to give warning of a danger which to us is manifest and alarming; and if the warning makes us the butt of ridicule, we must bear it.

Our protest is, no doubt, regarded by some as a piece of bigotry, and by others, as the dream of a nervous mind. Neither conjecture is correct; but we speak the words of love and soberness.

An American, who enquired of certain leaders in the "Down-Grade" what they thought of Spurgeon's conduct, was informed that sickness and age had weakened his intellect. This has been their contemptuous method all along; but facts are not to be set aside by such remarks.

Be the protester what he may, he declares his protest to be solemnly needful, and he begs for attention to it. It may be the old truth is in the

---

[27]From "The Charge of the Angel," *The Metropolitan Tabernacle Pulpit*, Vol. 34 (London: Passmore and Alabaster, 1888), 373–384.

minority, and that those who uphold it are thought to be troublers in Israel, and causers of false alarm: but we are none the less confident that, when good men return to their better selves, they will see differently. Bitterly will some regret that they allowed matters to drift, and drift, till they had wrought incalculable mischief.

We have spoken in saddest earnest. It is no pleasure to us to stand apart, and refuse complicity with what we judge to be a great crime. Our witness is on high. The Lord will judge between us and the enemies of the faith in his own good time![28]

---

[28]"Notes," in *Sword & Trowel* (February 1890).

APPENDIX 3

CHARLES FINNEY AND AMERICAN EVANGELICAL PRAGMATISM

Charles Finney was born in 1792 in Connecticut but lived most of his childhood in Oneida County, New York. His parents were not Christians, and Finney grew up largely ignorant of Christian doctrine. He remembered no preaching or gospel witness in that part of New York (which he called "a wilderness")—though the historical records indicate there was at least one strong evangelical church in the community.[1]

The religion Finney remembered as a child was, he said later, "of a type not at all calculated to arrest my attention."[2] He described the only preacher he remembered from his youth:

> I sat in the gallery, and observed that he placed his manuscript in the middle of his Bible, and inserted his fingers at the places where were to be found the passages of Scripture to be quoted in the reading of his sermon. This made it necessary to hold his Bible in both hands, and rendered all gesticulation with his hands impossible. As he proceeded he would read the passages of Scripture where his fingers were inserted, and thus liberate one finger after another until the fingers of both hands were read out of their places. When his fingers were all read out, he was near the close of the sermon. His reading was altogether unimpassioned and monotonous; and although the people attended very closely and reverentially to his reading, yet, I must confess, it was to me not much like preaching.[3]

---

[1] B. B. Warfield, *Perfectionism*, 2 vols. (New York: Oxford, 1932), 2:10.
[2] *Charles G. Finney: An Autobiography* (Old Tappan, NJ: Revell, n.d.), 78.
[3] Ibid., 6.

Finney characterized the pastor's content as "a dry discussion of doctrine," then added, "and this was really quite as good preaching as I had ever listened to in any place. But any one can judge whether such preaching was calculated to instruct or interest a young man who neither knew nor cared anything about religion."[4]

Finney decided to study law and took an apprenticeship in Adams, New York, where for the first time he became actively involved in a church. The local Presbyterian pastor, George W. Gale, a young man about two years Finney's senior, took an interest in the law student. Gale made Finney choir director in the church and began to visit him in the law office to converse about spiritual matters.

Then Finney began to notice references to the Bible in his elementary law textbooks, so he acquired a Bible and began to study it. But again, Finney says, the preaching was a stumbling-block to him. "[Gale] seemed to take it for granted that his hearers were theologians, and therefore that he might assume all the great and fundamental doctrines of the Gospel. But I must say that I was rather perplexed than edified by his preaching."[5]

Finney pressed the young pastor with doctrinal questions during their conversations in the law office: "What did he mean by repentance? Was it a mere feeling of sorrow for sin? Was it altogether a passive state of mind, or did it involve a voluntary element? If it was a change of mind, in what respect was it a change of mind?"[6] and so on. One gets the impression from the nature of Finney's inquiries that Gale's preaching could not have been as thoroughly tedious as Finney later portrayed it. The evidence suggests Pastor Gale's ministry was having the desired effect on Finney.

Indeed, while Finney was in Adams, he was spectacularly converted. Ironically, though Finney's conversion was dramatic, overwhelming, revolutionary, Finney never came to understand that conversion is wholly a work of God. In Finney's telling of the story, it becomes clear that he believed his own will was the determinative factor that brought about his salvation: "On a Sabbath evening in the autumn of 1821, *I made up my mind* that *I would settle the question of my soul's salvation* at once, that if it were possible *I would make my peace with God*."[7] Evidently under intense conviction, Finney went into the woods, where he made a promise "that I would give my heart to God or die in the attempt."[8]

---

[4]Ibid., 6–7.
[5]Ibid., 7.
[6]Ibid., 8.
[7]Ibid., 12 (emphasis added).
[8]Ibid., 16.

Finney was converted there in the woods. At first it seemed a normal conversion. Finney himself was unsure of what had occurred, except that he had yielded himself to the Lord. His mind was "wonderfully quiet and peaceful." The overwhelming conviction of sin he had felt was entirely gone. He even wondered if he had somehow "grieved the Holy Ghost entirely away."[9] But then later that evening, in the law office, Finney had an experience that he described as "a mighty baptism of the Holy Ghost. . . . The Holy Spirit descended upon me in a manner that seemed to go through me, body and soul. I could feel the impression, like a wave of electricity, going through and through me."[10]

Even after all that, however, Finney's state of mind that night was so confused that years later he wrote, "Notwithstanding the baptism I had received . . . I went to bed without feeling sure my peace was made with God."[11]

Finney's doubts were suddenly, mystically erased the next morning, however, and later that same day he decided God wanted him to preach and that he must begin immediately. "After receiving these baptisms of the Spirit I was quite willing to preach the gospel. Nay, I found that I was unwilling to do anything else. I had no longer any desire to practice law. . . . My whole mind was taken up with Jesus and His salvation; and the world seemed to me of very little consequence."[12]

It was, I believe, extremely unfortunate that Finney chose to pursue a preaching ministry immediately after his conversion. Devoid of any solid Christian influence in his early life, he was almost completely ignorant of the Scriptures and of theology. Finney had a brilliant mind, however, and had always been able to hold his own in a theological debate—even with a trained man like Pastor Gale. His legal training had conditioned Finney to think logically, but it had also saddled him with a world of wrong presuppositions. Finney's notions of justice, guilt, righteousness, transgression, forgiveness, responsibility, sovereignty, and a host of other terms were drawn from his legal studies, not from Scripture.

Wherever Finney preached, people responded enthusiastically. Immediate evidences of revival seemed to follow his wake. As his reputation spread, so did his influence. Finney boldly challenged conventional doctrine and persuasively championed his own rather novel set of doctrines. Finney began preaching wherever he could gather an audience, and it wasn't long before he began to make an impact on the established churches. "Here was

---

[9] Ibid., 17.
[10] Ibid., 20.
[11] Ibid., 22.
[12] Ibid., 25–26.

this young man, but two years a minister, but four a Christian, with no traditions of refinement behind him, and no experience of preaching save as a frontier missionary, suddenly leading an assault upon the churches. He was naturally extravagant in his assertions, imperious and harsh in his bearing, relying more on harrowing men's feelings than on melting them with tender appeal."[13]

It must be noted that when Finney came on the scene many churches had drifted from true orthodoxy to a cold hyper-Calvinism. *Hyper-Calvinism* is the belief that the gospel invitation is for the elect only. Hyper-Calvinists do not believe the gospel should be preached indiscriminately or that salvation should be offered freely to all. In essence, they oppose the very idea of evangelism. Many of the churches in Finney's day were stymied by hyper-Calvinist tendencies. Finney's own pastor, George Gale, may have had hyper-Calvinist leanings. Finney described Gale's preaching: "He never seemed to expect, nor even to aim at converting anybody, by any sermon that I ever heard him preach."[14]

Finney concluded that his pastor's belief in human depravity and divine sovereignty were incompatible with evangelism. He wrote: "The fact is, these dogmas were a perfect straight-jacket to him. If he preached repentance, he must be sure before he sat down, to leave the impression on his people that they could not repent. If he called them to believe he must be sure to inform them that, until their nature was changed by the Holy Spirit, faith was impossible to them. And so his orthodoxy was a perfect snare to himself and to his hearers. I could not receive it."[15]

Finney did not distinguish between Calvinist orthodoxy and hyper-Calvinism.[16] Consequently, he distrusted orthodox doctrine and rejected

---

[13]Warfield, *Perfectionism*, 2:21.

[14]*Autobiography*, 59.

[15]Ibid., 59–60.

[16]Finney wrote, "I have everywhere found, that the peculiarities of hyper-calvinism have been a great stumbling-block, both of the church and of the world. A nature sinful in itself, a total inability to accept Christ, and to obey God, condemnation to eternal death for the sin of Adam, and for a sinful nature, and all the kindred and resultant dogmas of that peculiar school, have been the stumbling-block of believers and the ruin of sinners." Ibid., 368–369. But the doctrines Finney enumerates are not doctrines unique to hyper-Calvinism; they are simple Calvinist orthodoxy—and in most cases, plain biblical teaching. Finney jettisoned them all—and thus repudiated the heart of biblical theology.

The unique theology Finney devised was fraught with problems—particularly in the area of sanctification. Finney developed a radical form of perfectionism, which in turn spawned many other fanatical ideas among his followers. B. B. Warfield wrote a thorough and devastating critique of Finney's theology in his two-volume work *Perfectionism*, 2:1–215.

What Finney failed to consider carefully enough is that the most robust revivals in eighteenth-century America—including the Great Awakening—all originated with Calvinist teaching. Jonathan Edwards, George Whitefield, David Brainerd, and the early Baptists were all strongly Calvinistic, yet zealously committed to aggressive evangelism. Unfortunately, Finney was all too eager to shed that heritage and devise his own brand of theology. The pragmatic approach that was part and parcel of Finney's system has endured until today, even among many Christians who would deplore Finney's doctrinal innovations.

Calvinism altogether. He studied doctrine only superficially and invented a unique system of theology that satisfied his own sense of logic. He applied nineteenth-century American legal standards to every biblical doctrine. "I had read nothing on the subject [of the atonement] except my Bible," he wrote, "and what I found on the subject, I had interpreted as I would have understood the same or like passages in a law book."[17] He concluded that God's justice demanded that He extend grace equally to all. He reasoned that God could not righteously hold mankind guilty for Adam's disobedience. In his opinion, a just God would never condemn people for being sinners by nature: "The Bible defines sin to be a transgression of the law. What law have we violated in inheriting this [sin] nature? What law requires us to have a different nature from that which we possess? Does reason affirm that we are deserving of the wrath and curse of God for ever, for inheriting from Adam a sinful nature?"[18] Thus Finney discarded the clear teaching of Scripture (Rom. 5:16–19) in favor of human reason.

Worse yet, Finney denied that a holy God would impute people's sin to Christ or impute Christ's righteousness to believers. Finney concluded that those doctrines—clearly taught in Romans 3–5—were "theological fiction."[19] In essence, he denied the core of evangelical theology.

Unfortunately, Finney's early success in preaching obscured the serious flaws in his theology. Finney himself admitted that when he was being examined by his church to be licensed to preach, the presbytery "avoided asking any such questions as would naturally bring my views into collision with theirs."[20] They were evidently intimidated by Finney's growing popularity as a revivalist. But one of the examiners did ask Finney if he accepted the Westminster Confession of Faith. Finney admitted later that he had never even read the Confession. But he answered the presbytery in a way that indicated affirmation of their doctrinal standards. "I replied that I received it for substance of doctrine, so far as I understood it."[21] Afterward, when Finney read the Confession, he was shocked to discover that it contradicted much of what he believed. "As soon as I learned what were the unambiguous teachings of the confession of faith . . . I did not hesitate on all suitable occasions to declare my dissent from them," he wrote.[22]

In rejecting hyper-Calvinist tendencies, Finney swung wildly to the opposite extreme. "There is nothing in religion beyond the ordinary pow-

---

[17]*Autobiography*, 42.
[18]Ibid., 339.
[19]Ibid., 56–58.
[20]Ibid., 51.
[21]Ibid., 51.
[22]Ibid., 59.

ers of nature," he wrote.[23] "A revival is not a miracle, nor dependent on a miracle, in any sense. It is a purely philosophical result of the right use of the constituted means—as much so as any other effect produced by the application of means. . . . A revival is as naturally a result of the use of means as a crop is of the use of its appropriate means."[24]

Finney was the first influential evangelist to suggest that the end justifies the means: "The success of any measure designed to promote a revival of religion, demonstrates its wisdom. . . . When the blessing evidently follows the introduction of the *measure itself*, the proof is unanswerable, that the measure is wise. It is profane to say that such a measure will do more harm than good. God knows about that. His object is, to do the *greatest amount* of good possible."[25]

Finney's influence on the American evangelical movement was profound. He was the first to ask converts to "come forward" in evangelistic meetings to indicate their acceptance of Christ. He is the one who first applied the term *revival* to evangelistic campaigns. It was Finney who popularized the after-meeting for inquirers seeking salvation. He also left his mark on the American preaching style, encouraging young preachers to be extemporaneous, anecdotal, more conversational, and less doctrinal than preachers traditionally had been. All of those ideas—pretty much standard fare in evangelicalism today—were part of the "new measures" Finney introduced.

Not all Finney's innovations were wrong, of course. He urged preachers to be direct, clear, cogent, earnest, and confrontive in their messages. He advised them not to speak about sinners in the third person, but to address them as "you" in order to target their consciences more directly. He stressed the need for immediate conversion, in contrast to the prevailing notion of that day, in which sinners were often counseled to wait on God to give them repentance and faith. Echoing Scripture and Jesus' own preaching, Finney called sinners to repent and believe—not to remain passive and hope God would convert them.

Finney's ministry was centered in western New York state. Even during Finney's lifetime, the area was known as "the burned-over district,"[26]

---

[23]*Revivals of Religion* (Old Tappan, NJ: Revell, n.d.), 4.
[24]Ibid., 5.
[25]Ibid., 211 (emphasis in original).
[26]Oddly, Finney himself may have helped coin this expression. In his memoirs, he referred to the area as "a burnt district," because of the resistance to his own revivalism he found there. *Autobiography*, 78. A fascinating secular analysis of the region and its history of revivalism has been written by Whitney R. Cross, *The Burned-Over District: The Social and Intellectual History of Enthusiastic Religion in Western New York, 1800–1850* (New York: Harper Torchbooks, 1950).

because repeated waves of religious fervor had seemed to erase any real concern for the gospel. But in his younger days Finney always seemed to be able to fan the flames at least one more time.

Before long, however, the excitement and fervor of the supposed "revival" gave way to hardened unbelief and widespread agnosticism. The "burned-over district" was scorched again and became harder than ever. In fact, since Finney's time that part of the country has *never* experienced another revival.

One of the workers who labored alongside Finney in the revivals wrote to him in 1834:

> Let us look over the fields where you and others and myself have labored as revival ministers, and what is now their moral state? What was their state within three months after we left them? I have visited and revisited many of these fields, and groaned in spirit to see the sad, frigid, carnal, contentious state into which the churches had fallen—and fallen very soon after our first departure from among them.[27]

B. B. Warfield wrote,

> No more powerful testimony is borne . . . than that of Asa Mahan [Finney's long-time friend and fellow worker], who tells us—to put it briefly—that everyone who was concerned in these revivals suffered a sad subsequent lapse: the people were left like a dead coal which could not be reignited; the pastors were shorn of all their spiritual power; and the evangelists—"among them all," he says, "and I was personally acquainted with nearly every one of them—I cannot recall a single man, brother Finney and father Nash excepted, who did not after a few years lose his unction, and become equally disqualified for the office of evangelist and that of pastor."
>
> Thus the great "Western Revivals" ran out into disaster. . . . Over and over again, when he proposed to revisit one of the churches, delegations were sent him or other means used, to prevent what was thought of as an affliction.[28]

"Even after a generation had passed by," Warfield notes, "these burnt children had no liking for the fire."[29]

Finney became discouraged when his methods failed. He accepted the pastorate of Broadway Tabernacle Congregational Church in New York

---

[27]Cited in Warfield, *Perfectionism*, 2:26.
[28]Ibid., 2:26–27.
[29]Ibid., 2:28.

City and later the presidency of Oberlin College in Ohio. He turned his energies to the development of his perfectionist doctrines and to the work of the college.

Later assessing his own evangelistic career, Finney wrote, "I was often instrumental in bringing Christians under great conviction, and into a state of temporary repentance and faith. . . . [But] falling short of urging them up to a point, where they would become so acquainted with Christ as to abide in Him, they would of course soon relapse into their former state."[30] Realizing his evangelistic methodology had failed, Finney, ever the pragmatist, concluded that his perfectionist teachings were the *real* key to successful ministry. Had he lived long enough, he would have discovered that the perfectionism planted seeds of spiritual disaster worse than the shallow evangelism.

A contemporary of Finney's said,

> During ten years, hundreds, and perhaps thousands, were annually reported to be converted on all hands; but now it is admitted, that [Finney's] real converts are comparatively few. It is declared, even by himself, that "the great body of them are a disgrace to religion"; as a consequence of these defections, practical evils, great, terrible, and innumerable, are in various quarters rushing in on the Church.[31]

So Finney's most enduring and far-reaching influence, unfortunately, is not from multitudes of souls saved or sinners reached with the gospel. Those effects, it seems, were almost wholly superficial, often vanishing as soon as Finney left town. Finney's real legacy is the disastrous impact he had on American evangelical theology and evangelistic methodology. The church in our generation is still seething with the leaven Finney introduced, and modern evangelical pragmatism is proof of that.

---

[30]Cited in Warfield, *Perfectionism*, 2:24.
[31]Ibid., 23.

APPENDIX 4

CARNAL VS. SPIRITUAL WISDOM

This appendix is excerpted and adapted into modern English from "A Soliloquy on the Art of Man-Fishing," by Thomas Boston. Boston was an evangelical pastor in Ettrick, Scotland in the early 1700s. He was a prolific author in the Puritan tradition, remembered for several important works, including Human Nature in Its Fourfold State and The Crook in the Lot, or The Sovereignty and Wisdom of God Displayed in the Afflictions of Men, both of which books are currently in print. The endurance of Boston's works is ample testimony to the timeless nature of the truths he dealt with, as is especially evident in this excerpt. Although the word pragmatism would not be invented for two hundred years, in this piece Boston delivers a powerful assault against the pragmatic approach to ministry.

Our Lord's command *"Follow me, and I will make you fishers of men"* (Matt. 4:19, emphasis added) implies a renouncing of our own wisdom. Human wisdom cannot be our guide (Matt. 16:24); we must deny ourselves. Paul refused to preach with the wisdom of words (1 Cor. 1:17)—nor did he follow the rules of carnal wisdom. Therefore, oh my soul, renounce your own wisdom. Seek the wisdom that is from above; seek to preach the words of the living God, and not your own. When you determine to take this direction, praying that you might not preach according to your own wisdom and natural reason, you receive God's signal blessing.

Do not take the way of natural reason or follow the rules of carnal wisdom. Its language will always be, "Spare yourself. Guard your honor and your reputation among men. If you speak freely, they will call you a railer and call your preaching reactionary. Every church will be frightened of you as a monster that would preach them all to hell; and so you shall never be settled. Such and such a man, who has a great influence in the church, will never like you. After all, direct preaching is not the way to win people; it unnerves them from the very beginning. Instead, you should bring them on little by little, being somewhat smooth—at least at first. For this generation is not able to abide such doctrine as what you preach."

But hear and follow the rules of the wisdom that is from above: "The wisdom of this world is folly with God" (1 Cor. 3:19). That which is in high esteem among men is nothing in God's sight. The wisdom that is from above tells us we must deny ourselves (Matt. 16:24; Luke 14:26). We cannot seek honor, reputation, acclaim, the applause of men, or other such earthly enticements. Heavenly wisdom tells us people may call us what they will, we must nevertheless "Cry aloud; do not hold back; lift up your voice like a trumpet; declare to my people their transgression, to the house of Jacob their sins" (Isa. 58:1). Divine wisdom says, "Not many wise according to the flesh, not many mighty, not many noble" are called (1 Cor. 1:26, NASB). "God chose what is foolish in the world to shame the wise; God chose what is weak in the world to shame the strong; God chose what is low and despised in the world, even things that are not, to bring to nothing things that are" (vv. 27–28). "You shall speak my words to them, whether they hear or refuse to hear, for they are a rebellious house" (Ezek. 2:7). God's wisdom will show you rules quite contrary to those of carnal wisdom. Consider then what carnal wisdom says, and what the wisdom from above says:

CARNAL WISDOM

Your body is weak; weary it not. It cannot abide toil, labor, and weariness. So spare yourself.

SPIRITUAL WISDOM

Your body is God's as well as your spirit; don't safeguard it from glorifying God: "You were bought with a price. So glorify God in your body" (1 Cor. 6:20). Paul said, "I have been in labor and hardship, through many sleepless nights, in hunger and thirst, often without food, in cold and exposure" (2 Cor. 11:27, NASB). But God "gives power to the faint, and to him who has no might he increases strength" (Isa. 40:29). This you have experienced.

CARNAL WISDOM

Work diligently for fluent and eloquent speech; fine style very much appeals to the learned. Without it they will think nothing of your preaching.

Attempt to be somewhat smooth and calm in your preaching. Do not attack the particular sins of the land, or of the persons to whom you preach.

It is dangerous to speak freely and deal with specifics: there may be more hazard in it than you are aware of.

You will be perceived as a fool, as a monster; you will be called a railer and so lose your reputation and prestige. You need to preserve that. Men will hate and abhor you; why should you expose yourself to such things?

SPIRITUAL WISDOM

Christ sent you "to preach the gospel . . . not with words of eloquent wisdom" (1 Cor. 1:17). Do not preach "with lofty speech or wisdom" (1 Cor. 2:1). Your message and preaching should not be "in persuasive words of wisdom" (v. 4, NASB).

"Cry aloud; do not hold back; lift up your voice like a trumpet; declare to my people their transgression, to the house of Jacob their sins" (Isa. 58:1). "Better is open rebuke than hidden love" (Prov. 27:5). "Be diligent to present yourself approved to God . . . accurately handling the word of truth" (2 Tim. 2:15, NASB).

"Whoever walks in integrity walks securely" (Prov. 10:9). "He who walks blamelessly will be delivered" (Prov. 28:18, NASB).

"If anyone among you thinks that he is wise in this age, let him become a fool that he may become wise" (1 Cor. 3:18). "We have become a spectacle to the world. . . . We are fools for Christ's sake" (4:9–10). "'A servant is not greater than his master.' If they persecuted me, they will also persecute you" (John 15:20). Who cares what people say about you? After all, many said of Jesus, "He has a demon, and is insane" (John 10:20). He said, "If anyone would come after me, let him deny himself and take up his cross and follow me" (Matt. 16:24). "If the world hates you, know that it has hated me before it hated you," says our Lord (John 15:18).

CARNAL WISDOM

If you are not subtle, your hearers will be irritated against you and may create trouble for you. And what a foolish thing would it be for you to speak boldly to such a generation as this, whose very looks are disagreeable!

Great people especially will be offended at you, unless you speak charmingly to them and court and caress them. And if you are looked down upon by great people who are wise and mighty, how will you have any self-respect?

Our people have just come out from under the oppressive hierarchy of a state church. They would not desire to have certain sins disclosed or especially old sores to be ripped open. They cannot abide certain doctrines. More agreeable doctrine will be better for them. Hold off negative things. Such doctrine may do them harm; it will do them no good.

SPIRITUAL WISDOM

"Whoever rebukes a man will afterward find more favor than he who flatters with his tongue" (Prov. 28:23). I have experience of this. "Like emery harder than flint have I made your forehead. Fear them not, nor be dismayed at their looks, for they are a rebellious house" (Ezek. 3:9). Experience confirms this, too.

"I will not show partiality to any man or use flattery toward any person. For I do not know how to flatter, else my Maker would soon take me away" (Job 32:21–22). "Have any of the authorities or the Pharisees believed in him?" (John 7:48). "Not many of you were wise according to worldly standards, not many were powerful, not many were of noble birth" (1 Cor. 1:26). "I will also speak of your testimonies before kings and shall not be put to shame" (Ps. 119:46). "If you show partiality, you are committing sin" (Jas. 2:9).

"You shall speak my words to them, whether they hear or refuse to hear, for they are a rebellious house" (Ezek. 2:7). "Whenever you hear a word from my mouth, you shall give them warning from me. If I say to the wicked, 'You shall surely die,' and you give him no warning, nor speak to warn the wicked from his wicked way, in order to save his life, that wicked person shall die for his iniquity, but his blood I will require at your hand" (3:17–18). "What the LORD says to me, that I will speak" (1 Kings 22:14).

CARNAL WISDOM

If you do preach such things, prudence requires that you speak of them very cautiously. If conscience says you must speak, do it somewhat covertly, so that you do not offend people too badly. This is especially important with respect to people who are young in the faith. Take your time exposing them to the hard truths and soften them as much as possible; you don't want to turn young believers away.

SPIRITUAL WISDOM

"Cry aloud; do not hold back" (Isa. 58:1). "Cursed be he that doeth the work of the LORD deceitfully" (Jer. 48:10, KJV). "[We] have renounced the hidden things of dishonesty, not walking in craftiness, nor handling the word of God deceitfully; but by manifestation of the truth commending ourselves to every man's conscience in the sight of God" (2 Cor. 4:2, KJV). Peter, preaching to unbelievers in the first sermon of the Christian era, told the Jewish inquirers, "You nailed [this Man] to a cross by the hands of godless men and put Him to death" (Acts 2:23, NASB). "We must work . . . while it is day; night is coming, when no one can work" (John 9:4).

Be especially pleasant to those who have the most influence in the church—at least until you are settled and secure with a comfortable salary. Otherwise, you may be always looking for work; for churches will be frightened away from you, and will not call you. How then will you live? Forthright preaching, therefore, may be detrimental to your livelihood. A more subtle approach might also afford you a broader ministry.

"To show partiality is not good, but for a piece of bread a man will do wrong" (Prov. 28:21). "Let the will of the Lord be done." (Acts 21:14–15). God has "determined [your] appointed times, and the boundaries of [your] habitation" (Acts 17:26, NASB). "My purpose will be established, and I will accomplish all My good pleasure" (Isa. 46:10, NASB). "God settles the solitary in a home . . . but the rebellious dwell in a parched land" (Ps. 68:6). "A faithful man will abound with blessings, but whoever hastens to be rich will not go unpunished" (Prov. 28:20). "The fear of man lays a snare, but whoever trusts in the LORD is safe" (Prov. 29:25).

Thus you see, oh my soul, how carnal wisdom—although it speaks convincingly and with a good deal of seeming reason—is quite contrary to the wisdom that is from above (cf. Jas. 3:15–18). It promises great advantages to those who follow it, but its promises are not always performed. It threatens great calamity for those who defy it, but neither do its threatenings always come to pass. It makes molehills mountains, and mountains molehills. Therefore reject the wisdom of the world, for it is foolishness with God.

Carnal policy would make us fear those who can only kill the body—and they can hardly do even that much these days. Worldly wisdom would make us cast off the true fear of God. Oh my soul, remember this, and use it to strengthen yourself: "The fear of man lays a snare, but whoever trusts in the Lord is safe" (Prov. 29:25). Never seek temporal profit by putting your soul in hazard; but "Wait for the Lord and keep his way, and he will exalt you to inherit the land; you will look on when the wicked are cut off" (Ps. 37:34). For his way is the safest way, though carnal wisdom may speak otherwise and call His way mere folly. Above all, remember that "the foolishness of God is wiser than men, and the weakness of God is stronger than men" (1 Cor. 1:25).

"God chose what is foolish in the world to shame the wise; God chose what is weak in the world to shame the strong" (v. 27). "Your faith [should] not rest in the wisdom of men but in the power of God" (2:5).

"The word of the cross is folly to those who are perishing, but to us who are being saved it is the power of God. For it is written, 'I will destroy the wisdom of the wise, and the discernment of the discerning I will thwart.' Where is the one who is wise? Where is the scribe? Where is the debater of this age? Has not God made foolish the wisdom of the world? For since, in the wisdom of God, the world did not know God through wisdom, *it pleased God through the folly of what we preach to save those who believe*" (1 Cor. 1:18–21, emphasis added).

"Fear not, for I am with you; be not dismayed, for I am your God; I will strengthen you, I will help you, I will uphold you with my righteous right hand. Behold, all who are incensed against you shall be put to shame and confounded; those who strive against you shall be as nothing and shall perish" (Isa. 41:10–11).